Praise for *Britain's Jews*

'[Freedman's] survey is detailed and fair ... For non-Jews, this explains us as well as is possible outside fiction.'

The Spectator

'Freedman, a prolific author of books on Jewish subjects, has produced something that could fairly lay claim to becoming the definitive guide to British Jewry...And as a portrait of a community at a particular moment, it is an exhaustive, impressive achievement.'

The Tablet

'The book is a great primer as an introduction to what makes Jews tick today.'

Jewish News

'[Freedman] writes clearly and knows the community inside and out.'

New Humanist

'Freedman's insider account of Britain Jewry...tells a story of "confidence", "maturity", even relative cohesion.'

Times Literary Supplement

Leonard Cohen: The Mystical Roots of Genius
Reason To Believe: The Controversial Life of Rabbi Louis Jacobs
Kabbalah: Secrecy, Scandal and the Soul
The Murderous History of Bible Translations
The Talmud: A Biography

BRITAIN'S JEWS

Confidence, Maturity, Anxiety

HARRY FREEDMAN

BLOOMSBURY CONTINUUM
LONDON · OXFORD · NEW YORK · NEW DELHI · SYDNEY

BLOOMSBURY CONTINUUM
Bloomsbury Publishing Plc
50 Bedford Square, London, WC1B 3DP, UK
29 Earlsfort Terrace, Dublin 2, Ireland

BLOOMSBURY, BLOOMSBURY CONTINUUM and the Diana logo are trademarks
of Bloomsbury Publishing Plc

First published in Great Britain 2022
Paperback 2023

A catalogue record for this book is available from the British Library

Library of Congress Cataloguing-in-Publication data has been applied for

ISBN: TPB: 978-1-4729-8723-5; eBook: 978-1-4729-8724-2; ePDF: 978-1-4729-8721-1

2 4 6 8 10 9 7 5 3 1

Typeset by Deanta Global Publishing Services, Chennai, India
Printed and bound in Great Britain by CPI Group (UK) Ltd, Croydon CR0 4YY

To find out more about our authors and books visit www.bloomsbury.com
and sign up for our newsletters

To Karen

CONTENTS

Introduction

Jews have lived in Britain longer than any other minority. They've been here so long, and are so ingrained in the national fabric, that they are often considered not to be a minority at all. Until a periodic outburst of anti-Semitism or a flare-up in the Middle East, or both, turns the spotlight on them once again.

Jews in Britain have done very well. They have risen to the top of nearly every profession, they run major companies, sit at the top tables in politics, make their voices heard in the media, are prominent in science and the arts. Of course, there is serious poverty and gross disadvantage, just as there is in any community. But by any objective measure British Jews have done well. Particularly when we consider where they came from, the impoverished, often oppressed lives that many Jews lived in Eastern Europe and the Ottoman Empire less than 200 years ago.

British Jews have another distinction too. They have lived safely and securely, continuously, in Britain longer than any other modern Jewish community has lived anywhere else in the world. They have organized themselves in a way that serves as a model both to more recent immigrant communities in

Britain and to Jewish communities elsewhere. Being British, they wear their distinctions lightly, and they don't trumpet their achievements; in fact, they rarely make a noise at all. But they give back quietly: established Jewish organizations help more recently arrived minorities to create their own structures; charities draw on the Jewish experience of dislocation and persecution to help oppressed people in the developing world; philanthropists support causes far beyond the boundaries of their own communities.

Like all minorities, Jews have been stereotyped, with adjectives applied to them to help fit them neatly into boxes. To those who are generous about Jews we are ambitious, educated, communally minded, charitable, loyal and so on. To those who aren't too keen, we are aloof, exclusive, self-interested and inward-looking. To the anti-Semites, that small, intellectually and ethically challenged rabble, the ever-present scab on the back of Jewish history, we are tight-fisted and grasping, united in a conspiracy to control the world and its institutions. (If nothing else, anti-Semites seem to have been branded with overactive imaginations.) These days, none of the stereotypes is pertinent; they don't resonate as even remotely accurate. Jews are as diverse as any other group in British society. Nevertheless, Jews are aware that their minority is scrutinized more intensely than most. Few Jews, even the most assimilated, are wholly oblivious to their Jewishness.

I spent a year or so speaking to Jews across the UK, from all walks of life, and of all religious and political outlooks, trying to find out what it meant to them to be Jewish. I asked them about their lives, their work, their religious outlook, their communities, their many opinions. In short,

I tried to construct a picture of what it means to be Jewish in Britain today.

One of the challenges of writing this book was in deciding who to speak to. There are many Jews in Britain doing remarkable things, and many more whose stories are worth telling. I couldn't speak to them all: I'd have ended up with an encyclopaedia, not a book. So to all the doctors, teachers, entertainers, politicians, journalists, artists, scientists, jugglers, academics, social workers, police officers, astronauts, tightrope walkers, builders, rabbis and everyone else I didn't get a chance to speak to – I am sorry we didn't have an opportunity to chat, but I hope this book will give you an insight into parts of Britain's Jewish world that you know less about.

I wrote the book while we were in the middle of the Covid pandemic. It meant I couldn't physically meet the people I was talking to: most of my meetings were conducted on Zoom. That didn't detract from the quality of our discussion at all – we are all used to virtual meetings these days. But it did feel a bit odd, talking one-to-one with getting on for 100 people without ever leaving my desk.

I begin the book by looking at one of the most striking developments in contemporary British Jewish life: the new confidence that many young Jews seem to have about who they are and what it means to them to be Jewish. They are very different from previous generations, who tried their hardest to keep their heads down and not to appear too strange in the eyes of their non-Jewish neighbours. This new generation is doing things *because* they are Jews, not *in spite* of being Jews. And some of the things they are doing are very interesting too.

Their confidence derives in part from the maturity of the Jewish experience in Britain, the certainties that come from being a long-established minority in a country where we feel as safe as we have felt anywhere else in our long history.

Confidence and maturity are positive aspects of Jewish life in Britain. But there is another side to the British Jewish experience. There is an anxiety among many British Jews, one that is often quite profound when it comes to anti-Semitism and the recently minted phrase 'Jew-hate'. Anti-Semitism has been in the news a lot over the past few years, and yet, as we shall see, there is reason to believe that the situation is not as grim as it is sometimes portrayed. Nearly everyone I have spoken to has agreed that Britain is a good place for Jews to live. Nevertheless the anxiety is real, and along with confidence and maturity, it characterizes Jewish life in Britain today.

One might have thought that religion would be the first chapter in the book. After all, Judaism is a religion, and unless one can understand the religion, how can one understand Jews? But Judaism is far more than a religion, and many people live as confident and identifying Jews without paying attention to the Jewish religion, without even giving it a second thought. That is not to diminish the importance or the centrality of religion in our culture, or the astonishing diversity of the people who practise its different forms, but – and here the rabbis will disagree – religion is not the essence of being Jewish. Judaism is an ethnicity. Like all ethnicities, we are not a pure race, but as some of the discussions in this book will assert, neither should we be thought of as only a religion. Census compilers please take note.

I spend a couple of chapters looking at the institutional side of the British Jewish community, because its organizations and support structures are what give Jewish life in Britain its heft. Without them, Britain's Jews would be little more than a disparate group. With them we become a community, although I will argue that the word 'community' is an inadequate term to describe the complexity of Jewish society. And, on the subject of Jewish society, I have devoted a chapter to what life is like for Jews outside London, for those in cities like Manchester and Glasgow, and for the very many Jews who live in small communities, often just a handful of people, all across the country.

Two of the most important Jewish priorities are education and the giving of charity. They have always played an essential part in Jewish life. For many Jewish people today philanthropy and social justice have taken on an almost mystical quality; they describe them in terms of saving the world. And Jewish schools are flourishing in Britain: there are many more than ever before, and a large proportion of Jewish children attend them. But not always for the reasons that their earliest enthusiasts imagined.

Jews are no strangers to migration. And over the decades and centuries Britain has welcomed Jewish migrants from almost every part of the world. I end the book by reviewing some of the more recent waves of migration of Jews into Britain, speaking to some of the latest immigrants about their experiences of settling in Britain and the challenges of maintaining their native traditions among a very different Jewry, with strong Anglo-Saxon traits.

While this book was being prepared for publication, Russia invaded Ukraine. It is a disturbing and terrifying event, one that resonates particularly with Jews because Ukraine is where so many of our families came from, and where so many were massacred in the Shoah. Jewish charities and communities have responded with alacrity, raising funds, helping refugees, showing solidarity however they can. For many of Britain's Jews the Ukraine war has touched a profoundly personal nerve. It has brought home the uncertainty of our lives, even in safe, secure Britain.

Since the hardback edition of this book was published a political crisis has erupted in Israel over the government's intended reforms to the judiciary. Many Israelis regard this as an assault on their democracy and the country is more polarized than at any time in its short history. Jews in Britain are similarly divided; it appears that a large majority are opposed to the far-right government's reforms. How the political crisis will be resolved and its impact on the attitudes towards Israel that we discuss in the last chapter of the book, remains to be seen.

When writing about Jews, it is never possible to please everyone; in fact, it's probably not inaccurate to say I may not have pleased anyone. Those on one side will say I am too far to the left; those on the other will say I am too far to the right. As for the centre – hopefully they will weigh what they read and come to their own conclusions. In the biblical book of Esther, after Mordechai had saved his fellow Jews from genocide and their memory from obliteration, after he had disposed of their enemies and won the favour of the king, who made him his second-in-command, we read that he got an approval rating from *most* of his people. That's about as good as it gets. And I haven't done any of the things Mordechai did.

I

The New Confidence

When Philip Roth's alter ego Nathan Zuckerman asks his non-Jewish, English wife what the British think about the Jews, she replies sharply: 'Why do Jews make such a bloody fuss about being Jewish? That's what they think.'[1]

Few topics dominate conversations between Jews more than their Jewishness. With little effort they can attribute every facet of their life, their lot in this world, their personality, to the fact that they were born Jewish. Not that they are all of one mind regarding the matter. Of all the stereotypes about Jews, and there are many, perhaps the most accurate is their argumentative nature, particularly when arguing with each other. Two Jews, three opinions, as the old saying goes.

Contemporary literature is full of stereotypes about Jews. Some lend themselves to great literature. Think how diminished New York novels would be without their opinionated, outspoken Jewish characters, forever in and out of therapy. The Israelis too are a writer's dream: brash, assertive, always right even when they couldn't be more wrong. But when it comes to British Jews, as Naomi Alderman writes, their fear of being noticed compounds their natural British reticence until they 'cannot speak, cannot be seen, value *absolute invisibility* above all other virtues'.[2] What on earth can be written about them?

Well, as it turns out, quite a lot. In our multicultural British society, Jews are a model of successful integration – unsurprisingly, since they have been here for so long. And they have changed substantially in the past two or three decades. Naomi Alderman's silent Jews are no longer silent. Or at least, they are a lot less silent than they used to be. Since the turn of the millennium, 2,000 years since the world's most famous Jew shattered his nation's private, exclusive relationship with their God, many of the old stereotypes that once applied to British Jews no longer seem relevant. Of course, it wasn't the magic number of the year 2000 that did this: Britain's Jews have changed in lockstep with British society. But the millennium is as good a reference point as any from which to mark that change.

One of the most noticeable things about today's British Jews is just how confident so many of them have become about being Jewish. Ray Simonson, Chief Executive of JW3 (of which more later), an ardent advocate of the new Jewish psyche, puts it like this: 'Growing up, I remember three words that Jewish adults said in hushed tones. They'd say: "Oh, you know the neighbours, have you heard they're getting *divorced*?" They wouldn't say it out loud in case it was contagious. They'd also say: "It's terrible news, you know she's got *cancer.*" And in a public space, they'd drop their voices whenever they spoke about someone being *Jewish.*'

They don't whisper the word 'Jewish' any more. Well, some still do, because Jews can't agree about anything. But many more of them are prepared to go out there today and celebrate their Jewishness. Or defend it. Or bemoan it in public, or deliberately draw attention to the fact that they are Jews. When the comedian Josh Howie started talking to predominantly non-Jewish audiences about being Jewish, in what he describes as 'quite an abrasive way, unapologetically, unashamedly Jewish', he says that he could feel the energy shift in the room, the audience reassessing him, as if 'we've now got to put you into a different box'. It even happened when he wasn't drawing attention to his Jewishness. He recalls doing a show in Edinburgh based on his teenage years, growing up in the 1980s, when HIV was constantly at the top of the media agenda. 'I deliberately didn't say anything in the show about being Jewish. But a reviewer wrote a piece about how I was Jewish, using my Jewishness like I was some sort of hypochondriac.'

Howie is part of a long tradition of British Jewish comedians, a star cast headed by the likes of Sid James, Peter Sellers, Bud Flanagan, and Marty Feldman. But Howie was one of the first to overtly trumpet his Judaism. Unlike in the USA, where Jews are much more visible and far less reticent about announcing their Judaism, earlier British Jewish comics were discreet about being Jewish. 'My grandmother's generation would say: "Assimilate, don't rock the boat." And in some ways that has served us well as a community. But I think there was a danger in that, being so quiet or silent lent itself to conspiracy theories and to people's lack of knowledge of the Jewish community.' Howie says that the events of the past few years, the political and media focus on anti-Semitism, have forced young British Jews to take a stand, to say unapologetically, 'I am Jewish and I'm not going to put up with this. We don't have to hide or apologize any more. And we demand recognition for ourselves in those spaces, around identity politics or wherever, where it is said that racism can't occur towards Jews. Maybe it doesn't come naturally to us, or we don't want to do it. And I don't know how older Jews or the Jewish community feel about it. But I guess what I'm trying to say is, we're more willing to pick a fight now.'

The growing confidence of Britain's Jews, at least among those under the age of 50, is partly a consequence of the zeitgeist. Identity matters today: we are supposed to be uninhibited in asserting who we are, our ethnicity, sexuality and origins. Jews, particularly young Jews, are no longer afraid to be proud of their identity.

But identity politics is only one factor in explaining the new confidence of Britain's Jews. More prosaically, Jews in Britain no longer feel as if they are an immigrant population. They no longer need to strive to establish themselves within the host community. It is nearly a century and a half since the great waves of Jewish immigration from Eastern Europe changed the British perception of Jews forever, and although many Jewish families in Britain arrived more recently, a good number trace their ancestry back to that time. Of course, it is too easy to generalize, and every family has a different story, but broadly the immigrant generations were too busy trying to keep their heads down and establish themselves to care about matters of identity. Anyway, they knew only too well who they were, they'd been outsiders in the lands where they were born, why should it be any different here?

Their children were different. They were ambitious. Shrugging off the old ways, they strove to improve themselves economically and to fit in socially, dragging themselves out of the inner-city, immigrant ghettos in London, Manchester, Glasgow, Birmingham and Leeds, propelling themselves towards the suburbs. They built their communities quietly, grateful for the freedoms of worship and expression that

Britain offered, rarely poking their heads above the parapet, raising their children according to the adage first coined in the nineteenth century: as Englishmen of the Mosaic persuasion. 'Come for tea, Come for tea, Oh my people,' they joked, deliberately misquoting Isaiah's 'Comfort ye, comfort ye.'[3]

Still, they could never just be British. Anti-Semitism at home, both interpersonal and institutional, then the rise of the Nazis abroad drove home the message that they were different. After the Second World War they listened with horror as accounts of what had happened during the Shoah gradually emerged, each report more devastating than its predecessor. Although the extent of the slaughter was already being reported in 1942, for reasons that Richard Bolchover eloquently explains in his book *British Jewry and the Holocaust*, few in Britain during the war years were able fully to grasp the reality of what was happening, to comprehend its horror or the extent of the devastation.[4] Even in the years immediately following the Shoah their inability to come to terms with the events was compounded by the incapacity of many survivors to disclose the full extent of their trauma. The trials at Nuremburg, Anne Frank's diary and the early writings of survivors like Primo Levi gave some sense of the enormity, but it took years for many of the personal stories to be told, and for the unspeakable depth of the tragedy to finally sink in.

British Jews' incomprehension was compounded by events in Palestine, where forces of the British mandate and Zionist paramilitary troops were caught up in a spiral of violence. In 1946, in a reaction to the wholesale round-up of Zionist agitators, Jewish terrorists from the terrorist organization Irgun Zvi Leumi bombed the British administrative headquarters at the King David Hotel in Jerusalem, killing 91 people. The following year the Irgun retaliated against the execution of three of their members by capturing and hanging two British sergeants. The British public reacted with fury. Anti-Jewish riots broke out in Manchester, Glasgow and Liverpool. British Jews were conflicted. How to reconcile the promise of an independent Jewish homeland with terrorism perpetrated by their kinsfolk against the nation that had given them shelter?

The distress of British Jews was made even worse when it transpired that the country which had offered so many of them a home was now turning away boatloads of Holocaust survivors from the ports of Palestine, sending them to displaced persons' camps in Cyprus, or in some cases back to the devastated Europe from which they had fled. Leon Uris's best-selling book *Exodus*, and Otto Preminger's subsequent, eponymous movie, are fictionalized accounts of what really happened to one of these boats.

And if all that wasn't enough for Britain's post-war Jews, the realization was slowly dawning upon them that they were witnesses to the unfolding of a 2,000-year-old dream. When the United Nations voted for an independent Israel in November 1947, they created the first independent Jewish state since the first century BCE. As Britain's Jews entered the second half of the twentieth century, they hardly knew what to make of it all.

It wasn't just the Jews who were experiencing change. Britain was changing too. The National Health Service was created and the Welfare State greatly expanded. Opportunities opened up and social barriers came down. As they fell, the new generations of Jews cast away the defences their parents had erected for their self-protection. Growing up alongside their British peers, educated in British schools, living and working in a multicultural society, these new Jews were comfortable in their skins. They knew who they were. They were British and they were Jewish. And whichever designation they chose to put first, whether they considered themselves to be British Jews or Jewish Brits, they saw no conflict between the two.

For Chief Rabbi Ephraim Mirvis, the story of Britain's Jews is an inspiration. 'We've gone through so much. We arrived here as refugees, we came with our hands tied behind our backs. There's been a lot of social mobility and so many different narratives. And for me, what stands out, and this is a story which repeats itself around the globe, is our adaptability. I can speak personally. As somebody who is now living in his fourth country: from South Africa to Israel, Ireland and now here. We are masters of integration. The Jewish story has been extraordinary in this country: as individuals, as families and as a community our contribution to society has been absolutely immense. While all the time being proudly British. We are British Jews. Yes, we have our challenges, we've got our quarrels, but those are details within an overall narrative, which is one of a highly successful, wonderful Jewish community.'

The confidence of today's new generations of Jews is not just a question of feeling more British or of fitting more easily into British society. The existence of the state of Israel has radically changed the ways Jews feel about themselves. It even asserts itself in the way they dress in public. It is a custom for religious Jewish men to cover their heads.[5] There is no religious imperative for a man to do so; it is a tradition, but one that is considered particularly significant. Indoors they wear a *kippah*, a small, unmistakably Jewish skullcap. Outdoors, until the late 1960s, they substituted a hat for their *kippah,* so as not to attract attention. The first time I saw a Jew wearing a *kippah* in the street was in 1967, a few days after Israel's rapid, decisive victory in the Six Day War. That victory, which many believed to be miraculous, kindled a new spirit of Jewish pride, a sense that Jews no longer needed to hide their Jewishness, that somehow little underdog Israel's victory against a coalition of mighty Arab armies had rubbed off on us all, that the meek, self-effacing Jew was no more.

Of course, subsequent events and the ongoing failure to agree a lasting peace with the Palestinians have dulled the euphoria. But a sense of Jewish pride, albeit more cautious, has remained. Paradoxically, the existence of Israel is in no small measure responsible for the new confidence of British Jewry.

There is a barmy theory about the word 'British'. Break it down into its syllables and we hear two Hebrew words, *Brit* and *Ish*. *Brit*, meaning 'covenant', is the name given to the Jewish ritual of circumcision, Abraham's covenant with God. *Ish* is the Hebrew word for 'man'. At the beginning of the nineteenth century a man named Richard Brothers published a book with the catchy title *Correct Account of the Invasion of England by the Saxons, Showing the English Nation To Be Descendants of the Lost Ten Tribes*. Among the proofs he offered for his claim that the inhabitants of Britain were the descendants of the vanished Israelite tribes was that the word 'British' can be translated as 'Man of the Covenant'. Very few people believed him. His British Israel movement did not flourish.

One of the most telling indications of the Jewish community's growing confidence was a public celebration held in London's Trafalgar Square in 2006. It was supposed to mark the 350th anniversary of the readmission of the Jews to Britain, when Oliver Cromwell is said to have reversed the decree of expulsion imposed on them by Edward I in 1290.

In fact, Cromwell never formally readmitted the Jews. But he did agree to a request from a group of Dutch merchants that they be given the right to worship freely in England. Many of the merchants were the descendants of *conversos* – secret Jews whose ancestors had nominally converted to Christianity in the 1490s to avoid being thrown out of Portugal and Spain, while continuing as best they could to live underground lives as Jews. Cromwell granted them his 'favour and protection', giving them the right to worship, to rent premises for a synagogue and acquire land for a cemetery. But he did not rescind the Edict of Expulsion. The formal readmission of the Jews, a hot political topic in the 1650s, never happened. But that didn't prevent an increasingly self-confident Jewish community from publicly celebrating its anniversary. 350 years is not a particularly significant number. Still, it provided the excuse for a party. They called the party *Simcha* – or 'Celebration' – on the Square.

Simcha on the Square wasn't without controversy. British Jewry may have come of age while keeping its head down on the national stage, but it had always been pretty good at quarrelling among itself. Traditionally its quarrels had been over religion and religious authority, but *Simcha* on the Square provided the community with an opportunity to demonstrate to the nation at large that it could argue with others just as vigorously as it could quarrel with itself.

The spat was with the then mayor of London, Ken Livingstone, a minor left-wing politician whose self-regard greatly outweighed his common sense, political deftness and likeability. Livingstone had already attracted the ire of the Jewish community for likening a Jewish journalist to a concentration camp guard, praising an Islamist supporter of anti-Israel terror as the world's most progressive Islamic theologian and generally making himself odious to people whose votes he had forgotten he would one day need. Livingstone was just about sensitive enough to realize that he should not show his face at *Simcha* on the Square, but his office had contributed £60,000 towards the event and he trumpeted his personal support for the event in a press release.

In an excoriating rebuke Henry Grunwald, President of the Board of Deputies, the representative body for British Jewry, accused Livingstone of a lack of sensitivity and understanding, and of a track record that failed to guarantee no further offence in the future. Other voices weighed in. The Jewish Music Institute, the main organizers of the festival, defended the mayor, saying they could find nothing of concern in his press release, but the Association of Jewish Ex-Servicemen and Women withdrew from the celebration in protest at the mayor's 'record of giving offence'. The London Jewish Forum said: 'The Mayor needs to build a relationship of trust with Jewish Londoners. This is not something that will happen overnight.' The following week Livingstone sent a letter to the *Jewish Chronicle* praising his own press statements, for which, he noted, the festival organizers had commended him. And so it went on.[6]

Perhaps the most newsworthy moment in the event itself came with the arrest of four members of the mock-subversive Jewish group Jewdas – themselves a testimony to a new spirit of Jewish self-confidence. They were arrested for distributing a leaflet suspected of being anti-Semitic. It advertised a party called 'Protocols of the Elders of Hackney'. The leaflet wasn't anti-Semitic, just stupid. Their true offence was in not understanding that good satire has to be funny. Their attempts at humour only improved marginally when they renamed the event 'Protocols of the Elephants of Zion'.[7]

Eventually, the police decided not to press charges against the four arrested in Trafalgar Square. Jewdas just weren't funny enough.

Reactions to *Simcha* on the Square were mixed. The organizers said that about 25,000 people turned up. For the Chairman of the Jewish Music Institute the event 'was testimony to the freedom to proclaim proudly and openly our Judaism in the heart of London'.

Not everyone was impressed. The historian David Cesarani z"l* had told his kids the event would be fun. 'When we got to Trafalgar Square, my heart sank ... It was typical of the way British Jews have integrated into this country that, instead of showcasing the huge talent we can boast, we got a half-baked event held under the shadow of a row with the mayor, unofficially boycotted by half the community. It could and should have been so much better.'

Simcha on the Square didn't become a permanent communal fixture; after a couple of years it fell victim to public funding cuts. But the idea of a public celebration had caught on, particularly among some in the Jewish evangelical community who saw it as an opportunity to promote their wares. They chose the ideal Jewish holiday to pin their rebranded celebration on. Of all the Jewish festivals, the one that most lends itself to spectacle is Hanukkah, an eight-day, midwinter interlude marked by candle lightings and the consumption of doughnuts and latkes. (Doughnuts and latkes played no part in the historical events that Hanukkah commemorates, but all Jewish festivals have their own traditional foods. As the saying goes: 'they tried to kill us ... let's eat!').

*z"l is a Hebrew acronym, similar to RIP. It means may his/her memory be for a blessing.

Inspired by the heroic triumph of a small group of Jewish resistance fighters over Greek invaders in the second century BCE, Hanukkah celebrates a victory over alien ideas and a lifestyle that threatened to overwhelm Judaism. The attention paid to Hanukkah today is a bit odd, because it is a minor festival, originally so obscure that the Talmud, compiled 800 years after the victory, had to ask, 'What is Hanukkah?' It is ironic then that Hanukkah has become a sort of Jewish Christmas, falling in December and often marked by the giving of presents. Candles are lit each night on an eight-branched candelabra known as a *hanukkiah*. It is impossible to travel in December through areas with a Jewish population of any size without seeing at least one giant *hanukkiah* glowing in the street, erected by the hasidic sect Chabad, as part of their programme of bringing Judaism into the lives of even the most non-observant of Jews. Hanukkah, the festival that commemorates Judaism's rejection of an alien culture, has been turned into a pseudo-Christmas to bring Jews closer to their own faith. Work that one out.

Hanukkah's other highlight, as far the public face of newly confident British Jewry is concerned, is a Sunday afternoon gathering in Trafalgar Square. Rabbis, politicians, tourists and several thousand Jews watch in admiration as a celebrity victim, a Jew who would probably baulk at climbing a stepladder at home, ascends in a cherry picker almost as high as Nelson on his column. Trying his hardest not to look down, he lights the *hanukkiah* and descends. The crowd audibly breathes a sigh of relief as he reaches the ground.

Simcha on the Square and the Hanukkah celebrations soon spawned other public events. Klezmer in the Park, also organized by the Jewish Music Institute, was British Jewry's understated response to Glastonbury, without the mud, portable loos or camping. Live music and entertainment by Regent's Park lake on a summer Sunday afternoon.

Jews have been singing and making music since biblical times. The Israelites sang a song as they crossed the Red Sea, fleeing from Egypt. Before he succeeded him as king, David calmed Saul's nerves by playing the harp. And the Levites sang David's psalms in Jerusalem's temple. Jews have made music ever since: Mahler and Mendelssohn among the composers, Menuhin and Barenboim among the performers, Dylan and Cohen among the rock stars. But Jewish music, as opposed to music made by Jews, was generally confined to weddings, celebrations and the synagogue. In Britain that started to change in 1984, when the Jewish Music Institute was founded. Today it puts on events and supports musicians through scholarships and education. Like all worthy institutions, it is perennially short of money and is run by the generosity of its volunteers. And it does have a mountain to climb. Describing it as an abyss of effort unredeemed by a grace of talent, the journalist Norman Lebrecht argues that the word 'Jewish' should never be uttered in the same sentence as 'music'.[8]

Food was celebrated too. Gefiltefest, rejoicing under the axiomatic slogan 'Celebrating Jewish Heritage through Food', ran for several years. Named in homage to *gefilte* fish, the distinctive fish balls of Yiddish cuisine, and consisting of cookery workshops, food stalls, demonstrations and tastings, the event was an epicurean's delight. Epicureans, according to the Talmud's somewhat skewed understanding of classical history, were the epitome of learned heresy. Gefiltefest showed just how far Jews had travelled in the 1,500 years since the Talmud was compiled.[9]

Public events are all very well, but they are over quickly. A far more in-your-face and, for some, a much more controversial demonstration of British Jewry's new confidence is the brash, glass-fronted community centre and venue JW3. Built on the site of a former Mercedes-Benz showroom on the ridiculously busy Finchley Road, with everything that is going on inside visible from the top of passing buses, it is not what a Jewish building is supposed to be. Jewish buildings tend to be discreet, barely visible, blending in with the environment, often concealed for security reasons behind high walls or fences. In the old days, synagogues would mimic the churches by posting biblical quotes on a billboard outside, to show that they weren't really so different after all.

JW3 does not have a biblical verse outside. Instead it has a large, unmissable, gaudy sign on its façade proudly proclaiming 'JW3: Jewish Community Centre London'. Inside, the extravagant, £50 million, four-storey building boasts an auditorium, library, restaurant, café, bar, classrooms, studios, offices and a cinema. The building's appearance may not be to everyone's taste, and when it was built in 2012 its very visibility was a worry to some. It is not like any other communal Jewish structure in London. It deliberately shouts, 'Look at us!' JW3's brash building is an essential part of its brand. It wants to be noticed.

Ray Simonson, JW3's chief executive, describes the uproar that preceded the centre's opening. 'We had emails, letters and phone calls telling us: "*They* (i.e. non-Jews) can see us. We're going to get blown up ...".' But now, he says, 'what we get is everyone saying: "I feel so proud when I go past on the top of the number 13 bus, when I see the giant *hanukkiah*, when I see the message that says Jewish Film Festival, Jewish Comedy Festival, Jewish Book Week, Jewish, Jewish, Jewish ..." And non-Jews don't bat an eyelid.'

Ray Simonson's vision is bold and ambitious. Energy, enthusiasm and quotable phrases tumble from him as he speaks. 'We are seeking to increase the quality, variety and volume of Jewish conversation,' he says. 'Too often in our community, the level of conversation in the public domain has become embarrassingly low. We want to increase that. We want to increase the quality of the conversation, we want to increase the variety. We're out loud and proud, we've got nothing to hide, and people respect that.

'JW3 offers multiple points of entry into Jewish life. If you want Torah, we've got it. If you want food, or cookery, we've got it. We've got dance, film, comedy, discussion. We cater for everyone, Jewish or not. In the summer we have a beach and in the winter an ice rink. I think we have genuinely had a transformational impact on the community. When we opened, we expected around 60,000 people through our doors each year. It's turned out that we get about 200,000.'

JW3 was the brainchild of the philanthropist Vivien Duffield, who based the idea on the Jewish Community Centres, or JCCs, that are such a prominent feature of American Jewish life. Ray says that Duffield was inspired by the JCC in Manhattan, where three things particularly seized her imagination. 'One was the building itself. It was very high-quality, it held its own against New York's other mainstream cultural venues. And the high quality of the building inspired a high quality of programming. The second thing she saw was many different types of Jews all in one place, a much broader range than you would normally see. And the third thing that really struck her was non-Jews coming into a Jewish space to use it not just for inter-faith events but for all sorts of activities, Jewish or not.'

This last point, he tells me, is particularly important. He says that that for the last few years British people have engaged with the word 'Jewish' almost exclusively through the lens of anti-Semitism, leading them to one of two views. Either they have sympathy for the Jews as victims or they have developed an antipathy, a sense that by complaining of anti-Semitism the Jews are causing trouble, stirring things up. 'So the idea of non-Jews just using a Jewish space, being in there mixing with Jews, brings us back to normality.'

JW3 runs social, cultural and educational activities, just like the JCCs in America do. But the larger American JCCs are far more than just event and meeting spaces: they are campus-based hubs that provide a home for the local Jewish communal organizations. As such, they have the potential to enhance communal life, create a bond between organizations and act as a unifying force within the community. JW3 doesn't have this advantage: space is at such a premium in London and property prices so high that it would be unrealistic to envisage a single campus headquartering all the city's leading Jewish communal organizations.

This raises the question of whether London's Jewish community really needs a building of JW3's scale and ambition. The city is full of synagogues and synagogue halls which lie empty for most of the week. There is no shortage of communal space for events; and the community organizations all have their own offices. So JW3 may be exciting and ambitious, but is it really necessary? Ray Simonson is quick to point out that JW3 was not a project demanded by the people; it didn't come out of focus groups. It was one person's idea, and Ray and his team are doing all they can to prove her right. So far all the evidence is in their favour. He told me that when they opened they set themselves a target of welcoming their millionth visitor by their 12th year of operation. They did better than that. The millionth visitor walked through their door one week before their fifth anniversary.

Perhaps the biggest threat to JW3's long-term success is the passive, reactive nature of the Jewish community. JW3 was an idea conceived and brought to fruition by a single enthusiast, a philanthropist with the passion, resources and influence to turn her dream into reality. Sooner or later there will be another big idea, a new, top-down initiative. Facilitated by big money and driven by the evangelism of a small, dedicated group, it will be uncritically accepted by a largely indifferent community, perhaps even overshadowing the work done by JW3. The Covid pandemic has shown us how easily the unexpected can bring about sudden change.

No cultural activity in the Jewish community has as high a profile as Jewish Book Week. It has been running for over 70 years, and is now one of the most important literary festivals in the country. It may be a Jewish event, but Claudia Rubenstein, the festival director, explains that 'we really see ourselves first and foremost as a book festival. We are about education, about engaging people in ideas. We are about talk, debate, persuasiveness.'

These are all the qualities that any good literary festival needs. But they are also the qualities that make Jewish Book Week quintessentially Jewish. Claudia tells me that they are very proud of the Jewish intellectual tradition. 'And it's important to us to showcase that, not just for the Jewish community, but also to the wider world. We're very aware that we are Jewish, and that we live in the UK. And I think the most interesting statistic to come out of our festival surveys is that up to 30 per cent of our attendees don't identify as Jewish. They come along because our events are of interest to them. We have a lot of non-Jewish fans who say that they like the openness of the discussion, the openness of the debate of Book Week, allowing people with different perspectives to have a platform.

It's very important, it's how we want to position ourselves. We are not just a group of Jews speaking to a group of Jews.'

Stimulating talks, packed auditoria, bustling crowds, book signings, bumping into long-forgotten acquaintances, a surfeit of energy: these are the things that draw people back to Jewish Book Week year after year. So when Covid hit in 2020, Jewish Book Week might have ground to a halt. Instead, just as so many other organizations discovered, the plague of Covid concealed an unanticipated benefit. Jewish Book Week went online, and it experienced a seismic change in how it interacted with its audience. The festival's reach mushroomed. Audiences tuned in from all over the world. Presenters expecting to speak to 250 people in an auditorium found they were addressing a digital audience of over 1,000 viewers, without even having to leave their living room. Jewish Book Week is no longer just an ambassador for Jewish culture in the UK; it is now a flagship for both Jewish and British culture across the globe.

I asked Claudia Rubenstein whether it is the fact of its Jewishness that has made Jewish Book Week such an important cultural event or whether it is simply the fact that she and her team are very good at organizing literary festivals. She said she thought it was both. 'I sit on very big shoulders, the history of the organization is phenomenal. It was set up by the visionary George Webber, who happened to have a very talented family, several of whom ran the festival, and it has managed to attract very high-calibre directors. Everyone has added their own stamp on to the festival, taking it more international, which is very important. You can become an echo chamber if you're just inviting the same people again and again, the same narrow group of people from within the community.'

Jewish Book Week has been through many changes since its founding in 1952. One of the most striking was when they moved the festival in 2012 from its former home in the Royal National Hotel, a spot that was beginning to look a lot shabbier than its name suggests, to Kings Place, an imposingly fresh, modern venue in the new King's Cross development. It wasn't just that Kings Place had better facilities, was more comfortable and felt like a much nicer place to be. Kings Place is a cultural centre in its own right and as such is a natural partner to Jewish Book Week. It brings Jewish Book Week to the attention of its own audience, enhances their PR and marketing and provides the logistical support to enable the festival to cater for hundreds of people in multiple simultaneous sessions, smoothly and seamlessly. Sometimes Kings Place and Jewish Book Week run events together. Claudia says that since they moved to Kings Place their audience figures have shot up, as has the number of names on their database.

Like all arts charities, Jewish Book Week is perennially concerned about money. It gets around one third of its funding from ticket sales; the rest has to come through sponsorship. But a key principle is that nobody should be denied access to a Jewish Book Week event because they can't afford it. And another is that children as well as adults should have access to Jewish Book Week speakers. They run a schools programme which Claudia describes as 'thriving', where they ask authors to go into schools to speak. It's free to the schools, and the authors don't charge.

'There are many wonderful authors,' Claudia tells me in conclusion, 'and it's been a massive pleasure to work with them. It feels like such a privilege to run this festival. It's the best job in the world.'

Limmud is British Jewry's other great success story. It is also a place of bustling crowds and long-forgotten acquaintances, of multiple events running side by side, of noise and chatter. Unlike Jewish Book Week, it is a residential event, and it is about so much more than books. From a low-key beginning in 1980 as a conference for 80 Jewish educators, Limmud has grown into a global, volunteer-led educational experience, with communities running events in over 40 countries. Nevertheless Limmud's flagship event remains its UK festival, the successor to the original conference, held during the Christmas break every year. Although it holds events all over the world, for most people the word 'Limmud' means its winter extravaganza.

It would have been inconceivable for previous generations of British Jews to put on an event like Limmud; its unabashed self-confidence is testament to the community's coming of age. Just as everybody else in the country is winding down, thousands of British Jews of all ages and religiosities gather for an educational, cultural and social retreat in a high-energy bubble, isolated from the rest of the world. Over the course of several days they choose from hundreds of sessions on the most diverse range of topics: lectures, comedy, dance, music, religion, creative workshops, film screenings, self-help sessions. The only thing connecting them is that they all fall under a very loose, Jewish rubric. The sessions are delivered by festival attendees who have come from all over the world, one of the principles of Limmud being that anyone can deliver a session if they want. Some are experts in the subjects they are lecturing on; others present sessions for no reason other than that they enjoy it. You don't have to be a professional presenter or educator; you don't even need to have any communication skills at all. Though if you are really no good, you risk people not turning up to your session, or getting bored and walking out.

For a long time Limmud was held on university campuses, where the residential and conference facilities were ideal for its still relatively young attendees. As the festival grew in popularity and its age profile widened, many of the older participants opted for the greater comfort of local hotels rather than the basic facilities provided by a university hall of residence. So Limmud moved to Birmingham's National Conference Centre, with its more upmarket hotel and conferencing facilities. It was more comfortable, but some felt the event had lost the informal intimacy of a university campus.

Apart from a very small professional team, Limmud is wholly volunteer-run. Everything is done by people freely giving their time. And the list of things to be done is formidable: everything from the allocation of accommodation to programme planning, dealing with contractors and logistics, providing meals for thousands of people, running children's activities, staffing the crèche, welcoming arrivals on site and, of course, recruiting more volunteers. Some enthusiasts devote years to volunteering at Limmud; others try it once and find it all too much. Limmud has won prizes for its volunteer-led leadership model; it has become a role model for other organizations hoping to learn from its example.

Limmud has now been running for 40 years. There is no indication that its popularity is beginning to wane. It is more than a global network of events, more than a flagship British winter festival. Limmud gives those who participate, whether as volunteers, presenters or just as attendees, a sense of belonging. Ezra Margulies has presented sessions at Limmud and has been involved for some time as a volunteer on the programming team. We were talking about how it felt for him, as someone who grew up in France, to be Jewish in Britain. He told me he liked being part of the Jewish community, but he didn't mean 'the community in the big sense of the term'.

What he liked was being part of an organization like Limmud or his local synagogue. 'It gives me a feeling of belonging.'

Jews in the UK have never been monolithic in their political opinions. Between the wars the predominantly working-class immigrants voted for parties on the left of the political spectrum, mainly for the Labour Party, though many chose to support socialist and communist candidates. But the families who had been here longer, who referred to themselves, only half in jest, as Englishmen of the Mosaic persuasion, did not share the immigrants' political concerns. Most Jewish MPs before the Second World War belonged to the Liberal or Conservative parties and represented constituencies not populated by the Jewish masses.

As the immigrants grew prosperous, and the former Englishmen of the Mosaic persuasion dissipated into the general population, the community's political attitudes changed. A Jewish Policy Research report published in 1996 showed that the political preferences of the Jewish community fell significantly to the right of the general population. This, said the report, was not surprising given the higher than average proportion of British Jews in middle-class occupations. But when middle-class Jews were compared with their peers in similar social and occupational groups, British Jews were consistently positioned on the left. Jewish professionals and business people still retained some of the left-leaning tendencies of their parents' and grandparents' generations, and were far less likely to vote Conservative than their non-Jewish colleagues.[10] The Labour MP Margaret Hodge pointed out to me that between the end of the Second World War and the 1970s around three out of every four Jewish MPs represented the Labour Party. Even now, she still perceives a radical cultural edge to being Jewish.

By 2010 the rightward drift was even more evident. Now the Jewish population was evenly split between Labour and Conservative, with younger people tending towards Labour and men more likely to vote Conservative than women. Seven years later support for the Labour Party had almost completely evaporated: 72 per cent of Jews intended to vote Conservative and only 17 per cent Labour. The anti-Semitism crisis in the Labour Party clearly had much to do with this, but it is likely that the rightward trend would have continued even if Labour's dull-minded anti-Semitic bigots had not emerged from obscurity.[11]

The dramatic shift in voting patterns over the course of the last generation or two can easily lead to the conclusion that the Jewish community has fully integrated into the middle classes. And there is no doubt that there are many prosperous middle-class Jews. But that is not the full picture. The former Labour MP Luciana Berger, who represented the voters of Liverpool Wavertree in Parliament for nearly a decade, says it is a mistake to describe the community as just being in the upper socio-economic bracket; she knows from her experiences as a constituency MP that many Jews experience the same financial and social pressures as everyone else. Jewish charities run food banks, and many synagogues hold weekly collections to support local families who are unable to manage financially. Poverty and deprivation are as endemic in the Jewish community as they are anywhere else.

Unlike the USA, where there has always been talk of the Jewish vote, Jews in Britain have never voted as a faction. But one of the consequences of Jeremy Corbyn's leadership of the Labour Party was that during the 2020 general election, for the first time in British history, there was clear evidence of a

Jewish vote. After the shocking treatment she received as a Labour MP, Luciana Berger stood for the 2020 election as a Liberal Democrat candidate. The Liberal Democrat Party assumed that if she ran in Finchley and Golders Green, the constituency with a higher number of Jewish voters than any other, solidarity and sympathy would propel her back into Parliament. They were banking on a Jewish vote. And they were nearly right. Many Jews turned out for her, and she soaked up the Labour votes, doing better than any previous Liberal Democrat candidate in the constituency – increasing the Liberal Democrat vote share by 25.3 per cent. But she was unable to win over enough Jewish Conservative voters. For many people the fear of splitting the Conservative vote and possibly helping Jeremy Corbyn to win the election was just too great. Dull-witted, far-left anti-Semitism had the last laugh, generating enough fear to keep a prospective Jewish MP out of Parliament.

The Jewish community's rightward drift was no doubt one of the factors that led Mayor Ken Livingstone to decide he could disregard the feelings of his Jewish constituents in 2006. Nevertheless, his boorishness came as something of a surprise. It was no secret that, like many on the left, he was an opponent of Israel, angered by the situation of the Palestinians. Indeed, many British Jews held similar views, even if they didn't go so far as to praise jihadi theologians. And it is no secret that, like other forms of racism, anti-Semitism has never been far below the surface in British society. But what nobody expected was that anti-Semitism would rear its vacuous head in a mainstream political party, particularly the left-leaning, avowedly anti-racist Labour Party. But it turned out that Livingstone's spat with the Jewish community over *Simcha* on the Square was just an early chapter in what would become a crisis of anti-Semitism that grew steadily worse once Jeremy Corbyn was elected Labour Party leader.

Corbyn, a man with few leadership skills and a track record of voting against his party in Parliament, never expected to be leader of the Labour Party. Ironically he was elected to the post on the heels of a fraternal struggle of biblical proportions five years earlier between two Jews, a battle for leadership of the party, in which Ed Miliband defeated his brother David. Ed, playing the role of Esau, had come to power on the back of trade union support even though David, the incarnation of Jacob in our metaphor, was generally regarded by party members and MPs as the divinely ordained heir to Labour's leadership, the man most likely to restore the party's crumbling fortunes. When Ed confirmed the popular view of his abilities by leading the party to yet another electoral defeat and resigned as leader, Corbyn surprised himself and the country by winning the contest to succeed him.

Of course, neither Ed nor David thought it ironic that after two Jews had battled for the leadership, the mantle was subsequently thrown over Corbyn. As Jeremy Corbyn himself explained, Jews do not understand British irony. He later claimed that he didn't mean all Jews, just Zionists. As if that made somehow absolved him of causing offence.[12]

Corbyn succeeded Livingstone as the politician British Jews most loved to hate. Like Livingstone, he had been critical of Israel and had expressed support for Palestinian terrorist groups. His candidacy to be Labour leader was criticized by pro-Israel politicians and by those in the Jewish community who immersed themselves in political affairs, but for most left-leaning Jews in the early days of his leadership the jury was still out. It wasn't until Jewish Labour MPs themselves complained about receiving anti-Semitic abuse from members of the far left, Corbyn's key supporters, that most people started to take notice. And it wasn't until Corbyn, devoid of empathy, proved reluctant to support his embattled MPs, that he was firmly identified as part of the problem.

To their horror, Jewish Labour politicians found themselves under attack for their ethnicity, reviled on social media, abused at local party meetings and insulted in public. Noticeably it was the women MPs who were attacked, rather than the men. Dame Margaret Hodge, one of those who bore the brunt of the attacks, puts it down to misogyny. She says she is regularly subjected to hate on three fronts, as a woman, as a Jew and because she is older. She quotes research carried out by the American data scientist Seth Stephens-Davidowitz which found that 60 per cent of threads that mentioned feminism on the far-right hate site Stormfront also mentioned Jews. She and Luciana Berger were mentioned on the site more frequently than any other Jewish politicians.[13]

The abuse, vilification and death threats directed at Labour's Jewish women MPs began with online attacks on Luciana in 2014. Six years later, the Equalities and Human Rights Commission published the results of an inquiry into the Labour Party that it had begun three years earlier. It found that the party had breached the Equalities Act on two occasions, and was responsible for unlawful acts of harassment and discrimination.

Margaret Hodge is no stranger to racial hatred. In the 2010 General Election, long before Corbyn damaged the Labour Party, she fought and dramatically won a bitter and unpleasant election battle against the neo-fascist British National Party. But her Jewishness had not been a particular factor in that fight. In fact, she says, she had always considered herself a Labour MP who happened to be Jewish. It wasn't until Corbyn came along that she found herself turned into a Jewish MP.

Ten years after Margaret's battle with the BNP, the anti-Semites on the extreme left of Corbyn's Labour Party made no bones about their similarity to the far right. They got hold of a flyer full of slurs and abuse that the BNP had used against her ten years earlier, and posted extracts from it on social media.

Margaret attributes left-wing anti-Semitism to a convergence of factors. 'First, if you're anti-capitalist, that's where all the tropes about Jews being really wealthy, from Shylock to the Rothschilds, come into play. And if you're anti-capitalist, and you have this trope about all Jews are rich, then it's very easy for that to morph into anti-Semitism. And because the ultra-left are anti-imperialist and anti-West, the Israel–Palestine conflict feeds into their outlook. It becomes a sort of totemic symbol of terrible Western imperialism. Again, that morphs very quickly into anti-Semitism. I think it's that mix, together with the fact that they just do not understand the unique nature of anti-Jew hate.'

She has developed strategies for dealing with the hatred. 'I've been in politics a very, very long time. And one of the bits of advice I give to young, aspiring people is that you've got to learn how to compartmentalize your life. It's one thing if it's about work, if people attack you because of your position. It's not personal, it's the position that creates the abuse.'

Luciana Berger detects a more personal dimension to the abuse directed at her and her fellow women MPs. It was the women, she said, who were most willing to put their heads above the parapet. She won't be drawn on why this was, but she is clear that the issue of not taking the concerns of Jewish members seriously started in the early days of the Jeremy

Corbyn leadership period, and that it fell to her and her women colleagues to protest against it.

As with Margaret Hodge, the Corbyn period was not Luciana's first political experience of hatred. She was confronted by anti-Jewish discrimination even before she was an MP, when she was first selected, at the age of 28, to stand as a candidate in Liverpool. She was the Director of Labour Friends of Israel at the time. When her candidacy was announced, those who opposed her selection seized on her political support for Israel (albeit with the left in Israel) to try to delegitimize her selection.

Luciana was brought up in a Jewishly committed family. An active member of a Jewish youth group, she says that one of her formative experiences was spending a week on a summer camp learning about *tikkun olam*. Literally meaning 'repair of the world', *tikkun olam*, of which we will hear more soon, is a contemporary Jewish term for social action. 'The whole concept of repairing the world is an important one, and we all play our part in different ways. Whether it's within our immediate families or our communities, or whether it's for our country, the world or the planet, playing my part was a value and principle that was instilled within me from an early age. I think about it often when I consider how my Jewishness might inform my involvement and engagement, and, perhaps in part, why I put myself forward to be a public representative.' She says she was always the person at school who took on the responsibility of organizing charity and community activities. 'I had sporty friends and drama friends, but I was the one that organized the charity days, and organized the visits to local old people's homes.'

The anti-Semitic abuse Luciana suffered, and the Labour leadership's refusal to deal with it, forced her out of the party.

She says she doesn't have any regrets about leaving the party that she had worked so hard for throughout her political career. 'I can look at myself in the mirror. And I knew that there was no way that I could go in good faith and knock on doors in any future election, and say, "Vote for me" and possibly get Corbyn into number 10.'

'There is no question' says Robert Winston, who sits on the Labour benches in the House of Lords, 'that Corbyn was a cataclysm; it was a catastrophe, the final nail in the coffin of the Labour Party. It had a radical effect on Jewish attitudes. And Corbyn doesn't understand it.' Nevertheless, he did not think of leaving the party during the Corbyn years; it did not change his fundamental attitude, 'Either you believe in a different kind of society from what you've got or you don't. And I felt also that Jews need to be inside the party to change it.'

Winston was created a life peer in 1995 and is a senior member of the House of Lords. He told me his being Jewish has been helpful, that he is respected for it. 'I think giving Jewish views and speeches, which I do a lot, as a non-rabbinical authority, is good. He spoke in support of the bishops when there was a question of whether they should remain in the reformed House of Lords. 'I argued that the bishops have a real place in our ethical judgements. And a lot of secular people in the House, friends of mine, thought I was ridiculous for supporting the bishops. I think supporting the bishops was worse than being Jewish.'

As a scientist, he finds that taking a religious attitude in Parliament leads to personal conflict. When there was a debate about assisted dying, he said he spoke against it, for non-religious reasons. But he abstained from the vote. He told his colleagues: 'I have a conflict because I'm Jewish.

And there's a Jewish view that assisted dying would not be acceptable. And therefore, I don't feel I can vote. Because I have a strong view that different religions should not be enforcing their view on a society which doesn't have the same religious conviction.'

If anything can be said in the Labour Party's favour under Corbyn's leadership, it is that none of his acolytes went so far as to try to vilify the Jews in Parliament. Unlike Alfred Raper, the Conservative and Unionist member for Islington East in 1918. In the wake of the Russian Revolution, Raper stood up in the House of Commons and reeled off the names of leading Soviet officials. 'Messrs Trotsky, whose real name is Bronstein; Zinovieff, real name Applebaum; Kamenev, real name Rosenfeldt; Radek, real name Sobelson, Steklov, real name Nakhamkes. ... Is it not a fact', he demanded, 'that the majority of these men are of Jewish origin, and further that these Jewish criminals, whom every decent Jew disowns, constitute the National Government of Central Russia?' Russia's government, Raper alleged a few days later, consisted of 'a band of discredited international Jews'.[14]

The roots of anti-Semitism stretch far back into antiquity. Most theories assume it began in the wake of the crucifixion and the early Christian notion of Jews as Christ killers. But there is evidence of anti-Semitism even before Christianity. In the biblical book of Esther, probably written in the fourth century BCE, the villainous Haman tells his king of 'a people scattered and dispersed among the nations ... whose religion is different from everyone else's, who do not keep the king's edicts. There is no benefit to the king in tolerating them ... let a decree be issued for their destruction.' He meant the Jews.[15]

We don't know whether the attitude of the quasi-fictional Haman was typical for his time, and it doesn't detract from the fact that it was the belief that the Jews killed Christ that fuelled Western anti-Semitism throughout history. But anti-Semitism soon became divorced from religion and took on a life of its own. The Second Vatican Council's *Nostra aetate* declaration in 1965, absolving Jews from responsibility for the death of Christ, had no impact on anti-Semitism. Modern churches are not bastions of anti-Semitism, and modern anti-Semites do not look to the Church to fuel their hatred.

Nor, it appears, did Alfred Raper. His hatred of the Jews was visceral – in his case, part of a wider political assault in the early twentieth century on 'alien' immigration, on foreigners contaminating British life with their unappealing ways. Raper's attitude was by no means atypical, and he was not the only prominent politician of his time to attack the Jews.

The early twentieth-century insults were largely met in silence by a Jewish community who still saw themselves as strangers on Britain's shores. Their silence didn't last long. By the 1930s, with the rise of the Nazi party in Germany, and fascism on the political agenda in Britain, Jewish opposition began to organize. In 1936, when the fascist leader Oswald Mosley announced that his Blackshirts would march through Stepney, the Jews and the Irish dockers joined forces to stop them, fighting a battle in Cable Street that has gone down in history as a turning point in the pre-war fight against fascism. And two years later Scottish Labour MP Manny Shinwell crossed the floor of the House of Commons to punch Commander Robert Bower in the face, after he had told him to 'Go back to Poland'. British Jews were learning to stand up to anti-Semitism. By the time Corbyn came along, they were ready.

The *Jewish Chronicle* led the media campaign against Corbyn. Week after week it published excoriating articles about what it termed the 'Labour Crisis'. In July 2018 it teamed up with its rivals the *Jewish News* and *Jewish Telegraph* to publish an identical front page, under the banner 'United We Stand', highlighting the threat that they feared would be posed to Jewish life in Britain should Corbyn become Prime Minister.

Most readers seemed to support the *JC's* stance, though not everyone was happy. A regular correspondent complained that the paper had turned a toxic social-media discourse and an intemperate discussion about the Middle East into an existential crisis for British Jews. Others accused the *Chronicle* of 'overstepping the bounds of measured and fair criticism', arguing that raising the spectre of Corbyn becoming Britain's first ideologically anti-Semitic Prime Minister went well beyond the evidence. One reader accused the *Chronicle* of making the Jews the story, rather than Corbyn and Labour. And another correspondent broadened the criticism, pointing to an unwarranted climate of fear among Jews and accusing the Board of Deputies, the Jewish Leadership Council and the Community Security Trust of missing an opportunity to reassure the community and allay fears. Many left-leaning Jews wondered whether Corbyn would have been reviled so extravagantly by the Jewish communal leadership if he had been a Tory.[16]

Stephen Pollard, the editor at large of the *Jewish Chronicle*, rejects such criticism. His fear was that if Corbyn's supporters could behave as they did in opposition, what would happen if they got into power? He speaks of having to strike a balance between hyping up the threat and scaring the community. 'I'm not saying we necessarily always got it right, but I think there was definitely a sense that the community as a whole was grateful to us for the way we campaigned on that issue.'

And he has no doubt about the vexed question of whether Corbyn himself was an anti-Semite or just a *nebbish* who found himself in a job bigger than he was. 'I don't see how you can surround yourself with anti-Semites, defend them, refuse to act against them and write and say the things that he has, and not be called an anti-Semite.'

Mark Gardner, chief executive of the charity the Community Security Trust, agrees. He describes how his perception of Jeremy Corbyn changed after the Enough is Enough demonstration in 2018, when hundreds of Jews were joined by Labour MPs outside Parliament to protest against anti-Semitism in the party. The demonstration must have shaken the Labour leadership, because for the first time Corbyn bowed to pressure and agreed to meet with a delegation of Jewish communal leaders.

Gardner speaks of going into that meeting thinking that Corbyn himself was not an anti-Semite and coming out believing the opposite. He says that Corbyn did not act reasonably. He makes the point that, when a reasonable, open-minded person is accused of saying or doing something racist, they will go out of their way to apologize and ensure that they don't repeat the mistake. But Corbyn did not do that in the meeting. He showed that he had no interest in the concerns that were raised. Gardner contrasts Corbyn's attitude with that of another Labour MP, Naz Shah, who apologized profusely after making an anti-Semitic comment, and went out of her way to learn and put things right.

And Chief Rabbi Mirvis says that he is in no doubt that the stance the community took during the Corbyn years 'has given inspiration not just to Jewish communities but to democratically minded people around the world to be tougher and stronger.

'The reality of anti-Semitism in the Labour Party would not have stopped the average British voter from voting for them, and if Corbyn had succeeded it would have had pretty negative consequences globally. I recognized very strongly that if we could succeed in our contributing towards stopping it, we would be acting in a highly responsible way. We were placed in a very pivotal historic role. I hear it from leaders globally. The former Canadian Prime Minister mentioned my role in stopping Corbyn. It's a huge compliment.

'And I get this hate stuff on social media every single day. They blame me for preventing Corbyn coming in. And they blame me for all the Covid deaths!'

Not all Jews disparage Jeremy Corbyn, and there are many who argue strongly against the charge that he is an anti-Semite. They tend to be on the left of the Labour Party, and they see the vilification of Corbyn as a right-wing media strategy that has no basis in fact. They dispute the idea that Corbyn's contacts and discussions with people from incendiary Islamist backgrounds is evidence of anti-Semitism.

Adrian Litvinoff is confident in his Jewish heritage and a supporter of Jeremy Corbyn. He grew up in an impeccably Zionist home; his father was the official biographer of both David Ben-Gurion, Israel's first Prime Minister, and Chaim Weizmann, the country's first president. But, like many supporters of Israel in the early years of the state, his parents became progressively less comfortable with Israeli politics as the 1960s progressed. He says he grew up with some of that awareness. 'The thing about Corbyn,' Adrian told me, 'is that he has always understood that we have to talk to our enemies to make peace. This idea that we don't talk to terrorists is just baloney. His relations with Palestinian leaders and organizations do not make him anti-Zionist, even less so anti-Semitic. He spoke to them because he recognized that sooner or later we are going to have to.'

If that is the case, I wanted to know, why did Corbyn get such a terrible press? 'We have to talk,' said Adrian, 'about the colossal distortion of public perception through the media that has been aimed at him, on a scale that I don't think any other politician in living memory has had to cope with.' He reminded me that, a few weeks before we spoke, a councillor in Yorkshire had posted a fake image suggesting that Corbyn was mourning the terrorist who had bombed the Liverpool Women's Hospital. The councillor had agreed to pay an unspecified amount of damages, which Corbyn said he would donate to charity. This, Adrian said, was just one of many deliberate misrepresentations of Corbyn in relation to terrorism. He told me about research which shows that up until 2015, until the time that Corbyn became the leader of the Labour Party, a ProQuest newspaper database on press articles mentioning Jeremy Corbyn and anti-Semitism, returned 18 responses, all reporting Corbyn opposing anti-Semitism. After 2015, once Corbyn was party leader, the same search returned 6,133 responses, the vast majority negative.[17]

Whether or not Jeremy Corbyn is personally anti-Semitic is not really the issue. We only have to listen to those Jewish Labour MPs who were abused by anti-Semites in their party to appreciate the depth of the problem. If we are generous, we can say that Corbyn was just not up to the job of being leader and was unable to stop the abuse. But we are not always generous, and we might ask, did he even try?

The Jewish community in Britain is becoming more polarized, both politically and in terms of religion. Louise Jacobs, the chair of the United Jewish Israel Appeal, which tries among other things to encourage young people to connect with Israel, feels that the chasm between the political left and right is growing within the community and is connected to religious outlook. She says that when she sits in educational seminars listening to young people from the progressive wing of the community and those from the more orthodox movements they have plenty in common, but she hears very different outlooks regarding their relationship with Israel. The progressive religious movements largely align with the political left and the orthodox with the political right. And this spills over into a wider political outlook that reflects the divergence of opinions in society at large. The different strands of the religious community are educating their children in ways that support different political outlooks; neither wing seems to be encouraging them to think critically for themselves, or to open up to divergent views and to make up their own minds.

Left-wing political thought has always had a minority place in the Jewish cosmos, and the Vashti website is one of its newest, most prominent outlets. The website's name is taken from the biblical book of Esther, the book in which the paradigmatic anti-Semite Haman features. In the book Vashti was a Persian queen who was put to death for refusing her husband's demands that she come to his all-male bacchanalia to show off her charms to his drunken friends. In biblical terms she is an independent-minded, feminist icon, willing to sacrifice her life for her dignity and values.

The website Vashti is edited by Rivkah Brown. Like many young Jews of her generation, she aspires to a Jewish identity that conforms to her values, satisfies her politically and spiritually, and reflects the person that she is. She was brought up in a middle-of-the road, observant family, attending a Jewish primary school, Jewish youth groups and summer camps. As a teenager she switched from the orthodox Jewish Youth Study Groups movement she attended and joined Noam, run by the more progressive Masorti movement. 'Religiously, I suppose, my progress through Judaism has been gradually more progressive, and now I identify, not denominationally, but as a very progressive Jew, a liberal Jew, but not with a capital L.'

She says she is now engaging with her Judaism eclectically, taking part in religious and political activities run by organizations she identifies with. Like Na'amod, a Jewish group who oppose the Israeli occupation of the Palestinian West Bank, and the subversive Jewdas, who describe themselves as an 'alternative diaspora'. When I spoke to her, she was just beginning to learn Yiddish with the radical, community language school Babel's Blessing. She describes the Jewish identity that she is now creating for herself as a patchwork.

'I guess, like many people of my generation, I've learned that the template for being a north London Ashkenazi Jew comes with quite a lot of things that I'm not comfortable with.' These include, she says, a quite unquestioning relationship to Israel and, until recently, a very critical attitude towards the Labour Party. 'Those things have alienated me from the Jews that I grew up with and the Judaism that I grew up around.'

Vashti, Rivkah says, is an answer to some of the questions that that Jewish people like her have been asking. 'It is an attempt to create, not just a politics of the left but a culture of the left. How do we create this kind of Judaism, make this patchwork of practice, political activism and social connections coherent?' She feels that the Jewish world suffers from a conservatism, a political stagnation that stems from a crisis of identity, an uncertainty as to how Jews should define themselves in the wake of the Holocaust and the establishment of Israel. Allegiance to Israel, she says, cannot be the sole secular definition of contemporary Judaism. Nor should anti-Semitism. Jews cannot siphon themselves off from other groups. They can't simply say, 'we are going to fight anti-Semitism.'

The challenge that Vashti faces is that, whereas old-fashioned Jewish radicalism was largely fought in the arena of class politics, today's radicals are faced with so many different issues that it is far harder to deliver a cohesive message. Vashti's potpourri of thoughtful, provocative articles embraces gender issues, the Israel–Palestine conflict, anti-Semitism, racism, workers' rights, the environment, religion, Islamophobia and much more. The range of topics indicates the scale of the challenge for people like Rivkah Brown, who are trying to create a space in which a self-identifying, Jewish left movement can convene and cohere, 'a Jewish left-wing culture that recaptures the spirit of Cable Street and the [nineteenth-century leftist-anarchist London newspaper] *Arbeter Fraynd*'.

There have always been Jewish radicals in Britain, Jewish activists on the left of politics, and they have always been a small minority in the Jewish community. They continue to be a small minority. But the interesting difference between the new Jewish radicals and those of previous generations is that in the past they were radical despite being Jews; today the radicals present themselves as such because they are Jews, a manifestation of their confidence in their Jewish identity.

Speaking to Rivkah put me in mind of something that Ray Simonson of JW3 told me. He and Rivkah operate in completely different spheres, with completely different agendas. But they have something in common. They are each creating ways to engage Jews in conversation.

2

Life

In the old days, until about the 1970s or '80s, if you wanted to eat a meal in a kosher restaurant, you'd have found your choices severely curtailed. Not just because there were very few such restaurants, but because those that you could find offered very similar, traditional, Eastern European Jewish menus. It didn't matter where you went, the options would have been largely the same: chicken soup, salt beef with latkes, chopped liver, *gefilte* fish, a choice of sweet, overcooked carrots or cabbage and, for dessert, *lockshen* (noodles) or *matzah* pudding. The food was homely, comforting and heavy, and the waiters usually rude; it was part of their charm. They knew better than you what you wanted to eat, and weren't shy about telling you, if they weren't too busy arguing with each other. If they spilled soup on you, it was your fault, you shouldn't have moved. If you said you were vegetarian, they would have been completely flummoxed.

Of course, things were little different in typical British restaurants at the time – apart from the rude waiters. The choices were just as limited: the standard dishes included meat and two veg, fish and chips, bangers and mash or steak and kidney pie. Vegetarians had to make do with a salad or an omelette. Standard Britain restaurants had a reputation for terrible food.

British dining out habits began to noticeably change in the late 1960s and 1970s. Restaurants serving Chinese and Indian food began to open up in the high streets; other cuisines soon followed. And it wasn't long before kosher cuisine started to diversify too. By the late 1970s it was possible to eat a kosher Chinese meal in London. And today, in most Jewish enclaves, you can get a kosher meal in almost any international cuisine, though there is a noticeable dearth of restaurants serving the old Eastern European menus. Our eating habits have changed. We are not so keen on cholesterol any more.

One of the key principles of kosher eating is that dishes containing milk, or indeed milk itself, cannot be eaten alongside meat. As a hedge against this happening, there are strict protocols to ensure that there is not even the possibility of milk and meat coming into contact with each other. Kosher meat-eating households keep separate sets of pans, crockery and cutlery: one for meat dishes, one for milk. And kosher restaurants tend to only serve dairy or meat dishes. Although it is theoretically possible for a restaurant to serve both, the logistics of keeping everything separate are so complex that very few establishments even try. Kosher restaurants are either meat or dairy. And their cuisines differ accordingly.

The days when kosher restaurants were few and far between are long gone. Between them, London's twin Jewish enclaves of Hendon and Golders Green contain something like 30 or 40 kosher restaurants, cafés and takeaways; it is impossible to be precise about numbers because they come and go at quite a rate. Up the road, Edgware has its fair share too. For those who fancy a meat meal, there are grills, burger bars, Chinese restaurants, American diners and delis. If you prefer dairy restaurants, there is Israeli and Mediterranean food: salads, pastas, pizzas, vegetarian dishes and fish. There are fish restaurants, falafel bars, sushi bars, pizza takeaways; nobody goes hungry in Jewish north-west London.

To be kosher, fish has to have scales and fins. So shellfish are not kosher. But kosher fish can be eaten in all restaurants, dairy or meat; as far as kosher regulations are concerned, fish is neither meat nor milk. It falls into the large *parve* or neutral category, alongside things like vegetables, fruit, hummus and falafel, all of which can be served alongside meat or dairy foods.

Until Covid there was even a kosher restaurant where tourists could get a shabbat meal. For decades one of the London Jewish community's most ignoble qualities was that, unlike many other cities across the world with far smaller Jewish populations, religious Jewish tourists could not get a kosher meal in a restaurant on shabbat, the one day in the week when eating well is an almost mandatory activity. Kosher restaurants did not open, because food cannot be cooked on shabbat, and money cannot be handled. So to serve shabbat meals, a kosher restaurant had to prepare all the food before shabbat begins at sunset on Friday, and take advance payment. For London's kosher restaurateurs, it was just too much hassle. And probably unprofitable as well. Why should they give up their day of rest?

An alternative was to go to a synagogue and hope that someone there would be hospitable enough to invite you back to their home to eat. But there was no guarantee. So religious tourists tended to buy food for their shabbat meals on Friday or have a kosher caterer deliver them and eat in their hotel rooms. But in 2018 the new Tish restaurant in Belsize Park, in what the *Jewish Chronicle* called a first for Britain, started offering shabbat meals. Sabbath-observant Jews do not drive on shabbat, and Tish is a bit of a walk from the central London hotels, but it was better than nothing. Unfortunately, Tish stopped offering shabbat meals during Covid, and at the time of writing they have not yet restarted. If and when they do, London will no longer be one of the most inhospitable Jewish cities in the world. As far as food goes, anyway.

Any restaurateur who adheres to the dietary laws can technically claim that their restaurant is kosher. However, most kosher restaurants choose to place their kitchens under the watchful supervision of one of the various orthodox synagogal bodies that certify the food is indeed kosher. Although an observant Jew is expected to believe anyone who says their food is kosher, the whole process of supervision has become so ingrained in Jewish life that very few people would fully trust a restaurant that claims to be kosher but is unsupervised. Supervision makes commercial sense.

Supervision is carried out by an inspector who checks that the ingredients sourced by the restaurant are fully kosher and that food preparation is carried out to the appropriate religious standard. In return, the supervising authorities issue a certificate of *kashrut*. Of course, there is a cost involved, which is invariably passed on to customers in the form of higher prices. Kosher food tends to be more expensive than any other, partly because of the supervision costs, partly because the market is small, with little opportunity for economies of scale. And partly because of production costs: animals are slaughtered individually in a very specific manner, not slung onto a production line in a factory-style abattoir.

Many Jews are not concerned about their food being strictly kosher. Some may eschew pork and shellfish, but they are relaxed about less onerous restrictions like the mixing of milk and meat. What they do want, however, is to eat an old-fashioned Jewish meal, the sort of cholesterol- and sugar-heavy cuisine we are all supposed to avoid. So although the old-fashioned Eastern European menus have more or less disappeared, there are a few so-called 'kosher-style' restaurants where you can get salt beef, chopped liver or pastrami and still have milk in your coffee afterwards. You can even get a cheeseburger – a dish that could never be served in a supervised kosher establishment. But these *faux* kosher restaurants seem to be a dying breed. Harry Morgan's in St John's Wood High Street, the most famous of London's kosher-style restaurants, closed its doors forever during the Covid pandemic.

Food is very important in Jewish culture. Every festival has its own signature dishes, as does shabbat, the weekly sabbath. On the table set for a shabbat meal on a Friday evening are two plaited, glazed, soft loaves of bread, known as *challah* (the word means 'loaf' in Hebrew). They are usually covered with a decorative cloth. The meal begins by removing the cloth, making a blessing if you are that way inclined, then breaking one of the loaves and passing the pieces around to everyone at the table. It doesn't really matter how religious you are: if you are planning a shabbat meal, then you will almost certainly go to the baker's on a Friday to buy your *challah*.

There are many Jewish bakers. Most specialize in cakes, biscuits, bagels and conventional loaves as well as *challah*. But it is *challah* that gives a baker its reputation. So much so that even in an area with several bakers there will be one, like Daniels bakery in Temple Fortune, which will have a queue stretching down the street on a Friday morning. No matter that you could get in and out of the quieter baker next door or down the road with your two loaves in the same time as it takes to progress even a few places in the popular baker's queue. Why this should be is not at all clear; there is not really that much difference between one baker's *challah* and another's, or indeed between their cakes and bagels. It must just be that some shops are better than others at understanding how to attract and retain customers.

Buying Jewish food has never been easier. Apart from the restaurants, delis and takeaways, there are the kosher superstores, where you can find almost everything that is stocked in a regular supermarket (apart from the bacon), but with a difference. There are two kinds of kosher store. There are those where the queue at the checkout stretches back as far as the eye can see, where, just as you are about to reach the front, someone will push in front of you saying, 'You don't mind, do you? I've only got a few things', while heaving a basket containing more than yours onto the conveyor belt. And there are those where customer service is taken to unimaginable extremes (for a Jewish shop), where every checkout has both a cashier and someone who will pack your purchases and, if required, carry them to your car. The queues in those shops can be just as long, because many more people prefer to shop there. But they move a lot faster.

If you are not used to kosher shopping, many of the brands will be unfamiliar. Like the food in kosher restaurants, the packaged, edible goods on a kosher supermarket's shelf have been prepared under religious supervision and they carry a stamp or logo showing that they have been certified as conforming to all the dietary laws. Because the kosher market in Britain is relatively small, most British food manufacturers do not even consider applying for kosher certification. So many of the goods come either from Israel, where nearly all the manufactured foods are certified as kosher as a matter of course, or from the USA. Apparently, over 40 per cent of all packaged food in the USA is certified as kosher, owing to an assumption that kosher means healthier, a somewhat exaggerated claim that the kosher food industry in the States is in no hurry to disabuse.[18] In the bigger supermarkets you may find fancy cakes and chocolates from France, where of course they know how to prepare food, and kosher wines from all over the world.

The blossoming of the kosher wine industry is a new phenomenon in the Jewish world. There is nothing in a normal bottle of wine that might inherently make it non-kosher, but the religious prohibition against wines of non-Jewish origin goes back to ancient times, when Judaism was battling against paganism and idolatry. In order to ensure that nobody drank wine that had been produced for use in an idolatrous ceremony, the Jewish legislators prohibited all foreign-made wines.[19] To be kosher, wine had to be produced by Jews, or at the very least, to come from a vineyard in which Jews had a commercial interest.

Most of us today have never come across a wine intended to be poured out at the feet of an idol, and in some orthodox circles opinion is divided over whether foreign wine is still prohibited. Nevertheless, kosher wine, containing no hint of idolatry (or indeed not contravening any other of Judaism's complex agricultural prohibitions), has become big business.

Even as late as the 1960s there was only one brand of kosher wine generally available in Britain: Palwin, bottled in London's East End by the Palestine Wine Company. The wine was only used for ritual purposes, to be drunk at the

Passover meal and for *kiddush*, the ceremony recited at the shabbat table just before the *challah* is passed round.

Palwin made several wines. Their varieties had no names, just numbers, which according to legend corresponded to the numbers of the bus routes that passed through London's East End. Palwin number 10, the only variety that survives today, is sickly sweet, because a bottle that is only poured out in one glassful on a Friday evening has to last for several weeks without turning to vinegar, and only a very sweet wine can do that. In time other sickly sweet wines came onto the market, followed during the 1970s by kosher French table wines. And then in the 1980s Israelis, who had previously imagined that their climate was not conducive to fine wine-making, began to discover that by using the right grapes and viticultural technology, they too could produce top-quality wines. Today the wine section of a kosher store, with vintages from all over the world, looks little different from any other supermarket. It's just that all the wines they stock are certified as kosher. So there is no need to bother learning about the historical or legal principles of what makes a wine kosher, or to ascertain just how lenient or severe the prohibitions against foreign wines really are, in an age where idolatry has long been forgotten.

The kosher meat industry has also revolutionized in recent decades. The basic regulations about kosher meat are that animals that do not have split hooves and do not chew the cud are prohibited. Famously this means that Jews do not eat pigs; less famously, they also do not eat rabbit, hare, wild boar, horse, camel or many other exotic foodstuffs. And even among those species that they do eat, they are not to eat the blood. When an animal has been slaughtered according to kosher requirements, it is then drained of its blood, rinsed, soaked and salted to draw out any residue. Each of these steps is minutely choreographed: the meat should lie in salt, for example, for a full hour. Liver, which is heavy in blood, needs further preparation, by broiling it over a flame.

In the old days, most of this was done at home. The slaughterer drained the animal of its arterial blood, and after that everything else was done by the consumer. I remember my grandmother beating slabs of liver even after all her other preparation, to make sure that every last drop of blood was wrung out. But today, unless you are particularly scrupulous, none of this is necessary. The kosher meat you buy will come ready prepared, all ready to cook. It has never been easier to buy and eat kosher meat.

Mass kosher catering is a specialist art, not to be attempted by someone unversed in the peculiarities of preparing a kitchen for kosher use, or the complexities of preparing kosher meals. It is a job for a kosher caterer, a small, specialist industry that comes into its own at celebratory events: weddings, barmitzvahs for 13-year-old boys, and batmitzvahs for 12-year-old girls. Even though many families are not too bothered themselves about whether the food is kosher, they are likely to use a kosher caterer, because the chances are there will be some guests who only eat kosher meals.

As at all such events, the number of guests, the menus and the venues will depend solely on the celebrants' budgets. Parties – or *simchas* – can range from a small, modest buffet in a synagogue hall to a lavish production, more an event than a meal, in a five-star hotel, or even in an aircraft hangar, film studio or sports stadium. The space will be completely transformed into whatever film, literary or sports theme the family has chosen; the entertainers will perform from a stage that makes the Oscars look cheap; the tables will be decorated with elaborate sculpted centrepieces; and there may be breakout rooms with play stations and TVs for kids who are getting bored, a kids' disco and adult dancing, the finest of fine wines and, of course, food and drink that surpass anything even your wildest imagination could conjure up. The chances of having a decent conversation with your neighbour, above all the noise and excitement, are pretty slim.

Of course, top-of-the-range *simchas* cost an extravagant amount of money to put on, so the market is restricted to those who can afford them and, in the case of barmitzvahs and batmitzvahs, to those who can afford to do the same for all of their children as they reach their age of majority. Putting on one of these events is not easy, not just because of the cost but also because of the competition. The kids who are celebrating will invite all their friends, and as they are all of a similar age, every child will go to every other child's barmitzvah, and so will their parents. And if you belong to a circle in which money is no object, and if you and your friends are all competitive by nature and you want to put on a spectacle for your child's barmitzvah or batmitzvah, then you dare not skimp on originality. Every parent who puts on a *simcha* wants theirs to be different, to be the one that stands out, the one that everybody remembers.

Lavish, over-the-top events, with costs running as high as a small mortgage, are fine for the very few who can afford them. But their son or daughter will invite friends, or family members, whose parents are not wealthy, who either can't afford to compete or, just as likely, are repulsed by the idea of splashing around so much money. Most families wouldn't even consider putting on an event of this scale. But even ordinary functions can work out very expensive, once all the trimmings – the photographer, entertainers, new clothes, hairdos and whatever else – are added to the catering costs and venue charges. They create tremendous pressure on families. So recently there has been a backlash to these opulent events. The Covid lockdowns, when large gatherings were banned, gave it impetus. Many people now choose to just have a small party in their home, or somewhere else equally modest, and very few find that their kids resent it.

Fully integrated into British society, Jews do the same jobs as everybody else. There are Jewish plumbers, scientists, removal men, musicians, engineers, care workers, beauticians, entertainers, jockeys; there is no secular career that is specifically Jewish, and there doesn't seem to be any area of work that Jews have not gone in for. But, perhaps for historic reasons, a greater proportion of Jews are self-employed than among the wider population.[20]

When the great waves of Jewish immigration took place towards the end of the nineteenth century, many of the new immigrants were religiously observant. They would not work on Saturdays or on Jewish festivals. Since Saturday working in those days was still very much a feature of British life, and flexible working had not yet been invented, religious Jews had to choose between giving up their observant lifestyle, looking for employment with a Jewish company that would give them Saturdays off or working for themselves. Those who worked for themselves included tailors, market traders, furniture makers, bakers and shopkeepers. Some of them established small family businesses; a few grew into household names.

Several of the early immigrants left London to become itinerant pedlars, selling their wares from door to door. Some, like Michael Marks, founder of Marks & Spencer, or, in the USA, Marcus Goldman and his son-in-law Walter Sachs, became tremendously successful. Most did not.

Goldman Sachs, Levi Strauss and, until its collapse in the 2008 financial crisis, Lehman Brothers are all examples of global corporations founded by Jewish traders. Marks & Spencer, Tesco and Burton (formerly Burton the Tailor) are the somewhat scaled-down British equivalents. Quite a few Jewish families will tell you with regret about an ancestor who turned down a request from Michael Marks to invest a small amount of money in his first shop. Either Michael Marks spent an inordinate amount of time tapping up potential investors or the story is a Jewish urban myth.

Jews do all sorts of jobs, but a disproportionate number are employed in white-collar, middle-class careers, often as doctors, bankers, lawyers or accountants. These are stereotypical Jewish careers, a stereotype that, according to a well-known online encyclopaedia, portrays Jewish lawyers as being greedy, exploitative and dishonest. As if non-Jewish lawyers weren't!

The story is told of the Jew who became Prime Minister. He told his mother, who shrugged, nonchalantly. He took her with him to meet the Queen. She went, reluctantly. The Queen said, 'Mrs Cohen, you must be so proud. Your son's the Prime Minister!' His mother shrugged again. 'Prime Minister? What's the big deal? His brother's a doctor!'

Medicine has always been a Jewish profession; in medieval times, when rabbis pursued their vocation unpaid, many earned their living as physicians. And in England, when the children of the immigrant generations won scholarships to university, a good proportion elected to study medicine. It was then that the problems started. They qualified as doctors, then found to their dismay that they could not get hospital jobs. They could get work as general practitioners, but it was almost impossible for them to find training as a specialist. The only doctors who got hospital jobs were those who hid the fact that they were Jewish, as indeed many Jewish doctors did.

David Katz, Emeritus Professor of Immunopathology at University College Hospital in London, told me the story, an apocryphal tale, he says, about Lord Max Rosenheim, a distinguished Jewish doctor who qualified in the 1930s and became president of the Royal College of Physicians in 1966. As a young man he applied for a job at University College Hospital. In those days appointments at the hospital had to be based on unanimous decisions by the senior medical staff; if any consultant dissented, the candidate would not be appointed.

Rosenheim was interviewed and given the job. 'Then two of the surgeons said: "We realized he was the best candidate; we had no option but to approve him. But we will never set foot in this place again." And they continued to stay on the staff but did not go into the hospital. And that was in the 1930s. The whole thing was sinister.'

David Katz was born in South Africa. He says that, when he came to Britain in the 1970s, there were quite a few Jewish medical organizations. He went to some of their meetings and came away disillusioned, feeling that their attitude to the British medical establishment was too obsequious. The final straw for him was when he heard a Jewish doctor defend a well-known member of the House of Lords, a pillar of the British medical aristocracy, against an accusation of anti-Semitism. 'He is not anti-Semitic at all,' this doctor said, 'he always sees the Jewish private patients I send him.'

20 years after he arrived in Britain, David was invited by Dr Lotte Newman, a pioneering London GP, to join a medical committee set up by the Board of Deputies.

Advances in medicine were throwing up new, religiously challenging, ethical issues; there were things that Jewish doctors needed to discuss. It would have been chaotic to try to coordinate these discussions among the plethora of Jewish medical organizations; what was needed was a single forum, consolidating all the different groups into a single body. Of course, the politics of bringing everyone together wasn't easy. But, as the head of an academic department, David was well placed to make it happen; he had a far broader overview than anyone else of the Jewish medical landscape. After much cajoling and persuasion, he and his associates achieved their aim. And so the Jewish Medical Association was born.

The Jewish Medical Association is not a religious body, and it doesn't try to impose ethical views on its members. But, like the members of other minorities, Jewish doctors are often asked, out of curiosity, to explain their faith's view on a particular medical or ethical issue. Such questions may be asked of any Jewish doctor, irrespective of their knowledge of Judaism, and the answers they give are not always correct. David told me about a highly eminent Jewish medical academic, with very little religious knowledge, who would confidently assert in public discussions that embryonic stem cell research was forbidden by Jewish law. He was wrong – it is not – and David says he had to put him right. So, alongside its primary function as a networking body and professional club that puts on events and lectures, the Jewish Medical Association also serves as an educational forum, a place where doctors can get to know a little more about their faith and its values.

The JMA is an example of how the British Jewish community has grown in confidence, no longer inhibited about standing up for itself. It provides a safe space in which medical professionals can express their opinions about Jewish issues, such as faith or Zionism, more robustly than they may feel they can do in public. They need that space: surveys of NHS staff indicate that Jews are subjected to greater harassment at work than other minority groups. Apart from the Muslim community, they experience religious discrimination more frequently than any other minority. Understandably, they may feel that the workplace is not the best place for them to discuss things that might open them up to anti-Jewish abuse.

Despite the harassment that many Jewish medical professionals experience, when the General Medical Council set up its Black and Minority Ethnic Forum, the JMA was not invited to join. David Katz says that the Forum's Chairman, Lord Singh, lobbied hard on the JMA's behalf but was rebuffed. 'They didn't see us as an ethnic group; in their eyes we were the establishment. They believed that we were the power group that oppresses them and that there is no discrimination against Jews for jobs. All of which is a joke. I did manage eventually to persuade them to accept us. The reason can be said in one word: Corbyn.'

The medical profession does seem to be more Neanderthal than most in the way it responds to the needs of minority groups. At a recent inter-faith forum attended by members of the JMA, a Muslim doctor presented several examples of how minority groups struggled to maintain their identity in the face of inflexible attitudes in the profession. Two of his examples concerned Jewish medical students who asked to be granted leave of absence from classes on the Day of Atonement, Yom Kippur. One was told that it was unacceptable for them not to attend classes, and, notwithstanding the fact that Jewish law prioritizes the saving of lives over religious observance, the student was told to think seriously about continuing the course and pursuing a medical career if religious observance was ever going to take priority over medicine. The other student was told by the course organizer that absence on Yom Kippur without a medical certificate would result in them failing the entire course. Their university refused to intervene.

One shocking example is that of a Jewish student who was six months pregnant. Her course organizer asked her, in front of her whole group, if she knew what gender her baby would be. When she said it would be a boy, he asked the group whether she should be allowed to try to kill this child, in the same way as she had tried to kill his older brother by circumcising him when he was eight days old.

Nicola Rosenfelder, a consultant oncologist at the Royal Marsden Hospital in London, recalls that, when she started working as a doctor over 20 years ago, she found herself reluctant to ask for Saturdays off, even though she was observant and would not usually travel on shabbat. She says that after working a Friday evening to Saturday morning night shift, she would sit in her on-call room in the hospital, on her own, reading a book until shabbat was over at nightfall, as it was too far to walk home.

Fortunately, things have changed now. Religiously observant Jewish doctors are generally able to negotiate working patterns with their colleagues, so that they can get the time off they need for festivals and shabbat.

Nicola told me about the experience that she and many Jewish doctors had in May 2021, when Hamas were firing rockets from Gaza into Israel and Israel was bombarding Gaza. As always happens when there is a flare-up in the Middle East, anti-Semitic comments started to appear on social media. Like other Jews, Jewish doctors found themselves on the receiving end of the abuse, often coming from other medical practitioners. They responded by creating informal WhatsApp groups, sharing details of the messages and reporting the abuse they received from other doctors to the statutory bodies that regulate the medical profession.

The WhatsApp groups also turned out to be very useful medically. Nicola describes them as an enormous multidisciplinary team meeting 'where you have many experts from different fields'. She says the groups were particularly helpful in the early stages of the Covid pandemic. The instant connections that the technology offers provided support for many of the group members. 'And if someone asks for a recommendation for a specialist, or an opinion on a clinical matter, they will receive lots of suggestions within moments.'

Medicine ticks all the right boxes for a Jewish career. It is a caring profession, well paid, thoughtful and prestigious. People respect doctors, and generally listen to them. Few are the Jewish parents who do not want their child to become a doctor or to marry one, or both. And yet the number of Jewish students choosing to study medicine is decreasing. Nicola Rosenfelder says that, when she went to medical school, she was the only Jew in her year.

In part this is due to a change in the demographics of medicine over the last few decades. Jewish doctors today are much more likely to be women than in the past; indeed more than half of the medical students today are women. Nicola talks about working in an environment that is frequently dominated by women. She thinks this may be due to the flexible working patterns that medicine offers, and the relative ease of part-time working.

Nevertheless, it seems that medicine has lost some of its appeal for Jews. Parents do not encourage their children to become doctors in the way they once did. Nicola told me that when she trained to be a doctor, every other doctor she spoke to, with the exception of one woman, told her that if they had their time again, they wouldn't go into medicine. 'I think the pattern of medicine passing down from generation to generation may be less prevalent nowadays. I wonder why that is and whether it is due to the degradation of the profession, in terms of working patterns and paperwork.'

Robert Winston trained as a doctor before going on to do medical research, pioneering new treatments to improve in vitro fertilization, helping thousands of childless women to have babies. He developed methods of screening embryos for genetic diseases and presented BBC TV programmes on science and medicine for many years. He is now Professor of Science and Society at Imperial College. I asked him how being Jewish had influenced his career.

His short answer was that being Jewish had affected his ethical approach to science and the way he communicates it; he said he sometimes illustrates his lectures to students with Talmudic quotes. He gave his long answer by telling me a story about the 1985 Parliamentary bill which, if passed, would have restricted embryo research and would have seriously impeded work on treating and improving fertility. He spoke against the bill in Parliament and led the opposition to it in the press, radio and TV.

'What actually stumped many of the opponents to this research was that I said: "I come from basically the same religious root as you, albeit a bit older. And you use the same liturgy as we use. And you have the same principles about the protection of life that we have. But we don't believe that the embryo actually is a full human being."' He quoted

Talmudic examples that stressed the Jewish concern for pregnant mothers and their unborn children, pointed out that Thomas Aquinas had adopted a similar position and used religious arguments from the Catholic background. 'And they were completely nonplussed. They couldn't deal with it. I said, 'This is a pluralistic society. I'm not trying to enforce my religious views on you, you shouldn't be trying to do it with me either, if we're to have a proper democratic society. It was a very powerful argument. And I think being Jewish was very helpful.'

He told me about a visit to his lab by the former Chief Rabbi Immanuel Jakobovits. He spoke to the 60 or so scientists there, only one of whom was Jewish. 'He argued about the status and ethics of the human embryo and he was obviously quite conflicted about whether or not it was human. It was interesting that the Chief Rabbi was showing that there is no certainty about any of this stuff. He was arguing something which was deeply rational, very persuasive, and it was extraordinary how much respect the atheists in the group gave him.'

Although there are thousands of Jewish doctors, nobody in modern Britain has ever accused the Jews of controlling medicine in the same way as they are falsely accused of controlling the media or the banks. Even the most stupid anti-Semite is unlikely to refuse medical treatment just because their doctor is a Jew.

The old canard that Jews run the world's banking and financial systems has roots at least a thousand years deep, going back to a time when the Church prohibited Christians from lending to each other on interest, and local rulers excluded Jews from most trades and professions. Christians in need of a loan were forced to turn to the despised, infidel Jews, and the Jews, in desperate need of a livelihood, lent them money on interest. Nobody likes repaying loans, and often it is difficult to do so. Debtors grew to resent their Jewish creditors, piling hatred upon hatred until the image of the Jew became synonymous with that of a crooked, depraved usurer. As the centuries passed and the financial system grew in sophistication, so did the stigma attached to Jewish financiers, until they were accused not just of usury but of controlling and manipulating the entire financial system.

It's nonsense, of course. Richard Bolchover, who started working in banking before the Big Bang of 1986, when the way the City worked was irrevocably changed, gave me a potted history of Jewish involvement in Britain's financial sector. He says that prior to the Big Bang there were relatively few Jews in the City (compared, for instance, with Jews in law firms servicing the City), partly because there were pretty rigid sectarian divisions in the way the sector was organized. Jews had opportunities like everyone else, but these opportunities were constrained. 'If you were a Jew, or even, in fact, if you were Catholic, you would probably go to one of the Jewish firms, basically Rothschild, Warburg or Samuel Montagu if you were a banker, Smith New Court if you were a jobber, Strauss Turnbull if you were a broker and so on. Very few Jews would be employed by firms like Schroeder or Baring; they just really didn't employ Jews. Everyone in the city, apart from those in the Jewish firms, seemed to have come from four schools, either from Harrow and Eton or from two East End comprehensives, so-called barrow boys, who knew how to trade.'

Then the Big Bang happened, when Margaret Thatcher shook everything up. 'She said: "This is ridiculous, we're doing away with all of that, anybody can own anything, even foreigners." And there was this mad scramble, the Americans came in, Goldman Sachs and JP Morgan, everybody was bought and it all changed. More Jews arrived. But arguably it had been more Jewish before then, because there had been these identifiably Jewish institutions, of which only Rothschild's remains today as an independent.'

Richard began his career at Samuel Montagu, a bank created in 1853. Born in Liverpool, Samuel Montagu, the bank's founder, who later became Sir Samuel and eventually Lord Swaythling, was a profoundly religious man, whose Judaism, according to his daughter, was a discipline from which he did not stray 'for a single instant'.[21] Three decades after he established his bank he entered Parliament as the Liberal MP for the strongly Jewish constituency of Whitechapel. A member of the 'Cousinhood', the few wealthy, almost aristocratic Jewish families who ran the community's institutions in the nineteenth century, he worked tirelessly for the poor immigrant families. In 1903 he set up a dispersion committee to ease the overcrowding in Whitechapel by offering jobs and subsidies to families who were willing to move to smaller towns around the country. He has been described as the poor man's Rothschild.

Richard says that when he worked at Montagu, the bank still retained an echo of its Jewish origins but the firm was hardly characterized by its Jewishness. The only real concession to its history was that Jewish members of staff who requested it were given employment terms that allowed them four days off for Jewish holidays, in addition to their normal holiday allowance. 'It was specified in my contract, that I was entitled to these four days off as paid leave: two for New Year, one for Yom Kippur and one for the first day of Passover.'

Of the few City institutions that were thought of as Jewish, Rothschild's was probably the one that least conformed to the stereotype. And it is even less visibly Jewish today. Bernie Myers spent most of his career there. He says that the external perception of the bank as Jewish hardly matches reality. When he started at the bank, every member of the staff was given a turkey for Christmas, with kosher turkeys being given to the few Jews who worked there. The only visible concession to the bank's Jewish heritage was that every year at Passover no bread was served in the dining room. Nor was pork ever served, even though the dining room wasn't kosher. Of his six former colleagues on the senior management team only two were Jewish. And the bank had an office in Abu Dhabi long before it had one in Tel Aviv. He says it was different, though, in the bank's New York branch, which, like the city itself, was full of Jews. He said that everyone he walked past looked like his cousin or his uncle.

Bernie's journey towards a career in the City was fairly typical for his generation. He was born during the war, one of three brothers. His parents were not particularly well off, and he says that they only had one aim for their children: to get an education and enter a profession. His mother wanted him to be an actuary; his headmaster predicted he would become an accountant. His headmaster was proved right. Bernie studied at the London School of Economics, toyed with becoming an academic and then joined a large accountancy firm in the City. Then he was headhunted to run the corporate finance department of a newly arrived American bank. When he told his boss that he was leaving, the reply was: "I'd like you to stay, but if you're going, go somewhere that will teach you, rather than you teaching them. Go to Rothschild's, go to Warburg's, go to Samuel Montagu."

And he actually set the interviews up for me. Out of all of them, Rothschild's was the one that was appealing.'

Of course, there are many Jews who work in the City, in the banks, hedge funds and private equity. But there are people there from every background; all they have in common is that they are bright and ambitious. And if Jews really do control finance, how come there have only been two Jewish Chancellors of the Exchequer in modern times? One of whom had the misfortune to preside over the 1987 financial crash?

It seems that today the City is losing its appeal even for the smartest and most ambitious. Technology has become the sector of choice for those who would once have gone into finance, Jews included. Those Jews who go into the City today, who work for firms like Goldman Sachs, tend to do so almost as a rite of passage, as a credential to enhance their CV, before moving on to more eclectic careers. Because, like many others today, most young Jews are more interested in a career that gives them a good work–life balance than one which pays a fortune but works them to the bone. Bernie says that he will be very surprised if his grandchildren have the same sort of career that he had. 'My guess is that the Jewish world will not be vastly different from the wider world. The City was for a period the place to be. I don't think it is necessarily seen to be that any more. There's logic in that; I don't think the money will be there as it was before. And the City is a tough life.'

Alan Jacobs qualified as a solicitor and worked for a large, very English law firm before moving into banking. He agrees that the City is not dominated by Jews, but he does think that they wield an influence in finance that is disproportionate to their numbers. 'The internationalization of flows of capital generally has benefited the Jewish community, because we are international by our very nature. We see that by the number of Russian Jewish oligarchs, a strong influence from the Swiss Jewish community and also South African Jews who have come to the UK and are very international in their outlook.'

Alan's first job in banking was at J. Henry Schroder Wagg & Co., a firm with German origins. He describes seeing himself, probably unfairly, as one of a handful of 'token' Jews in the firm at the time. In 2000 Schroder's became part of Citigroup, one of the largest financial institutions in the world, which, owing to the intricacies of various acquisitions, was run by a Jewish management team. 'So, if you were really looking for a Jewish conspiracy, you could say "Here's one", because the company became progressively more Jewish.'

I asked Alan whether what he had told me gave credence to the admittedly mindless accusation that there is an international Jewish conspiracy to control money. He was scathing in his reply. 'No one controls money. It's quite clear from what happens in the world that even countries don't have control over money. No individual bank does. It's a nonsense to suggest, in a world where capital moves around as quickly as it does, that there is a conspiracy or that anyone has control. It's undoubtedly the case that being Jewish does give you a certain number of automatic connections, like it does with anything in business. You're part of a club. But, on the other hand, being part of that club means you're not part of other clubs.' And there are many clubs in the City: old school networks, college alumni, masonic lodges. Any Jewish networks in the City are just a few among many.

One aspect of the club mentality is a willingness to help others succeed. Alan sees this as a defining attitude among those Jews who move in financial circles. 'It seems to me that Jews in the City are well disposed to help fund the next generation, the generation after that and their businesses. It's a recurring cycle. I see young people coming in and raising money to do things or have people backing them. There is a desire to ensure that prosperity continues into the future.'

There is no international Jewish banking conspiracy, and Jews do not dominate any of the professions. But it does seem that a disproportionate number of them do become high achievers in their fields. The corollary of a history of dispersion is that most Jews have something of an international outlook, with relatives and friends across the world. A network that transcends national borders, one that knows and has access to the right people in the right places across the world, is a great boon in a globalized economy. But it comes with an insecurity, a repressed but occasional worry that the country we have always assumed to be our home may one day turn out to be just another temporary sojourn on the journey to who knows where. And that insecurity is a factor in the complex psyche of the high-achieving Jew. Status and reputation may count for nothing when the knock comes at the door. But striving to achieve helps. Success is a powerful antidote to fear, but fear still stalks British Jewry. One only has to pick up a copy of the *Jewish Chronicle* to see how much anxiety there is still about anti-Semitism, even though most Jews have had no direct experience of it.

The *Jewish Chronicle* is the oldest Jewish newspaper in the world. First printed in 1841, it is widely considered to be the newspaper of record for Britain's Jewish community. Once affectionately known to Britain's Jews as '*The Chronicle*', these days it calls itself the *JC*. For over 60 years its masthead pronounced that it was the 'Organ of British Jewry'. They removed the slogan when the zeitgeist turned it into a double entendre.

The *JC* has reported on all the major events in British Jewish history. It has often played a pivotal role in shaping those events. During the First World War, when the future of Palestine was an international subject of debate and a divisive topic in British Jewry, the *Chronicle* sided with the pro-Zionist lobby. In an article headed 'A Grave Betrayal' it attacked a manifesto published by the anti-Zionist presidents of the Board of Deputies and Anglo-Jewish Association, accusing them of being at odds with the mass of Jewish opinion in the country, which was staunchly pro-Zionist. The *Chronicle*'s condemnation led to the resignation of the president of the Board. When the British government committed itself to supporting a Jewish state in Palestine, in a document that became known as the Balfour Declaration, the announcement was timed so that it could first be proclaimed to the world through the *Jewish Chronicle*.

It was the *Chronicle* that first alerted the nation to the extent of the slaughter in Nazi Germany. On 11 December 1942 it brought out a black-bordered issue with the headline 'Two Million Jews Slaughtered. Most Terrible Massacre of All Time'. Over the next three years the paper campaigned for the opening up of Palestine to refugees and for a Jewish army, and in 1944, when it became clear that the Allies would neither bomb the railway tracks leading to Auschwitz nor take decisive action to prevent the deportation of Hungarian Jews, it declared, in a voice of frustration. 'Slaughter Passes Unnoticed'.

Despite presenting itself as the 'Organ of British Jewry', the paper had no inhibitions about taking sides, when it suited it, in communal disputes. It played an influential role in the Jacobs Affair of the 1960s, British Jewry's most damaging dispute, when Rabbi Dr Louis Jacobs was ostracized by the mainstream orthodoxy body, the United Synagogue, for his theological views. William Frankel, editor of the *JC* and a friend of Jacobs, ensured that the controversy remained in the public eye week after week. It has often been said that without the *JC*'s intervention, the controversy might never have happened at all. The *Chronicle* would certainly have sold fewer papers.[22]

Most recently, the paper led the communal campaign against Jeremy Corbyn. Stephen Pollard, the paper's editor at the time, believes that, although the affair was unpleasant, it had the effect of bringing the community together, helping its members to realize that, notwithstanding its internal divisions, the outside world does not distinguish between different types of Jews 'other than, in their view, good Jews and bad Jews'.

The Corbyn controversy dominated the *JC*'s pages for over five years, from before his election as leader of the Labour Party until well after his trouncing at the ballot box and subsequent resignation in 2019. Without the controversy, the *JC*'s content would have been far less interesting. Pollard, who is now the paper's editor at large, suggests that all his journalists would have had to write about would have been the changing nature of British Jewry: the growth of the *haredi* community and its implications for communal life.

It is not easy running a Jewish newspaper. Within their community Jews are notoriously fractious, unafraid to state their opinion, quite happy to argue for their point of view. There will always be readers who disagree with editorial decisions, who think a particular story shouldn't have been run or that an article should not have been framed in a certain way. They have no qualms about expressing their discontent. Stephen says that, if there was a story on the front page about a Jew doing something bad, he would get at least half a dozen complaints accusing him of washing the community's dirty linen in public. They would tell him that he should know that 'they' hate the Jews already, that he shouldn't give 'them' more ammunition. He says he got that a lot. But he accepts there is a fine line that he had to be sensitive to. There is little doubt, he says, that, however unfair it may be, stories about the most egregious Jewish malefactors can affect the way that Jews are perceived in the outside world.

Shortly after he was appointed editor there was a news story about a *haredi* child abuser. 'And to me, it was definitely a front-page story. Because, you know, it was pretty horrible. And I remember somebody in the newsroom saying "No, don't put it on the front page. We don't do that sort of thing." And I remember thinking, "I'm afraid you do now."'

Stephen Pollard says that editing a newspaper is about as much fun as one can have: 'It's a bit like having a grown-up train set.' The job does have its stresses, though. 'Especially if you're writing for an audience each one of whom thinks that they could do a better job than the *schmuck* who is actually editing it. Still, a lot of the reactions I get are sweet, meant only for the best of motives. Walking down the street, it would never occur to people not to come up and talk to me. Even if I'm just out with the kids, and we just want to go on the swings. They want to come and talk about the latest news or this, that or the other. I can't say, "I'm busy."'

As his reaction to Jeremy Corbyn shows, Stephen is very focused on the dangers of anti-Semitism. But the threat to today's Jewish community is not just from outside. There is also the arguably more insidious, internal threat of assimilation, of British Jewry gradually dissipating and disappearing as it becomes absorbed into the mainstream of national life. It happens on an individual and family level the whole time; it doesn't take much ingenuity to imagine that a tipping point may be reached, after which the decline becomes irreversible.

Assimilation and intermarriage are almost universally regarded as the greatest contemporary threat to the continuity of Judaism. But assimilation is nothing new, and it is useful to look at it in context. In his acclaimed biography of the philosopher Martin Buber, Paul Mendes-Flohr quotes a letter that Buber received in 1908 from a Jewish law student in Prague. The letter was an invitation for Buber to speak at an event being put on by Prague's Jewish Students' Association, aimed at assimilated Jews in the city. The writer of the letter bewailed 'the lamentable process of defection that was particularly rampant among Jewish denizens of Western European urban centres'.

Although we have no data to compare past rates of assimilation with today, the chances are that the level of atrophy is far greater now than previously. But assimilation has been going on throughout Jewish history, it is not necessarily something to despair about. It may be painful for families to see their kids abandon their identity and traditions, but erosion of minority cultures is a natural process. And Jewish life seems to have resisted the consequences of assimilation far better than other minorities; there are many examples of the children and grandchildren of those who have left the fold seeking to reconnect with their roots. The same cannot be said of other early immigrant communities. These days we never meet a Huguenot or a Palatine. Buber himself married a Catholic woman, although she did eventually convert.

I asked Stephen which he saw as the greater threat: anti-Semitism from outside or assimilation from within. He told me that as a newspaper editor he has to focus on the real threats, rather than those that so far only exist in potential. 'I think it's entirely appropriate that people worry about people marrying out and that kind of stuff, if they define Judaism, as a lot of people quite rightly do, through the religious aspects of it. But I think that if people assimilate and the community does get smaller, there is a still a baseline that we will not go beneath. I'm less worried about that myself.'

Jonathan Freedland has been writing for the *JC* since 1998 and is the most politically left-wing of the paper's regular columnists. He recognizes that his political perspective differs from other opinions in the paper, but sees little point in hiding his views. And he praised Stephen Pollard as a genuinely pluralistic editor. 'He didn't change a word I wrote. When I'd pitch an article that I knew was the opposite of his view, he'd say, "Great, that's really good." Often he'd give it the prime slot and trail it on the front page. Even though I knew it was not his view.'

For much of its history the *JC* was the glue that held the community together. Ostensibly a news medium, arguably its more important role was as to connect people in an age that had never heard of social media. For years it scattered two-line bulletins across its pages, reporting on the medical progress of communal figures who were known to be unwell. The *Chronicle* was where you found out who had been born, who was marrying and who had died, its 'Social and Personal' announcements sometimes running to three or four pages of small, closely spaced print. These were the pages that most readers turned to first when it dropped through the letterbox on a Friday morning. But, like most print media, the *JC* struggles to thrive in an age of digital communication. Today it sometimes carries only enough personal announcements to fill a quarter page of large, widely spaced type. Its circulation has fallen dramatically, from a peak of 63,000 in 1989 to just over 20,000 in 2017. Though it is still the case that each copy is read by more than one person.

The decline in the *JC*'s circulation is not just due to digital media, nor is it because of increased competition. It reflects the dissipation of the Jewish community, the fact that assimilation into the wider social sphere has loosened the communal bonds. For many British Jews, although their Jewish identity is important to them personally, taking an interest in the wider Jewish community, reading about it in a newspaper, is no longer central to their lives.

When those who accuse the Jews of controlling finance want a bit of variety, they are likely to accuse them of controlling the media. It's an absurd charge. But there is no doubt that Jews are astonishingly over-represented in the media. As someone who has spent much of his career working in the media, Stephen Pollard is well aware of this. 'You can't get away from that. But it's not *because* we're Jewish. It is because we're *Jewish*. It's because some of the characteristics of Jews are the characteristics of people who end up in certain professions. Look at the law. Look at all kinds of different professions. There are more Jews than you would expect, given our relative population. It's because Jews revere education; the whole of Judaism is built on study. We are beginning to see the same phenomenon in some Asian communities, who are becoming disproportionately represented in the professions as well.'

Jonathan Freedland, who is also a *Guardian* journalist and the longest-serving columnist both there and on the *JC*, has a theory about why Jews might punch above their weight in the media, with Jewish journalists accounting for a solid chunk of the opinion pieces published in the quality British press, even though Jews constitute only around 0.5 per cent of the population. He says it's because Jews are somehow liminal, living to some degree on the borders of mainstream society. 'And there is a perspective, a kind of insight, that you have when you are ever so slightly on the edge, when you are on the outside looking in. There is something about that vantage point that does equip Jews, I think, to be programme makers, correspondents, commentators.'

I asked him if he felt that Jews in Britain see themselves in that way, as being on the edge, as different from everyone else. He agreed that was probably the case, although the cultural make-up of British society today is such that everyone feels different in some way. There is little embarrassment or shame in feeling different now, in contrast with the experiences of earlier generations of Jews. Jonathan's father, the late Michael Freedland, was a pioneer in Jewish broadcast journalism. In the 1970s and 1980s he hosted a programme on BBC Radio London called *You Don't Have To Be Jewish*. Yet, although there were many other Jews working at Radio London at the time, Jonathan says that his father was the only one there who was 'out' as Jewish. 'I remember him saying that the other Jews on the radio station were really uncomfortable with his programme, and worried it would sort of rub off on them, that it would somehow make people think "Oh, shouldn't you be working on the Jewish programme?" They didn't like it.'

The change that Jonathan describes, between Jewish self-perception in his father's generation and today, where most Jews feel no different from any other minority, is yet another indication of the theme that I kept coming across as I was writing, that British Jews today are far more comfortable with who they are and far more prepared to stand up for themselves, to celebrate their Jewishness, than previous generations. It's not just because Jews have changed: it reflects an evolution in Britain too, the budding of a mature multicultural society. And if Jonathan is right, it is a process of which we are only at the beginning: 'I've seen a perception among the young, those of university age, that one can only claim moral authority if one is some kind of outsider or even victim. It's a way of saying, "Look, I'm not of the mainstream establishment."' If this holds, it means that Jews' historic experience of being victims will no longer be a source of shame for some Jews, but will be something that can be admitted and even valued.

Jonathan Freedland noticed the change in Jewish self-perception when he returned to Britain after living for some time in the USA. When he had been at university, he says, the logo for the Union of Jewish Students was three lower-case letters: ujs. 'It was very discreet. It didn't say what it was, you had to know what it was.' When he returned to England from the USA, a new logo had found its way onto T-shirts. 'The word "union" was in small letters. Then in huge, banner-high letters, the word "Jewish". Then "students", again in small letters.'

This change took place over the course of around 15 years. And then there was Corbyn. And like so many others that I have spoken to, but perhaps even more significantly because he is a respected political commentator, Jonathan sees the Corbyn years as profoundly empowering for Jews. 'It's one of the great ironies, that one of Corbyn's most lasting contributions will have been the binding and unifying effect he had on British Jewry. I think that's going to be of interest to historians, because that period banished the quietism of the Cable Street period, once and for all.'

He says that he has seen evidence of this generational change on the *Guardian* too. When he started there, he was almost always the only journalist on the paper who felt comfortable raising Jewish issues or explaining things in a Jewish context. Now he has other Jewish colleagues, who have no inhibitions about expressing their Jewishness.

Hadley Freeman told me that Jewish journalists on left-wing papers get a lot of abuse. It comes from two directions: from the hard left, whose opposition to Israel contains more than a smattering of anti-Semitism, and – to a much lesser degree – from Jews themselves who regard the *Guardian* as prejudiced against Israel. She says it feels easier to be a Jew in the right-wing press than on the left. 'It's funny to me,' she says, 'because the early twentieth-century Jews were seen as very Bolshevik, very left-wing, Jewish communists. And now, working on a left-wing paper with a lot of very left-wing readers, I find that Jews are seen as right-wing, they're seen as capitalists.'

It is, she told me, strange being a Jewish columnist on a left-wing paper at this time. 'If you do have a connection to Israel, and if you believe in Israel's right to exist, it is complicated.' She has family in Israel. One of her cousins ran a school for Israeli and Palestinian children, helping to foster relations between the two communities, until he was targeted by both sides and had to flee.

Hadley told me that she had to go to the police a few years ago because she was getting so much anti-Semitic abuse that she was worried about her family. 'I started getting a lot of abuse from anonymous accounts, you know, telling me to go into the ovens, you know, all the Holocaust stuff.' But she emphasizes that, when she wrote about anti-Semitism in the Labour party, she was the target not of abuse but of anger. 'I don't want to confuse the two. For me, abuse is anonymous accounts telling you to go to Auschwitz. But people shouting at you, or just disagreeing perhaps unnecessarily strongly, not accepting that two people can see things differently in good faith, that's just anger.'

Even so, she was surprised to receive abuse from the left. She says she can deal with right-wing attacks, and with sexist attacks, but because she considers herself as being on the left she wasn't prepared for attacks from her own side. 'I think that was the big surprise.'

She says it's interesting that the same people who are so supportive of the Black Lives Matter movement were the ones who were dismissing Jews when they were saying, 'Hang on, this Corbyn guy looks quite anti-Semitic.' It's as if identity politics has nothing to do with Jews. 'I think Jews feel a strong sense of identity. But the idea of identity politics is all about supporting minority groups who are generally oppressed. And I don't think people see Jews in that way.' It is almost as if Jews have been in Britain for so long, and have established themselves so well into the fabric of the society, that they are no longer seen as a minority community. Until, of course, the zeitgeist changes and hatred once again rears its head, as has happened in recent years. She says that she understands why Jews are not seen as vulnerable. 'As minorities go, we are pretty well off. But that didn't protect Jews in Germany in 1930.'

Hadley takes issue with the blanket assertion that Jews are not oppressed. She says it depends on what one means by 'oppressed'. If it means that one's life chances are reduced or social mobility stifled, then Jews are not oppressed. But if it is that one gets abused because of one's minority status, then Jews certainly are. 'Any Jew who puts themselves forward is going to get some anti-Semitic abuse; it happens all the time.

I don't feel like I'm oppressed. But that doesn't mean other people don't try to oppress us.'

Being Jewish invites other criticisms too, attacks that are not necessarily anti-Semitic. She has interviewed Woody Allen a couple of times and written articles defending him against accusations of sexual abuse. Readers wrote to her saying that she defended him because she was Jewish. 'Even though I have written pieces condemning people like Weinstein, Epstein, Madoff, all our "great" representatives, I still get "You defend Woody Allen because you're Jewish." I get a lot of that from Michael Jackson fans, because I've interviewed his victims. And Jackson fans turn round and say "You condemn Michael Jackson, but you defend Woody Allen, because you're Jewish."' She thinks that, because she has written so much about being Jewish and about Jewish culture, there are some readers out there who are just looking out for her to write something that gives them a reason to pounce.

Hadley Freeman was born in New York, where Jews and Judaism are ubiquitous. She arrived in the UK when she was 12 and lived in west London, where Jews are far thinner on the ground than they are in other parts of the city. The contrast between New York and the part of London she lived in, the fact that she had to go out and look for Jewish life and culture rather than having it all around her, has shaped her perspective of what it means to be a Jew. She describes herself as a 'terrible Jew', by which she means that she is not particularly religious. But of course, there are many ways to be a good Jew, only some of which involve religion. And she does belong to a synagogue, sends her children to Hebrew school and enjoys being part of a Jewish community. 'I love Jewish culture and how it has shaped the modern world, whether it's in literature, in the cinema or in music: the three titans, Dylan, Leonard

Cohen and Paul Simon. I just think it's fascinating. I love that whole cultural side of things. One of my favourite recent pieces was writing about the representation of Jewish women in American movies. That stuff just thrills me. I love it. And if I'm seen as the Jewish female voice on the *Guardian*, well, that's fine. That is who I am.'

Like any newspaper that serves a small constituency, the *JC* has always struggled financially. When it hit trouble in 2019, it was bailed out by a consortium of donors put together by the then Jewish Leadership Council (JLC) chair, Jonathan Goldstein. Stephen Pollard told his readers that the future was assured. 'Here's to the next 178 years', he wrote.[23] But a year later, when the Covid pandemic hit, the country was locked down and advertising revenues dried up, it was apparent that the bail-out funds could not do the trick. The paper went into liquidation. So did its nearest rival, the freesheet *Jewish News*.

But Jews are nothing if not enterprising. The owners of the two papers put their heads together and came up with a plan to buy the papers back from the liquidators, and to merge them into a single journal. They were pretty confident that their bid would succeed; they had adequate funds, and they knew that nobody else was likely to be interested: who would be foolish enough to buy two struggling titles in the middle of a pandemic?

To their great surprise they were pipped at the post by the most unlikely of consortiums, backed by money the source of which was not declared, and fronted by Robbie Gibb, Theresa May's former Director of Communications, who is not Jewish. The victorious consortium promised to pay all creditors in full, and to declare the origin of their funding in due course. Stephen Pollard insists that the funding comes from a Jewish source, and that the consortium, which now comprises the board, is there to make sure the paper is efficiently run. But he concedes that the old model, under which the *JC* was run as a business, is no longer viable, that the consortium have followed through on their pledge to invest heavily in the paper, even though they will not get it back. The *JC* has joined the ranks of every other Jewish community newspaper; it is now supported philanthropically.

The takeover at the *JC* caused some concern within the community. That the bail-out funds came from an anonymous donor did not sit well with those who felt that a community newspaper should be transparent and chaired by a member of the community. In April 2021 the *Sunday Times* reported that, although the consortium had promised to repay all the paper's creditors in full, a year after the takeover there were still 300 contributors who had not been paid and the source of the funding had still not been disclosed. It rhetorically asked Robbie Gibb if he would care to comment, and quoted Alan Jacobs, the *JC*'s former Chairman, who at the time of the takeover had accused the consortium of a 'shameful attempt to hijack the world's oldest Jewish newspaper'.[24]

Alan Jacobs is now a trustee of the *Jewish News*, which has been bought by the group that failed in their bid for the *JC*. They bought the *Jewish News*, he said, because they felt that there was a need for a newspaper that was lighter, and 'less fixated on the Labour Party'. So that if the *JC* did drift rightwards and slip into what Alan described as 'we're not quite sure this represents us territory', there would be 'another newspaper up and running with more of a focus on the centre of the community'.

The rightward drift that Alan anticipated does seem to have taken place. The paper appears little more amenable to the Labour Party than it was in the days when it was battling Jeremy Corbyn. This strengthens the view that the *JC*'s new owners bought the paper as part of a political strategy. There are various opinions on where the paper's funding comes from: the name most frequently heard is that of the late Sheldon Adelson. Adelson, who died in 2021, was an American billionaire who donated generously to many Jewish causes. He was also Donald Trump's largest backer, reportedly giving hundreds of millions of dollars to the ousted president's re-election campaign. The rumours about Adelson may be wrong, there are other candidates in the frame. But whoever it is, the secretiveness is not reassuring. It all feels a little over the top. It's only the *JC* after all.

Richard Ferrer is the editor of *Jewish News*. He was disappointed that the merger with the *JC* did not proceed; he felt that yoking the *Jewish News*'s community focus to the *JC*'s historical brand would have resulted in a very powerful combination. Richard was disappointed on a personal level too; had the merger proceeded, he would have edited the new paper. He says he was appointed as editor on a Tuesday and then on Thursday 'one of, we believe, Sheldon Adelson's associates came along with a higher offer. Since then it's veered to the right, in a very odd way.' He knows that this shift in the *JC*'s editorial focus should create an opportunity for his paper but is sanguine in accepting that it is hard to prevail over nearly 200 years of history.

When *Jewish News* began publication in 1997, it was known as the *London Jewish News* and was seen as something of a mouthpiece for the centrist orthodox United Synagogue. Richard, who joined the paper in 2009 expecting to only stay for a few months, has moved it to a religiously neutral position, where, he says, he will publish any view, whether it's to the left or to the right, 'as long as it is rational'. It is a reasonable policy, probably the only way to represent the totality of Jewish views in a community that is becoming increasingly amorphous. 'There has been a great expansion among the younger generation of Jews who have no affiliation towards Israel, and who seem inclined towards left-wing politics. And as a result, the right has also expanded greatly. To the point where I don't quite know what the term "Jewish community" means any more.'

Richard is not the only person I spoke to who finds it hard to define what the Jewish community is, who has difficulty in tracing its contours and boundaries. But as the editor of a paper that aims to cater for this shapeless thing called the Jewish community, his dilemma is far from academic. It affects the very style and content of his publication. He recalls that when he was in his teens, in the 1980s and 1990s, it was pretty much taken for granted that one's affinity to the Jewish community went more or less hand in hand with one's affinity to Israel; the two were pretty much symbiotic. That is no longer the case. The bond between Britain's Jews and Israel has weakened, particularly among those who are not involved with Jewish organizations or who do not have kids in Jewish schools. Israel is no longer a vulnerable, pioneer enterprise, reliant on the diaspora for financial support. And the novelty of a Jewish state has worn off; it no longer seems as remarkable as it did a generation or two ago. These things serve to weaken the commitment of British Jews to Israel. And then, Richard says, 'you've got those *haredim* who do not even accept the idea of a secular Jewish state'.

Richard identifies weaknesses in the infrastructure of British Jewry as another factor in the incoherence of that which we call the Jewish community. 'The Board of Deputies is anathema to many, especially to the younger generation.

Try sitting through a plenary session and keeping your sanity; it's incredibly difficult. I have to do it, unfortunately. And again, in the whole Corbyn debacle, they seemed to be very backwards in coming forwards. The JLC uses its money for influence; the Board is unwieldy and out of date. And everyone's talking about merging the Board and the JLC. The JLC would like it, but the Board would like nothing less. So I can't see it happening.'

Richard Ferrer is one of what seems to be a growing number of committed, identifying Jews who see no reason for religion to be a factor in their Jewish identity. This matters. Not because Richard is any more correct in his opinions than are the most fervently religious Jews; we live in an age of diversity and there is no right and wrong when it comes to matters of the heart or the soul. But it matters in terms of how Jews are seen by broader society and indeed how they identify themselves. When the 2021 census was issued in England and Wales, the section on ethnicity contained no 'Jewish' option. Although it was possible to write the word 'Jewish' in the 'Other' box, it was clear that the Office of National Statistics, and hence officialdom at large, did not consider that being Jewish is an ethnic category. They did, however, have 'Jewish' as an option under religion. But for a growing number of people, their Jewishness has nothing to do with religion. Like Richard Ferrer, they regard themselves as cultural or ethnic Jews. Of course, the problem really lies in definitions. Jewishness is as much an ethnic identity as it is a religion, although in actuality it is a bit of each and not fully either.

Richard says that the fact that he is not religious does not stop him being a passionate member of the Jewish community. 'What appeals to me is Judaism as a brand, with its emphasis on education, on culture, on care for the elderly, on charity, on family values, on all these things that we need now more than ever. It's not a devout belief in a higher being or the relentless praying or not eating bread for eight days. It's not that at all. But what I find most alarming about British Jewish life today is that we just don't have the courage. We don't have the courage of our convictions to scream this stuff from the rooftop. We're still very cowed. Still very quiet and apologetic.'

Richard is right. Although the Jewish community is much more confident these days, that confidence asserts itself in our willingness to confront anti-Semitism, or to take pride in our identity alongside all the other minorities in multicultural Britain. But we rarely shout about our values. We stand up for our rights, but we do not yet have the confidence to celebrate how we discharge our responsibilities. He believes that Jews should not define themselves through anti-Semitism, or prejudice, or stereotypes. 'We define ourselves by our accomplishments and the contribution we make to British life.' He says that, on reflection, the community probably overreacted to Corbyn. As a newspaperman he says he holds his hand up, saying that at times the hyperbole was too much.

Almost without realizing it, British Jews have achieved a unique standing in national life. They are, he says, a working example of how minority communities can assimilate to their host society while retaining their culture and traditions, even though the other side of the coin is that assimilation creates anti-Semitism. 'They regard us as chameleons. "You look like us. We can't see you. We don't know you. So we'll be scared of you." But at its best, the Jewish community is very much out there. I mean, if you look at things like Limmud, or JW3, dare I say even the *Jewish News*? This is a modern Jewish-British brand.'

There is no room for complacency in Richard's vision of his British-Jewish brand. For all its new sense of confidence, of standing up for itself, there are still big issues to be addressed, not least the shifting demographics that are polarizing large chunks of the community and further undermining the already shaky notion of a British Jewish community. The growing intolerance within the community, between those with differing political views, is another matter of concern. It comes to the fore in arguments over Israel and Palestine: for example, a campaign to exclude the pro-peace advocacy movement Yachad from the Board of Deputies was driven by those who disapproved of its political stance. The political split in the community was visible too when the Labour Party was mired in its anti-Semitism crisis, with Jewish Voice for Labour seeing little evidence of anti-Semitism anywhere in the party and the Jewish Labour Movement seeing it everywhere. And then there are the battles over the International Holocaust Remembrance Alliance definition of anti-Semitism. The Department of Hebrew Studies at University College London was instrumental in persuading the university to reject the definition; it led to a backlash from Jewish students and communal leaders. Richard goes so far as to suggest that the political discourse between left and right in the Jewish community is now as hostile as it is in national life.

Of course, Jews have always argued, it is part of the vibrancy of Jewish life. But their arguments now seem to mirror those in the secular world: the price for successful integration into mainstream society is to reap its disadvantages alongside its benefits.

There are social issues too, that the Jewish community has ignored for far too long, issues of sexual and domestic abuse and mental health. And then there is the vexed question of

Jewish–Muslim relations. Richard speaks of a lack of moderate Muslim voices, saying that 'what passes for moderate in the Muslim community is quite chilling. I think Muslim–Jewish ties in the UK are big, a big thing that needs to be dealt with. I know of a couple of imams who will happily speak moderately and charmingly on a TV show, and then preach at their mosques that Jews are the Antichrist. The whole issue is fraught.'

I asked Richard what he, as a newspaper editor, is doing about these issues. His answer was, 'We campaign. We do events. We try and work with communal organizations to give them a voice in a bigger platform. If you look at the last three or four years of front pages, you can see there's a constant thread there.' With a dig at his rival the *JC* he added: 'I would never put Israeli politics on the front page.'

What British Jewry lacks is a serious, thoughtful journal that tackles some of the issues inherent in British Jewry together with those current in the Jewish world. A journal that offers the British community the opportunity to raise the level of its own discussion and make its voice heard in global debate. The *Jewish Chronicle* played that role in its heyday, when everyone read newspapers, when community journals were a forum for their readers, when they were more than just purveyors of news.

And there was also the *Jewish Quarterly*, a remarkable journal created in the 1950s by the indefatigable Jacob Sonntag, whose magazine provided a platform for Britain's Jewish thinkers, creatives, academics and intellectuals. Sonntag believed so strongly in his magazine that he would go out onto the streets and sell it to people standing in theatre and cinema queues. The *Jewish Quarterly* continued as the pre-eminent, serious Jewish publication long after Sonntag died, a testament to the quality of thought inherent in the British community. But it met a sad end. Like almost every other quality journal, it always suffered from financial problems and was forced to cease publication a couple of times.

Eventually it was 'rescued' by an incompetent management team who appointed an American editor who knew nothing of the British community and had no concept of their tastes or political leanings. He was sacked after two editions, reinstated, then left and the magazine closed once more. An Australian publisher has now taken it over; he has restored some of the quality and has incorporated one or two British voices, but the *Jewish Quarterly* is now a global publication with little or no relevance to the British community and not much to distinguish it from its global peers. With nothing to recommend it over other publications, it bears no relation to what the *Quarterly* was in its prime. And although there are usually one or two other small magazines circulating on the fringes of the community (*Jewish Renaissance* comes to mind), British Jewry is once again without its own unique, thoughtful voice. The motivation, and the funding, no longer seem to be there.

It's a shame. British Jewry is an educated community with some eminent thinkers and highly capable writers. The fact that we cannot even maintain our own cultural print publication, that there is no appetite to establish one and no market crying out for it, stands in sharp contrast to the energy and creativity that are so evident among some younger British Jews.

3

Religion

You don't have to be religious to be Jewish, but Britain's Jews still categorize themselves by religious affiliation. Even secular Jews do: you may hear them say something along the lines of 'I am Jewish, but I am not religious.' Conversely, there are very many non-religious British Jews who belong to a synagogue and who, if pressed to declare their religious affiliation, would say that they are orthodox.

The reason is, that even if you never go to synagogue at all, or if you go no more than once or twice a year, you may choose to join an orthodox congregation and to consider yourself an orthodox Jew, albeit a non-observant one. This is one of the unique features of British Jewry. The word orthodox means 'correct belief', and in Jewish communities elsewhere to be orthodox means to live a religiously observant lifestyle. But in Britain it is possible to call oneself orthodox despite being largely unobservant and paying little attention to religious beliefs. The reason has very little to do with religion. It has to do with death.

Synagogues are places of worship, but the need for a place to pray is often far from the minds of those who join them.

You don't need to be a synagogue member to attend a service, other than on the two or three days a year when the building is full to capacity. But you do need to belong to a synagogue to be buried in a Jewish cemetery, unless you are willing to have your heirs pay through the nose for your funeral. Most synagogues in Britain offer a funeral expenses scheme, a savings-type plan, collected with the synagogue membership fee, that covers the eventual cost of your funeral. The scheme is convenient and inexpensive; it removes any concerns about saddling one's heirs with the cost of a funeral, and it benefits the synagogues by encouraging people to take out membership. It sounds ideal. But, like all good ideas, it is not quite as perfect as it seems.

The biggest problem is that funeral expenses schemes are generally non-transferable. Unlike a savings plan, you can't get your money out when you leave. In that sense it is more like a life insurance policy. You can spend your life paying into a burial scheme run by one group of synagogues, and then one day decide to join a different group of synagogues, who operate a different burial scheme. The money you have paid into the original scheme will not be transferred across. You could still be buried in a cemetery belonging to the original scheme, but that's no good if you have moved to the other side of the country. It's what happened in a case in 2017. A couple had contributed to a scheme in Southend for 45 years, and then they moved to Devon. When one of them passed away, the Southend scheme refused to cover the cost of the Devon funeral.[25]

There is also a growing issue over the linkage of burial schemes to synagogue membership. Fewer people these days are willing to join a synagogue just to be part of a burial scheme. But it doesn't mean they don't want a Jewish funeral.

They may have no interest in religion while they are alive, but they may want to hedge their bets in death. Burial is one of those things where a connection to one's heritage suddenly feels important. But since the Jewish cemeteries are owned and managed by the synagogue-based burial schemes, if you want a Jewish burial, there are only two options. Either you join a scheme or you hope that your heirs will pay a lump sum to have you buried in a Jewish cemetery when you die.

Sooner or later, as the numbers swell of those who want a Jewish burial without having to join a synagogue, an entrepreneur will step in. They will buy a piece of land, get the appropriate statutory permissions, consecrate it as a Jewish cemetery and set up an independent burial scheme which anyone can join, irrespective of synagogue membership. If and when that happens, it is likely to hit synagogue revenues hard. There may be an exodus of all those inactive members who joined to be part of a burial scheme and who make very little day-to-day demand on the synagogue's resources. It's a potential crisis that has been brushed aside so far by the synagogue bodies. They may not be able to ignore it forever.

It is the existence of burial schemes that has led to the rather odd but somehow quite touching idea of British, irreligious orthodoxy, of belonging to a synagogue whose beliefs you don't share. People join orthodox synagogues for historic reasons – maybe it's where they got married or perhaps it was the synagogue their parents belonged to. Maybe they just liked the tunes they heard on the few occasions they attended, or perhaps they were flattered by the attentions of a charismatic rabbi. Whatever the reason, having joined and signed up to the burial scheme, it makes sense for them to stay. It is comforting to know that, whatever happens to them in life, their burial will be taken care of.

Irrational it may be, but the United Synagogue, the oldest synagogue group in the country and the largest in Europe, has turned the all-inclusive British version of orthodoxy into an ideology. They are committed both to orthodoxy and to 'the maximal inclusion in a non-judgemental way of every Jew irrespective of their level of Jewish observance'.[26] It is a seemingly contradictory mission, but as a blend of Jewish optimism and British muddling through it works quite well. That their membership numbers are falling is more to do with demographic and social trends than it is to do with religion. But their financial stability does depend heavily on people keeping their membership active, in order to remain part of the burial scheme.

The British community, for most of its history anyway, has managed to project a unified image to the outside world. Largely because of the dominance of the United Synagogue and that strange British Jewish institution, the Chief Rabbinate.

Britain is unique among world communities in having a Chief Rabbi who exerts – or, more accurately, is widely believed to exert – ecclesiastical authority over the Jewish community. This is nothing to do with the personality of the Chief Rabbi; it is the system over which he presides that grants him this authority. The roots of the system itself lie in the formative years of Jewish settlement in Britain, when the community was beginning to organize itself. The leaders of the community in the nineteenth century, the so-called Cousinhood, the small group of wealthy, interconnected families who were instrumental in leading the charge towards full Jewish emancipation, were determined to show that British Jews could conform to the norms and expectations of English society, both in their manner of behaviour and in their communal institutions.

Seeking to establish themselves and their families as respectable members of genteel society, the Cousinhood were reluctant to be embarrassed by their co-religionists, newly arrived from Eastern Europe. They didn't want to be associated with their indecorous, 'foreign' behaviour, or with the sort of religious anarchy that was likely to take hold in the absence of a well-ordered system of ecclesiastical authority. They were perhaps still bruised by what the diarist Samuel Pepys had written nearly 200 years earlier, when visiting a service at Bevis Marks in the City of London, Britain's oldest synagogue.

Pepys had probably not been told that he was visiting the synagogue on the festival of *simchat torah*, a joyful occasion celebrating the completion of the annual cycle of reading the Torah, marked by dancing, singing and exuberant behaviour, He probably thought that he'd turned up at the synagogue on a normal day. He was not impressed:

> But, Lord! to see the disorder, laughing, sporting, and no attention, but confusion in all their service, more like brutes than people knowing the true God, would make a man forswear ever seeing them more and indeed I never did see so much, or could have imagined there had been any religion in the whole world so absurdly performed as this.[27]

The United Synagogue was the Cousinhood's attempt to formalize the Jewish religion in Britain. Established by Act of Parliament in 1870, it was modelled closely on the Church of England, with a Chief Rabbi as its Archbishop of Canterbury. There had been a de facto Chief Rabbi in London since the beginning of the eighteenth century, but in 1844 representatives of communities from across the country elected Nathan Marcus Adler to a new formal position as Chief Rabbi of the United Hebrew Congregations of the British Empire. When, at his instigation, the United Synagogue was formed, he became its senior cleric. And although the foundation document of the United Synagogue refers to '*a* Chief Rabbi', as far as the outside world is concerned, the United Synagogue's Chief Rabbi was, and remains, *the* Chief Rabbi, even though he only formally represents the centrist orthodox community.

It is not easy to be portrayed as the religious representative of a community, particularly when that community values discussion and debate, and doesn't shy away from challenge and dissent, and even more so when many of its members don't accept you as their representative. The current Chief Rabbi, Ephraim Mirvis, is conscious of the historic gravity of his role but is open and accessible in conversation. He quotes the nineteenth-century ethicist Rabbi Israel Salanter: 'If I am a rabbi and everybody loves me, I'm no rabbi. And if I'm a rabbi and nobody loves me I'm not a *mensch* [a person of integrity].'

I asked him whether he believed his influence extends beyond his core, centrist orthodox community: whether, for example, secular Jews might look to him for leadership. He said that, although in his role he is recognized as being a voice for Jews and Judaism, he certainly does not claim to be the only voice, nor does he have the right to represent every single Jewish person. 'My hope is that the stances that I take do represent the interests of all Jews and Judaism. And I often take counsel with people in respect of what the issue of the day is, in order to ensure that the stand that I'm making is one that will, broadly speaking, be supported by Jewish people. I feel the weight of responsibility very heavily on my shoulders, that I am not there as an individual, but I'm carrying all Jews of this country with me. One cannot aspire ever to get everybody's support.'

Chief Rabbis can't help being compared to their predecessors, particularly by the Jewish media. Rabbi Mirvis's predecessor was Jonathan Sacks z"l, who passed away in 2020. Rabbi Sacks was recognized by many as British Jewry's most articulate representative, a man who was as much involved in national ethical debates as he was in his own community. Ephraim Mirvis has a different style. He says that the reason he had an impact during the Corbyn crisis is because his voice was not heard every day. And he has, as much as possible, kept away from communal conflict, in a way that Jonathan Sacks, largely due to the provocation of others, was sometimes unable to do. Rabbi Mirvis says he was determined to come into office ensuring a constructive and harmonious relationship with leaders across the religious spectrum. 'I'm a cricket fan. Basically, my message is we should all be batsmen not bowlers. Our aim should not be to bowl the other team out but to be proud of what we stand for, to score single runs, two, threes, get some fours, and hopefully get some sixes here and there. We need to define ourselves by what we are championing and not by what we are against. And we shouldn't feel insecure because of anyone challenging us.'

Rabbi Lord Sacks's tenure as Chief Rabbi was not without its intercommunal difficulties, tensions between the various religious streams periodically running high. But while he was in post, and even more after he retired, he established a reputation on the global stage, through his books, broadcasts and teachings, as the religious voice of any faith who was most in touch with the ethical and spiritual issues confronting the world today. Lira Winston, who suddenly and tragically passed away shortly after I spoke to her, was a trustee of the Rabbi Sacks Legacy Trust. She told me that the British community owe him a tremendous debt, that he made people proud to be Jewish. She said that he made his biggest impact on the community by putting education at the top of his agenda. His book *Will We Have Jewish Grandchildren?*, published in 1994, put the challenge of assimilation on the communal agenda, placed the focus firmly on education and accelerated the push to build Jewish schools that had been started by his predecessor Rabbi Immanuel Jakobovits.

Henry Grunwald is the chair of the Rabbi Sacks Legacy Trust. He says that, in the wake of Rabbi Sacks's death, the aim of the Trust is to promote his teachings. 'There are a number of things that we have planned. The website will be redeveloped into a complete digital archive. So that students will be able to go on and see everything he said and wrote. He developed educational material for Jewish schools, which was incredibly popular in the USA. It is used here as well, and we hope to make it available in Israel. But the States is where he really was big, even bigger than here.'

The religious spectrum, like its political equivalent, runs from right to left, and the United Synagogue, the largest denominational umbrella body, occupies the middle ground, known as Modern or Centrist Orthodoxy. The London School of Jewish Studies, or LSJS, as it is better known, is Modern Orthodoxy's principal adult education centre in Britain. It offers undergraduate and postgraduate degrees in Jewish Studies, trains teachers for Jewish schools and partners with other organizations in offering rabbinic training. Its Dean, Rabbi Dr Rafi Zarum, has an unusual background for a rabbi. He has a PhD in quantum chaos theory and began his career as an academic before deciding to change course and study for the rabbinate.

Although unusual, Rafi's background is not as unlikely as it would have been 30 or 40 years ago, when it was not uncommon for orthodox rabbis to maintain that a postgraduate degree, or even university education at any level, was unnecessary. Spending time in secular study was seen as a distraction from Talmudic learning. Fortunately, such views are less prevalent today. Rafi told me that some of the rabbis in the United Synagogue these days entered the profession having started out in other careers, often with doctorates or Master's degrees. In that sense they are more like their grandparents' generation, when having a PhD was regarded as an enhancement to a rabbinic career.

LSJS's roots go back to its founding in 1855, when it was called Jews' College, a name it kept until 1998. The original aim of the college was to train rabbis and teachers, to give them a professional qualification and, as they often came from immigrant families, to make sure they did things in an English way. Jews' College wanted its graduates to reflect the culture and mores of the society in which they lived, and to show that being Jewish and being English were fully compatible. This, Rafi says, 'included learning how to speak with an eloquent English accent and being civilized; it was basically a Judaism for modern England'. LSJS, he says, 'epitomizes the English version of Modern Orthodoxy, which enables educated people to learn as much as they can about the world around them, while being deeply rooted in their religion'.

In other words, LSJS's mission is not to make people religious. That's where it differs from an outreach organization or a synagogue. Rafi is very clear about where his organization sits on the evangelical spectrum. He says that one of the commandments of Judaism is to study Torah, which means to be intellectually engaged in the pursuit of knowledge. 'That is a value of its own, it's important and it's what we're encouraging.' He says that if people then go off and become more religious, that's great. But it's not what LSJS is there for.

For decades, English rabbis were trained almost exclusively at Jews' College. But as Israel emerged as the religiously vibrant centre of world Jewry, offering a far livelier lifestyle and much better weather, more and more English rabbinic students chose to study and gain their ordination there. Eventually, Jews' College hit a funding crisis. So Rabbi Zarum says that 'a bunch of us came and did a pitch to the Chief Rabbi, Jonathan Sacks, saying that we value the idea of merging the best of the academic world with the traditional *yeshiva* [rabbinic college], that we want to run an adult education programme in that style and have lectures and courses that will help to rebuild our academic credibility. And he was very supportive of it. We got some funding from the community, and it's grown ever since.' Rafi says he sees himself as a community academic, offering the best of academia that's relevant to the modern world, in the same way as his mentor Jonathan Sacks did.

Like so many people I have spoken to, Rafi believes that much of the change taking place in the British community today can be attributed to Jonathan Sacks. 'He realized that the way to make change in the community is either through power or through influence. Power would come through the application of Jewish law and control, and by making statements. Influence comes through teaching. He made a pragmatic choice. He saw that if you go for the authority approach, you're going to have lots of wars and battles with people who disagree. But if you take the influence approach, it allows much more room. So that's the path he went along. He didn't focus on Jewish law; instead he preached an open-minded Judaism.'

That comment led us into a discussion about where the British community is heading. There is no reason, of course, why it should be heading anywhere, but from all the conversations I have had there is no doubt that change is in the air. Rafi puts the change down to shifting social attitudes, but he fears that the United Synagogue may not be evolving fast enough for the next generation. 'With the relaxing of norms and expectations, and with the death of deference, parenting today is different. Thirty years ago children would have done what their parents said, in a way they don't now. And religion would come along as part of that. But not any more. Now we need more compelling reasons to continue this tradition. The LSJS approach is to voice a reason where Judaism has more meaning today than it ever did.'

He gave the example of what he calls 'switch-off shabbat', the religious requirement to turn off all electronic devices for 25 hours over the sabbath. The sabbath, shabbat in modern Hebrew pronunciation, is the centrepiece of the Jewish week, observed with varying degrees of rigour by Jews of almost every shade of religiosity. For the orthodox, shabbat is a day of ritual and restrictions, a time of rest during which all work is forbidden. But what constitutes work is closely defined: many of the prohibitions of shabbat, such as writing, driving and switching on electric lights, seem onerous and over-restrictive to most people. But for those who keep *shabbat* they are far from restrictive; they create a framework of sacred time, in which the cares and hassles of daily life are suspended, in which family life, socializing, synagogue attendance and relaxation come to the fore.

Not using electronic gadgets is just one shabbat restriction, but one with obvious benefits to those who spend much of their life glued to a screen. So it is a custom that some non-religious people have also adopted: hence the idea of 'switch-off shabbat'. Rafi uses it as an example of how Judaism is evolving so that those who are not observant are able to find meaning in it. 'In one sense it's about rebranding our religion. For modern people to recognize that Judaism has something to say about the psychological, emotional, political and organizational challenges of the 21st century.'

So where, I wondered, is God in all this? Rafi believes that God is there underneath. 'The rabbis of the Talmud talk about renewal. You could call it branding and therefore imply that it's not so religious, that it's distant from tradition. But I'd argue that tradition was always about renewal; the voice of God is just hard to hear with so much other material and so many needy voices out there. And so we have to work hard to show that the voice of God is still relevant to our world.'

Not everyone has such a laid-back attitude towards God. For the past century and a half, the question of what Jews are supposed to believe, and how it should impact on their religious observance, has led to the some of the most intractable disputes in British Jewry. The biggest dispute of all, which split the community in the early 1960s, was over the question of who wrote the Torah, the Five Books of Moses. Rabbi Dr Louis Jacobs, probably Britain's leading rabbinic intellect of the twentieth century, was condemned by the orthodox establishment for maintaining that there was a human element in the authorship of the Torah, that it had not been dictated word for word to Moses on Mount Sinai. Jacobs, who had expected to be appointed as Principal of Jews' College, the forerunner of LSJS, was denied the job, and when he applied to return to his old synagogue as its minister, the Chief Rabbi at the time forbade him. Virtually the entire membership of his synagogue resigned in protest and set up their own independent congregation. The dispute led to the foundation of the Masorti movement, one of British Jewry's religious streams, which sits somewhere to the left of Modern Orthodoxy.

Disputes and disagreements have been responsible for the formation of all the streams in British Jewish life. Louis Jacobs was not the first British rabbi to challenge the traditional belief that the Torah was divinely dictated. And Masorti was not the first movement to be founded on what it described as a non-fundamentalist theological platform. Rabbi Tony Bayfield, who was the head of the Movement for Reform Judaism from 1995 to 2011, told me that Reform Judaism broke away from what had become the conservative view in the nineteenth century, when the study of Judaism became a lively subject of intellectual discussion.

'If one goes back into history, the period from 150 BCE to 200 CE was a truly defining time, an age of enormous upheaval. Out of that period emerged two major Jewish religious parties, Christianity and Rabbinic Judaism. Rabbinic Judaism was founded on a doctrine of the dual Torah, that not only did we receive the written Torah at Sinai but we also received an oral Torah. It was a dynamic and enormously fruitful insight that created a faith which, more than perhaps any other, emphasizes inquiry, interrogation, debate, discussion and disagreement: an uncompromisingly intellectual expression of religion.'

But in the nineteenth century this founding doctrine came into conflict with the intellectual developments of the modern world. A new discipline, the academic, or scientific, study of Judaism, emerged, which sought to understand and explain the development of the religion. It placed a particular emphasis on the authorship of the Bible. Tony describes how nineteenth-century orthodoxy insisted on retaining a literal interpretation of the dual Torah rather than seeing it as a crucial, dynamic metaphor, holding firm to the doctrine of the oral Torah, 'even if the Enlightenment challenged it. Whereas other expressions of Judaism emerged, that wanted to engage with the ideas of the modern world. And Reform came out of that.' In fact, it wasn't until the emergence of Reform that Orthodoxy got its name. Traditional Judaism became known as orthodoxy to distinguish it from Reform. Today Reform Judaism is the second largest denomination in British Jewry, after Orthodoxy, comprising about 20 per cent of the Jewish community, though they may soon be pushed into the third place by the *haredim*, whose numbers are growing rapidly, owing to their high birth rates.

Rabbi Bayfield summed up Reform Judaism for me as 'an expression of Judaism which does not believe in a God who zaps the wicked and rewards the good, who does not heal through miracles or intervene in human life by suspending the laws of nature, who does not believe that the Torah came flying through outer space and landed at Moses's feet'. Like his teacher Rabbi Dr Louis Jacobs, whose theology inspired Masorti, Tony asserts that the Torah emerged with the imprint of history upon it. 'God's fingerprints, or voiceprints, are all over the text. But they aren't the text.'

The only religious group never to have suffered an ideological split is the long-established Spanish and Portuguese, or Sephardi, community. Founded by those Jews who Oliver Cromwell allowed to enter Britain in the seventeenth century, the small community built the stunning

Bevis Marks synagogue in the City of London. Opened in 1701 and the jewel in the crown of Britain's synagogues, Bevis Marks is the only synagogue in Europe to have held services continuously for over 300 years.

The Spanish and Portuguese community sits on the orthodox side of the religious spectrum, and although its members are as diverse in their personal religious practices as any other middle-of-the-road orthodox community, they have never experienced an ideological breakaway. Other than in 1840, when some of their members joined with those from two Ashkenazi congregations to establish the West London Synagogue, so as to have a more decorous and modern service.

The West London Synagogue would eventually become Britain's first Reform congregation. And it suffered its own split at the beginning of the twentieth century, when a group broke away, complaining that the synagogue had stagnated. They called themselves the Jewish Religious Union and saw themselves as an intellectual response to the pressing religious and ethical issues of the time. The Union's founders aimed to stimulate a resurgence of interest in Judaism by holding services mainly in English, with organ music and full equality between the sexes. They held their services on Saturday afternoons to cater for those, particularly women, who worked a six-and-a-half-day week and could not get to synagogue in the mornings. Eventually their movement became known as Liberal Judaism. Rabbi Charley Baginsky, the Chief Executive of Liberal Judaism today, says that they adhere to the same ethos as their founders, structuring their services so that they are far more accessible to those who cannot read or understand Hebrew. They have more or less dispensed with the Saturday afternoon services because working patterns have changed. With the exception of their

Central London congregation, where Saturday afternoon services are still held.

Even Orthodoxy, which sees itself as the guardian of tradition and the authentic voice from whom the other movements broke away, is riven into factions. On the right are the Strictly Orthodox, or *haredim*, whose cloistered lifestyle is a consequence of their belief in the literal truth of the Bible and their unyielding interpretations of Talmudic law. To their left is Modern Orthodoxy. Between the two sit the Traditional Orthodox.

Creationism is the outstanding example of their divide. Most *haredim* take the biblical account of creation literally and follow the ancient rabbis who calculated the age of the universe by adding up all the lifespans listed in the Bible. According to the rabbinic computation, this book will be published in the 5,783rd year since creation. In contrast, most adherents of Traditional Orthodoxy will generally accept the scientific account of creation and evolution as correct. They will try to find a way of reconciling it with the biblical account: for example, treating the seven days of creation as seven aeons of unequal and indeterminate length. It is an approach that holds up until one examines the sequence of creation in the Bible and discovers that it doesn't match the evolutionary sequence. The Modern Orthodox, and all points to their left, therefore reject this view. They see no conflict between science and the Bible; as far as they are concerned, the biblical account of creation is an allegory, and was never meant to be accepted as scientific fact.

Rabbi Michael Harris, one of the most articulate proponents of Modern Orthodoxy in Britain, describes it as 'the attempt to combine full commitment to Orthodox Judaism with openness to the modern world'.[28] Of course, this definition masks all sorts of questions, not the least of which is how open one should be to some of the more disturbing aspects of the modern world. Fortunately it is a question that lies well beyond the scope of this book.

There is no end to the propagation and division of Jewish denominations, and the names they give to themselves. Leonard Cohen sang about finding ourselves on opposite sides of a line nobody had drawn.[29] Chief Rabbi Mirvis is more prosaic: 'Labels are man-made. *Haredi*, Modern Orthodox, Open Orthodox, Centrist Orthodoxy. Masorti, Reform. We are Jewish. We are human. I don't believe that when I get to heaven the question will be, "So what did you do for the United Synagogue?" The question will be, "What did you do for humanity?" That's the question.'

Openness to the modern world sounds like a reasonable idea until it comes into conflict with deeply rooted traditions. Reconciling the two is not always easy, notably when it relates to the conflict between the role of women in contemporary society and the orthodox religious tradition.

All orthodox streams subscribe to the system of Jewish law based on the Bible and the Talmud. One of the principles of this legal system is that women are not obliged to perform religious acts that must be carried out at specific times. The ancient reasoning behind this was that women were too busy as mothers and homemakers to commit themselves to time-bound religious duties. So women are not obliged to recite those prayers which are to be said at specific times of the day. And if women are not obliged to recite those prayers, then they cannot lead the congregation in prayer, since leading the congregation can only be done by someone who is obliged to pray themselves. As a result, participation in synagogue services throughout history was exclusively male. Women sat in a separate, segregated area, apparently so that the men could not find their presence a distraction.

Those principles still apply in orthodox synagogues. Men and women sit separately. In some synagogue buildings women sit upstairs in a gallery; in others they sit on the same level as the men but separated by a screen. They do not lead services. That's how it was for centuries. But during the second half of the twentieth century, as the status of women in wider society began to change, there were calls for change in Britain's more contemporary-minded orthodox synagogues too. Women began to demand a greater role for themselves in synagogue life.

Changes came about slowly. Within the United Synagogue the first significant change was that women were admitted to the boards of management in their congregations; then some years later they were allowed to chair the board. They started to join in the recital of the *kaddish*, the prayer said by those who are recently bereaved or are commemorating the anniversary of a relative's death. The batmitzvah ceremony, which a girl celebrates at the age of 12, became more prominent. At first all the 12-year-olds celebrated their batmitzvahs in a group on a Sunday afternoon, then gradually the ceremony was moved to a shabbat morning, with different congregations finding their own ways of incorporating the ceremony into the morning synagogue service. Today, in most Modern Orthodox synagogues, batmitzvah girls deliver an address to the congregation. Sometimes they have their own service, conducted exclusively by women. But unlike boys, who celebrate their barmitzvah, girls in male-dominated orthodox services never read from the Torah or play any other liturgical role.

There was a moment in the 1990s when it looked as if regular women-only services might become a permanent trend. But it didn't last long. The longest-running women's service, in Stanmore, eventually shifted its emphasis from prayer to learning. Although those few rabbis who supported women's services were able to make perfectly cogent legal cases to justify their position, few women were prepared to learn the skills to lead a service, and those who did have the skills generally preferred to attend services in more progressive denominations, where the ethos was altogether more egalitarian.

Recently, however, in a few progressively minded orthodox circles there has been a move towards more egalitarian services. The legal reasoning that determines how these services are run is complicated, but these quasi-egalitarian or 'partnership' services conform to orthodox strictures, including the separation of men and women and the requirement for ten men to be present. But they rely on lenient legal opinions as to which parts of the service women are obliged to participate in, and therefore to function as a service leader. Most mainstream orthodox rabbis oppose these services, arguing that they have no validity within Jewish tradition or law. But they are conscious that Jewish law has always developed in response to changing social conditions: it is just that the pace of change tends to be glacial. And as the experience of women-only services shows, change is not always lasting. The partnership services regard themselves as a new, permanent development, but it may be some time before they will know for sure.

JOFA, The Jewish Orthodox Feminist Alliance, was set up in Britain in 2013. Inspired by the American organization of the same name, it aspires to expand the religious and political opportunities of women, within the framework of orthodox Jewish law. Eve Sacks is a co-chair and trustee. She says that she thinks that the United Synagogue has tried somewhat to accommodate women, within the boundaries of what they are able to do, but that there are still big barriers to women's participation in orthodoxy. A member of the United Synagogue, she says she struggles to identify as orthodox. She agrees that Modern Orthodoxy in Britain aspires to be inclusive but fails to cater to women who feel strongly about their feminism. They are particularly likely to notice the difference as their daughters approach the age of 12 and they realize that the batmitzvah they will celebrate in the synagogue will not have the same status as the barmitzvah for boys. 'They've made a barmitzvah for their son. Now it's their daughter's turn. She wants the same opportunities as her brother, she has been brought up in a world where girls can do everything boys can do, so why can't she now? If they're not religiously observant, they will go to Progressive or Masorti synagogues. Because why not?'

Why not indeed? One might ask why women who expect full equality with men would bother to remain members of an orthodox congregation. The answer is that they consider orthodoxy as their home; it belongs to them as much as anyone else. Since so much of religious practice is based on emotion, on doing and experiencing what feels familiar and comfortable, why should they give up everything they enjoy because the orthodox rabbinate will not budge on the question of women's involvement? Particularly when, they say, Jewish law is flexible enough to accommodate their needs. Their rabbinic opponents, of course, disagree.

Rabbi Bentzi Sudak, one of the leaders of the hasidic Chabad movement in Britain, thinks that the questions over women's involvement in religious services has come about because

Judaism has been reduced to the synagogue, or *shul*. 'Judaism is an all-encompassing religion. It's a lifestyle, something that happens every day of the week, continually. But we have changed the emphasis from Judaism to *shul*-ism. *Shul* is an important part of the Jewish religion, where predominantly men would go once a week, or once a day or three times a day, to reconnect with God. But it is only one part of Judaism, it's not the only place we experience religion. In Christianity, religion is experienced in the church. In Judaism, religion is experienced everywhere, not necessarily in the synagogue. But in our age we've taken one, male-dominated part of the Jewish religion and made it the dominant focus of Judaism.'

Many orthodox women would agree with that. They will say that the synagogue is a man's domain, that orthodox women connect with Judaism in other ways, ways that are as meaningful for them as the synagogue is for their men.

Other women – and men – would not agree. They may acknowledge that Bentzi Sudak is correct in saying that the synagogue is just one component of the lifestyle we call Judaism. But, with the exception of the most committed and the orthodox, they will say that the synagogue is the place where most people connect with their Judaism. The synagogue's centrality to Jewish life today may be the fault of modernity, or history, or some other factor, but it is what it is. The synagogue has become synonymous with Judaism, and many British women want an equal role there, just as they have in every other aspect of their lives.

Matthew Anisfeld, who looks at the British community through the lens of someone who has lived and studied in the USA, thinks that the centralized communal structure in Britain prohibits flexibility within individual communities.

By not applying Jewish law constructively to the contemporary changes in gender roles, he fears the orthodox community risks alienating its membership.

Of all the issues that confront women in orthodoxy, none is more harrowing than that of the *aguna*, the 'chained' wife who cannot remarry. It is a global problem that affects women in British Jewry as much as anywhere else in the world. The root of the problem lies in the fact that Judaism accepts the idea of divorce on demand, as long as it is the man who is making the demand. If a man refuses to give his wife a divorce of his own free will, then the couple remain married. And if she gets into a relationship with another man, and they have children, those children are regarded as illegitimate, and are severely restricted in terms of who they can marry under Jewish law.

Many solutions have been proposed over the years, short of the obvious one, which is to change the law, or at least to find an unobjectionable workaround. But orthodox rabbis will tell you that a change in the law is impossible unless all rabbis agree. Otherwise a woman whose divorce is validated by a rabbinic court which accepts the change in the law may find that, if she remarries and has children from her new marriage, those children may be treated as illegitimate by a court that refuses to accept their mother's divorce. And this in turn may impede the possibility of their marrying the person they want. The whole situation sounds absurd and archaic. It is.

In the past few years attempts have been made in Britain to turn to the national courts for a solution, but for reasons that only lawyers and rabbis seem to understand, no guaranteed, fail-safe solution has yet been found. In Israel recalcitrant husbands can be imprisoned until they consent to give their wives a divorce. In Britain the religious courts may order them to be ostracized by their community, a remedy that only works for those who care. It is not unheard of in some places for vigilantes to beat up men who won't give their wives a divorce. And although a divorce is not valid unless it is given by the husband of his own free will, there is a simple solution. They harass or even imprison him, or worse, until he consents of his own free will!

Reform and Liberal synagogues have none of these gender issues. Their more flexible approach to Jewish law, and their prioritizing of the ethical values of Judaism over the law's intricacies, allow them to resolve problems that orthodoxy shies away from. Women play a full role in these denominations. Their congregations have mixed seating as a matter of course, men and women participate equally in leading services, and the sermon, weddings and funerals are just as likely to be delivered by a woman rabbi as a man.

Britain's Liberal and Reform movements are also known as Progressive Judaism. Their names are a little confusing because Reform Judaism in the USA tends to equate with what we call Liberal in the UK, while there is no Liberal strand in America. But in the UK, Reform and Liberal are two distinct movements, although they share many of the same values and theological approaches. They work closely together, and in April 2023 the two movements agreed to merge – to share resources and expertise, and to capitalize on the growing numbers of those who share their values.

Rabbi Tony Bayfield told me that Reform Judaism is for people who are interested in an expression of Judaism that is not merely secular and for those who do not 'label secular ethics as social action or *tikkun olam* all the time. Rather, they are interested in the radical ideas and values of Rabbinic Judaism and wish to deploy them in an engagement with the world and people around us today.'

I asked him to explain his apparently throwaway remark about *tikkun olam,* since it's a topic that seems to define Judaism for so many of the people I have been speaking to. He said: 'If it's *tikkun olam* which is rooted in a real knowledge of Jewish ethics, of distinctive Jewish ethical teachings, then it's wonderful. But if it's merely contemporary secular values with a superficial Jewish label attached, then it's a betrayal of Jewish tradition. An evasion of Jewish tradition.'

In his recent book *Being Jewish Today* he noted how far the phrase *tikkun olam* has shifted from its medieval, early kabbalistic meaning. It has shifted still further from its even earlier status as a piece of legal terminology. 'I see no problem,' says Rabbi Bayfield, 'with people who cannot find their way to a belief in God, but who are true Jewish humanitarians, not secularists. Who take on the values that are so central to our ethical traditions, the rabbinical and the prophetic, that make a distinctive contribution when we share them with the world.' His concern is that the phrase *tikkun olam* has become secularized; no longer resonating with Jewish values, it is often used as a synonym for Western ethical conventions to which so many pay lip service.

Just as the meaning of *tikkun olam* has shifted, so have the priorities of the Reform movement. Another Reform leader, who did not want to be identified, told me that the movement is 'broken', that it had lost its vigour since Tony Bayfield retired as its head. They said that all the work that Tony had put into developing the movement has now dissipated and that a chasm has opened up between the synagogues and the movement. 'Tony got us into a position where really talented volunteer leaders wanted to join the leadership of the Reform movement. Because it was something exciting, going somewhere. And all that's gone.'

With 1,300 adult members and 700 children, Finchley Reform Synagogue is one of the largest in the country. When I spoke to its Senior Rabbi, Miriam Berger, it was close to completing a major rebuilding project to free itself from the constraints of its 1960s building, which could no longer accommodate everything that the community does. Things like hosting a weekly homeless shelter during the winter months, accommodating the local Somali community for Ramadan prayers after their own building was burned down in an arson attack, supporting the disadvantaged and vulnerable in their own community, running summer schemes and, of course, the ubiquitous educational programmes that every synagogue of any size runs for its members.

We think of synagogues, like churches, mosques or temples, as places of prayer. And prayer is indeed one of the things that go on in a large congregation like Finchley Reform on a shabbat morning. But it is not the only thing. If you walk into the building on a Saturday morning, you can't just sit down and join in the service or surreptitiously chat to your neighbour, as is the custom in many synagogues. Instead you have to decide what you want to do. You can attend the main prayer service, go to an educational session or go to what Miriam described to me as their 'fresh services, or alternative services, where you might only do one piece of liturgy during the whole service, but you spend the time discussing it and contemplating it, thinking about where it takes you'.

The basic principle in a Reform service, Rabbi Miriam explained, is to make the liturgy meaningful. Jewish prayers stretch back over thousands of years. Some, like many of the Psalms, are beautiful, inspirational poetry. Others are dry and repetitive, archaic in the ideas they contain. Making liturgy meaningful requires a direct engagement with the text, dwelling on its content and meaning and understanding how it may be relevant to our lives today. It is a different approach to an orthodox service, where prayer, which is only one component of an all-embracing Jewish lifestyle, is a familiar and unchanging stream of words, texts and contemplations that draw ideas and insights in their wake as they are recited.

Rabbi Miriam says that someone from an Orthodox congregation entering a Reform synagogue on a shabbat morning would recognize the vast majority of the prayers. But they are unlikely to hear all the prayers that they are used to, or not necessarily in the same order. The synagogue service is divided into sections, and whereas in an orthodox synagogue the whole of each section is recited, in a Reform community the prayer leader will select individual prayers or biblical passages to concentrate on.

Most of the spiritual leadership team at Finchley Reform are women. And while orthodoxy still struggles to harmonize tradition with the status of women in the twenty-first century, Reform has moved on to address some of the other inequalities that have been hard baked into Judaism over the course of the past 3,000 years or so. One of these is what to do when a couple of mixed heritage die – when two people, only one of whom is Jewish, pass away and want to be buried together. Under Jewish law, Jewish cemeteries are only for Jews. And although in principle Reform would have little difficulty in erasing that rule, it is hard to do so in an existing cemetery; there are too many other sensitivities involved to suddenly introduce a change in burial policy. Reform has got round this problem by building a new woodland cemetery. It meets the requirements of those who want an organically sustainable burial. And because it is a new cemetery it can start off with new policies. Couples of mixed heritage can now be buried together.

Liberal Judaism embraces change as enthusiastically as Reform but the perspective feels slightly different. Charley Baginsky says that they take the concerns of their founders very seriously, 'almost sitting alongside Torah in terms of our identity. We remain a very ideological, intellectual movement, holding on to the founders' deep pragmatism and sense of social justice.' But where the founders were concerned about the emancipation of women and issues of social justice in the early twentieth century, Liberal Judaism today campaigns on contemporary ethical and moral concerns, against the social ills that contaminate Britain and the world today.

Charley describes the Liberal stream as a political Judaism. They support a change in the law over assisted dying, campaign on behalf of refugees and are working with the Harwich Kindertransport Memorial Appeal, using the campaign as a platform to speak about child refugees and migration.

I put it to her that Liberal Judaism's focus on national political change seems to differ from the aim of the movement's founders, which was to create an expression of Judaism that was relevant to disenchanted Jews. 'I think they are the same thing,' she said. 'I think they go together.' Disenchanted Jews, she seems to be saying, will be energized and attracted by campaigns for social justice. That may be the case for those on the left of the political spectrum. One has to wonder if it is the same for those on the right.

Most of the 40 Liberal congregations in Britain are in locations where there is not a large Jewish population, and many of their members live in places where there are no Jews at all. This wide geographical spread presents the movement with challenges, but also creates opportunities, as Charley and her rabbinic colleagues discovered during the recent Covid pandemic.

Before the pandemic, the Liberal movement was grappling with how to bring such a widespread group of people together. How to make those who lived outside London feel as involved as those who were able to attend synagogue services and events, and how to make sure that the multiplicity of voices which are part of the ethos of the Liberal movement could all be heard. They had already begun to develop educational programmes that could be delivered remotely so that, when Covid hit, they found they were largely prepared to take advantage of the new reality. They now conduct services online as well as in their synagogues and are developing the use of technologies to support their communities and to address the issues on which they are campaigning.

Liberal Judaism has always been radical in dealing with the question of who is a Jew. Under Jewish law, a Jew is someone who was born to a Jewish mother or has converted to Judaism. The children of Jewish fathers, where the mother is not Jewish and has not converted to Judaism, are not recognized by the orthodox as Jews. This, understandably, can cause much grief and heartache to people whose orthodoxy is important to them, who find that their own communities do not consider their grandchildren to be Jewish. Particularly since conversion to Judaism under orthodox auspices is a lengthy and rigorous process.

Liberal and Reform Judaism long ago tried to ameliorate the situation by making conversion to Judaism easier than in orthodoxy, but this didn't always help. Sometimes the non-Jewish partner doesn't want to convert. Even if they do convert, orthodox authorities do not recognize the validity of

Liberal or Reform conversions, storing up problems for the children if they want to marry someone from an orthodox family, in an orthodox synagogue.

Liberal Judaism bypassed the difficulty by accepting the principle of patrilineal descent: declaring that the children of Jewish fathers and non-Jewish mothers are Jews. More recently the British Reform movement has followed their lead. Rabbi Miriam Berger told me the Reform and Liberal movements recognize the importance to their members of having Jewish grandchildren, whether or not the mother is Jewish. She said that, as long as a child from a mixed heritage family is brought up Jewish, they can apply to the Reform *bet din*, the rabbinic court, to have their Jewish status recognized. I asked her how the *bet din* would know if a child has been brought up Jewishly. She said that the rabbi of their synagogue has to advocate for them in the *bet din*. And if they don't have a rabbi, that will be because they don't belong to a synagogue. And if so, the assumption will be that they haven't been brought up Jewishly.

Liberal Judaism tries to stay attuned to the behavioural changes taking place in society at large. They conduct same-gender and non-binary marriage ceremonies and they offer blessings to mixed-faith couples. The reason why they do not perform mixed-faith marriage ceremonies is that British law does not allow it. If and when the law changes, there is little doubt that the Liberals will be the first in line to oblige. In the meantime, their rabbis have the discretion to offer mixed faith blessings under a *huppa,* the traditional wedding canopy, if the couple request it.

I asked Rabbi Charley if she thought that the Liberals' willingness to go it alone on matters of personal status might prove to be problematic. The long-term consequence of people being considered as Jewish only by some Jewish streams and not others might lead to a situation in which there are two or more pedigrees of Jews, one of which does not recognize the validity of the others. 'It's been a concern that people have had for generations. My mum did a progressive conversion. And I remember growing up there was this big worry, you know, about us being recognized or not. And it hasn't come to fruition. People have said for generations that Liberal Judaism or Progressive Judaism would weaken the Jewish community. But I don't see the evidence for that.'

Historically, relationships between the orthodox and progressive streams of Judaism have been tense. Charley says that as a result of both Covid and Corbyn, these tensions have eased, at least for the time being. The different communities have learned to unite around their common interests. During the peak of the Covid pandemic, when the different streams were being briefed together at round table meetings by the government, they were obliged to speak to each other, to discuss common responses to issues as they unfolded. 'I've seen such a shift,' she says, 'since I came into the rabbinate. There are people in the *haredi* community who I can pick up the phone to now, to ask what their response is to this or that. I meet fairly often with other denominations, and they all call me rabbi, even the Strictly Orthodox. I think relations are getting better, rather than worse.'

'We worry too much about speaking with one voice. I hear it all the time, "There's so few of us, we must speak together." But there's a difference between feeling together as a large community and having to say the same thing all the time. That's the biggest worry, I think, for people, that we're not going to be saying the same thing. But we all work together, better now than at any time I can remember.'

Others have told me similar things. There has always been a certain amount of tension at leadership level between the different religious streams; sometimes it has spilled over into outright dispute. But the double crisis – first Corbyn, then Covid – has brought the leadership together, even if it only turns out to be temporary. In Chief Rabbi Mirvis's words, 'We are more united today than we have been a long time. I see it in the relationships between different religious groupings and in other areas: huge politics, but we are more united. I think the threat brought us together. It affected us all.'

Masorti, the newest of the four main streams of British Judaism, straddles the divide between Modern Orthodoxy, on one side, and Liberal and Reform, on the other. Like Modern Orthodoxy, Masorti tries to reconcile traditional observance and belief with modern scholarship. Unlike Modern Orthodoxy, it does not accept the traditional belief that the Torah was given to Moses in the wilderness; it regards the Five Books of Moses as divinely inspired but humanly authored. The theological distinction between Modern Orthodoxy and Masorti sounds cut and dried when it is put like that, but the reality is more ambiguous. Many Modern Orthodox thinkers doubt the Mosaic origins of the Torah, and a fair few Masorti congregants are uncomfortable with giving up the age-old literal belief in the revelation on Mount Sinai, when Moses received the Ten Commandments.

David Newman, whose father was a United Synagogue rabbi, grew up in Britain and moved to Israel when he married. He sees British Jewry with the objective clarity that only someone familiar with it but living outside it can have. 'British Jewry,' he told me, 'has never got over its theological hang-ups. I think it's because it's a small community. In America, where you've got a million or two of every denomination, who cares whether one lot recognize the other? The moment you don't care about it, you can go and speak to them. But here, everybody treads very gingerly.'

Theology is not the only point of difference between Masorti and Modern Orthodoxy. Modern Orthodoxy sometimes finds it hard to reconcile its wish to remain within the orthodox camp with its desire to update archaic or politically incorrect aspects of Jewish law and practice. Its adherents do not want a schism within orthodoxy and are often accused of 'looking over their right shoulder', fearful of innovation lest the *haredi* rabbinate disapproves. Masorti, which burned its bridges with the *haredi* world long ago, is far more liberal in its interpretation of Jewish law, sometimes to such a degree that one might wonder why they continue to call themselves Masorti, a Hebrew word meaning 'traditional', or 'Conservative', as the movement is known in the USA.

Instinctively Masorti rabbis tend to associate with their Reform and Liberal colleagues, because they do not feel that they judge them in the same way as the orthodox might. Orthodoxy by its very definition cannot be pluralist; it cannot accept the validity of any other denomination of Judaism. Masorti, Reform and Liberal are all pluralist movements; they may not always agree with each other ideologically, but they do accept that Judaism can be expressed in more than one way.

When I spoke to her, Leonie Fleischmann was a co-chair of Masorti Judaism, the movement's umbrella organization. She had been a member of the Masorti youth group Noam and says that she found a community there that she never wanted to let go of. She joined the board and was elected as co-chair just before Covid struck. She told me that the pandemic gave the movement a purpose. 'Because all the congregations were struggling with how to respond, they didn't know what to do. We were able to bring everyone together to share ideas and run online events. And now one of the main areas we are focusing on is on looking for groups of young people who are forming their own communities, to see how we can support and empower them.'

One of the most visible differences between Masorti and Orthodoxy is in the role of women in the synagogue. Because Masorti sees Jewish law as dynamic, as a framework sufficiently flexible to respond positively to social and technological change, it has managed to mirror the changing roles of women in wider society far more easily. 30 years ago their largest synagogues still held to the traditional model of men leading services, with women sitting separately. Today their services are nearly all egalitarian, although their largest synagogue still offers the option of gender-segregated services, for those men and women who prefer it. And Masorti now has women rabbis.

Zahavit Shalev was one of the first two English women to serve as a rabbi in a Masorti congregation. She grew up in a committed, orthodox family and spent her gap year at an orthodox seminary in Israel. It is not unusual in orthodoxy for girls to spend a gap year at a seminary, or for boys to do the same at a *yeshiva*. This year of advanced residential study is one of the defining differences between an orthodox and non-orthodox lifestyle. Rabbi Zahavit describes her seminary experience as mind-expanding, adding that she was very happy there. But overall she felt embattled within orthodoxy: 'I felt that being a girl in the *frum* [religious] world was quite insulting at times, I was very much a secondary citizen.' It was not until she went to Limmud, where she met a lot of what she describes as 'very interesting people', that she began to feel that religiously she was moving in the right direction.

She left university with no intentions of becoming a rabbi; she didn't even start thinking about it until she was married and her first child had been born. By this time she had left her early career in publishing and was involved in a number of Jewish activities, teaching on an international adult education programme, running a conversion course at the synagogue she attended and working part-time with young adults for the Reform movement.

Her job at the Reform movement came to an end just as one of the rabbis in her synagogue was leaving, and they were about to begin the process of recruiting his successor. She approached Jonathan Wittenberg, the inspirational Senior Masorti Rabbi and the leader of her synagogue community. 'I said to him, "I've got a bit more time. I thought I'd give you first refusal." And he said, "Well, the salary and the job spec are in place, so we should think about employing you." And then, quite quickly, I said, "I don't want to do a rabbinic job without qualifications. If you're going to hire me to do rabbinic work, I'd like to be a rabbi."'

I asked Zahavit to explain to me the difference between Masorti and orthodoxy. She told me that Masorti is closely attached to the same liturgical traditions as orthodoxy, and that the services are similar. 'And I think there's a commitment to *halacha* [Jewish law] even though we know that the majority of our community are not massively moved by it. It feels important that we are committed, and help our members to understand what that commitment is, even if they choose not to adhere to it.'

But there is a noticeable difference of outlook between Masorti and orthodoxy. Zahavit says she thinks Masorti is more open, and more outward-facing. And although some in orthodoxy might challenge that analysis, it is certainly the case that Masorti is more willing to recognize diversity, in terms both of moving towards gender parity and of absorbing issues into the religious purview that are not exclusively Jewish – things like climate change and the hostile environment many refugees face.

And yet, despite its commitment to openness and diversity, Masorti, like any community of people, includes in its ranks those who are not able to commit fully to changing circumstance. Zahavit speaks, with a sort of amused resignation, of congregants with whom she has built up a relationship, perhaps teaching them or helping them out in some way, who tell her they are getting married. 'That's marvellous,' she says, and they reply, 'Yes, and we want our wedding to be conducted by a man.'

Even though most British Jews had little interest in the theological issues of the Jacobs Affair that led to the foundation of Masorti, the dispute opened up questions about religious authority within the community, and about the attitude of the orthodox rabbinate towards dissent. Many of the early members of Masorti were left-leaning, intellectually minded, traditional Jews who saw their movement as challenging the status quo in the community, refreshing it with new ideas and injecting it with new vigour. Times have changed, and the religious issues that concerned Masorti's original founders no longer excite strong emotions, but the radical ethos has remained. And that ethos is itself now being challenged by the pace of social change. By the realization that some of the issues about which its older rabbis were radical ten or 15 years ago have now entered the national discourse, and are themselves being superseded.

There are new changes afoot, changes that lie not only beyond the experiences of the older rabbis but even beyond those of rabbis of Rabbi Zahavit's generation.

'I'm not young,' she says. 'But I am young to the rabbinate. And because I am not an older man, I tilt slightly towards the younger set of Masorti rabbis. And there are all kinds of things on the agenda today that were not things that my older colleagues had to think about, but which we, their younger successors, will have to think about.'

The challenges that she sees as confronting Masorti in the coming years include, of course, issues over gender, which Zahavit describes as massively complicated, 'because gender is such a contested place these days'. But there are also new topics on the horizon. She gave the example of the Jewish psychedelic movement, in which, according to one website, 'chemically assisted mystical encounters are a normative part of Jewish spirituality' (instead, some of us might say, of being a normative part of growing up).[30] Then there are those whose spiritual quests involve blending other religions into Judaism. This is not a new phenomenon: there have always been those Jews who have been drawn to other spiritual systems, particularly oriental religions, and sought to embed them back into Judaism. But the pace and variety of such syncretistic quests are increasing all the time, throwing up new challenges for those rabbis who want to engage with Jews beyond the mainstream, who believe that Judaism has to be relevant to all Jews. 'If we're going to stay relevant, we have to be listening to what people are asking and what they're interested in. It's not that Torah is not interesting. It's just that it's going to be reflected through a whole bunch of other things that are important to people, people who are quite strident in their identities.'

Ask any member of the Strictly Orthodox, *haredi* community to tell you what Judaism is, and you are likely to be told that, far from being just a religious faith, it is an all-embracing lifestyle. They will tell you that Jewish law mandates every aspect of human behaviour, from the way one ties one's shoelaces to the way we are supposed to treat one another. From the imperative for men to worship three times a day with at least nine others to the blessing of God which one recites when seeing a rainbow or hearing thunder. There is hardly an aspect of human activity that falls outside the purview of a *haredi* lifestyle.

The *haredi* world may look monolithic to an outsider, but it is composed of many different communities. Some of the *haredim* are *hasidim,* members of distinctive sects that trace their roots back to a fervent spiritual movement that captivated eighteenth-century Eastern European Jewry. Those who are not *hasidim* are the descendants of the *misnagdim,* meaning 'opponents', so-called because their forebears fought against the hasidic movement when it first emerged. They felt that the hasidic approach was too innovative, too ready to favour the experiential and the mystical over Judaism's traditional legalism. Today those divisions are largely forgotten; *hasidim* and their opponents all coexist under the strictly orthodox *haredi* umbrella.

The word *haredi* comes from a phrase in the Book of Isaiah describing those who quake or tremble at God's command. *Haredim* and Quakers take their names from the same source. Britain's largest *haredi* community is in Stamford Hill, in north London, from where they are spreading out into adjoining areas as their numbers increase and local property prices rise. There are also substantial *haredi* communities in London's Golders Green, in north Manchester and in

Gateshead, where a *yeshiva* that was established in the 1920s sits at the centre of an expanding pious community.

One of the features of *haredi* life is the amount of time spent studying Talmudic and religious texts. Most *haredi* men will spend a few hours each day studying, either listening to lectures or learning together with study partners. The Gateshead community has grown rapidly in recent years. Partly as a result of an influx of *haredi* families in which the men, who somewhat unusually have professional jobs, want to spend part of their day working and the rest of their time absorbed in religious study. They need cheaper housing. Gateshead is ideal for them, and they, it seems, are ideal for Gateshead. It caters for them intellectually, and housing is far cheaper than in London. Whereas Stamford Hill is regarded, even by *haredim* in other cities, as closed and insular, Gateshead is seen as more open, engaged and learned. It was described by its former rabbi as 'the Oxbridge of the UK Jewish community'.[31]

Haredim are generally recognizable by their distinctive garb. The men wear large black skullcaps or dark, broad-brimmed hats. They wear their sidelocks long: the boys and younger men may curl them ostentatiously into ringlets, while older men tend to tuck them behind their ears. Their suits are dark and over their white shirts many wear a sort of slip-on, sleeveless vest, with knotted tassels hanging down from each corner, in fulfilment of a biblical commandment. Many religious Jews wear these fringed garments beneath their shirts, but *haredim*, who have nothing to hide, wear them on top. On festivals and sabbaths, those who come from the hasidic sects are likely to revert to elaborate eighteenth-century Polish attire, which may include a round fur hat, silk robe or kaftan and white socks. Every sect has its own dress code.

The women are less constrained in the colours they wear, but they all cover their hair in public, with either a wig, scarf or snood. They wear modest clothing at all times, their sleeves extending down to their wrists and their skirts and dresses to their ankles. They do not wear trousers; those are men's garments, and the biblical prohibition against cross-dressing is strictly observed. Unsurprisingly, when the secular media are writing about Jews, the accompanying photo is often of *haredim*. Even if the story they are writing is wholly unconnected with religion.

Haredi Jews tend to live in close proximity to one another: it is not easy to live a *haredi* lifestyle on one's own. Their communities are largely self-sufficient. They have their own support networks and schools, read their own newspapers and buy their food in shops that sell kosher produce approved by rabbis from their wing of orthodoxy. If they need a doctor or dentist, they will, wherever possible, go to one who is either *haredi* or has close contact with the community. Those who are economically active, often in property or jewellery, will come into contact with other Jews and with the world at large. But many, particularly those who spend their lives in full-time education, supported by family or the community, will have no contact with anyone beyond their immediate, Yiddish-speaking circle.

Because all *haredim* dress so similarly, it is easy to fall into the trap of thinking that they are all the same as each other. In a sense their uniformity in dress is intentional: individualism and the cult of the self are antipathetic to the *haredi* value of modesty. But it can also mean that those who are not *haredim* do not see the person whom the clothes conceal. It is easy to imagine all *haredi* Jews as being as identical in thought and personality as they are in dress, to consider them as an alien tribe who not only have strange ways that are embarrassing to other Jews but who also, because of their high birth rate and rapidly expanding numbers, are seen as a threat to the conventional, middle-class image of British Jewry.

Of course, this perception is nonsense. As individuals, *haredim* are as diverse as any other group of people. It's just that they have a different outlook on life, and they seem to be better at not flaunting their egos. Generally.

When I spoke to David Newman, who has many friends and family in the *haredi* community, he described them as 'different shades of one colour'. He told me of three brothers he knows, all *haredi* Jews, all growing up in the same environment. One is now a member of the supreme religious authority in Israel; he dresses in the same way as all other *haredim*, but unlike most *haredim*, he is a religious Zionist. Another brother is a member of Chabad, the hasidic group focused on outreach, and the third belongs to the inward-looking Satmar hasidic sect. Three brothers, all different, each looking the same as the other two.

Nevertheless this perception of a homogeneous *haredi* community does persist. I put it to Rabbi Herschel Gluck, perhaps the least likely of all Stamford Hill rabbis to conform to the prejudiced stereotype of a *haredi* Jew. Awarded an OBE in 2012 for services to inter-faith understanding, particularly for his work with the Muslim-Jewish Forum, which he founded, Rabbi Gluck's personal network stretches far beyond the Jewish world. I told him that there was a perception in centrist British Jewry that the *haredi* community was something of a threat to mainstream Jewish life. He burst out laughing. 'The *haredi* community offers a lot to Anglo Jewry. On many levels, as far as Torah study is concerned, as far as acts of kindness and caring for others are concerned. I think that to be able to communicate Judaism in an intellectual, passionate manner is something that Anglo Jewry can derive a lot of benefit from. If you go through this neighbourhood, and you see how many Jews go to synagogue three times a day, how many Jews go to the study house to learn, how many do acts of kindness and how they put themselves out to live a scrupulous life, it is phenomenal. For them, Judaism is a way of life, not just a hobby. It is the essence of being.'

Rabbi Gluck founded the Muslim-Jewish Forum after serving on the executive of JCore, the Jewish Council for Racial Equality. He was working with Muslim immigrants, helping them to settle in Britain, when he was approached by the Next Century Foundation, an NGO working in the field of conflict resolution. He agreed to become involved in some of their global peace and reconciliation projects. And he began thinking about what was happening in Britain: 'I was doing this work all over the world. And I thought to myself, "What about my own backyard? Is everything perfect here in the UK? We have a lot of good relations with the Muslim community here. But is it good enough? And is it strong enough? And do we have organizations that will be able to withstand the stresses that might be in store in the future?" This was in the year 2000, so before 9/11. That's when I started the idea of the Muslim-Jewish Forum, which was the first time that Jews and Muslims, uniquely, had come together, to work together.'

He says that in the Forum they speak about anything other than politics and religion. Its members see each other not as mirroring the Middle East but as neighbours living side by side in Britain. They have invested their lives in the UK and they have shared concerns about being able to continue living and educating their children here, as members of the Jewish and Muslim faiths.

It is that faith which drives Rabbi Herschel Gluck. He is unusual in the *haredi* world for directing so much of his tremendous energy beyond his community, but all his work reflects the Jewish value of *gemilut hasadim,* 'acts of kindness', a value to which the *haredi* community attach tremendous importance.

One of the features of *haredi* life, which derives directly from their conviction that Judaism is an all-embracing lifestyle, is their warm and supportive communal life. Small things that would seem quite extraordinary in mainstream society are taken for granted. Families will announce a wedding and issue a general invitation for anyone who wants to come and join them at the celebration. When a baby is born, the local community is encouraged to call in to the new parents' house on a Friday evening for a drink and to welcome the child. *Haredi* life is a communal affair, and the obligation to rejoice is taken very seriously.

Of course, it is not idyllic – nothing is – but there is no doubt that the community has many more strengths than are generally recognized by those who do not know it. It sets an example to Anglo Jewry not only in its commitment to religious education but also in its charitable endeavours, in its support for its less prosperous members and the strict adherence of most *haredim* to the principle that one tenth of their income should be given to charity. Its volunteer-run organization Hatzola responds to medical emergencies, working closely with the NHS to respond to crisis calls, and its Shomrim security patrols serve both Jews and non-Jews alike. *Haredi* Judaism today is a far cry from its old image of a blinkered, isolated movement, trying its hardest to distance itself from the world around it.

But some of that still remains. *Haredi* Judaism may be modernizing, but there are still many within the community who are deeply distrustful of the outside world. Even though they acknowledge that Britain is a *malchus shel hesed*, a benevolent kingdom, where they are unlikely to be persecuted, those *haredim* who continue to look inwards are nevertheless deeply distrustful of the outside world. In a 2020 blog post Eli Spitzer, who we shall meet shortly, noted that:

> Any conscious *haredi* is aware that our current situation in a *malchus shel hesed* is, by *golus* [exile] standards, remarkably good and none of us want it to be otherwise. However, our basic perception of reality is one where gentile ambivalence is normal, hostility is frequent and benevolence is an occasional welcome novelty. The kind of shock and disgust felt by Anglo Jewry at the exposure of Jew-hatred spouted by Labour councillors and activists, just has no analogue for *haredim*. Lots of things in life are surprising, but a *goy* [non-Jew] hating a *yid* [Jew] isn't one of them.[32]

The Holocaust hit their world disproportionately badly; there are few *haredi* Jews in Britain who did not lose close relatives in the extermination camps. For them, anti-Semitism is not something to protest about; it is what they expect. Their paranoia is exacerbated by the fact that visually they are far more of a target, because of their dress and the tight, densely populated neighbourhoods in which they live.

Those at one extreme of *haredi* life regard themselves as the authentic remnant of Israel who, cast into exile 2,000 years ago, are now patiently trying to bring about the messianic age through faithful adherence to the precepts of Judaism. They live a lifestyle that they imagine has remained unchanged for 2,000 years. They are oblivious to the fact that *haredi* Judaism is as much a product of the modern world as any other Jewish stream. The very existence of an ultra-orthodox faction, or indeed any faction, in what was once a largely religiously undifferentiated Jewish world, is a consequence of the Enlightenment. The contemporary *haredi* ideal, that a young man who is not a rabbinic prodigy can aspire to a lifetime of unwaged Torah study, was inconceivable when even the most observant of Jews were concerned with the imperative of putting food on the table. And the transnational structure of *haredi* society, in which rabbinic rulings handed down in Brooklyn or Jerusalem affect what goes on in north London, Manchester and Gateshead, could never have happened when people lived in European ghettos and villages where communication was poor.

Not all strictly observant Jews are *haredim*. The traditional orthodox are just as religiously observant, but they engage with the wider world and are part of what, for want of a better word, we call the mainstream British Jewish community. They don't wear *haredi* garb, but they dress conservatively and the women conform to the same perceptions of modesty as their *haredi* sisters. They are conservative both in religion and politics, are likely to attend synagogue three times a day and when their children leave school they will typically spend a year or more in a *yeshiva,* a college for advanced Talmudic study in Israel. But unlike the *haredim,* far fewer will remain in full-time, lifelong religious education. Some do, but most of them are likely to go to university or start a career. Traditional orthodoxy, in Britain at least, does not require withdrawal from the world.

Like every other community in Britain, the *haredim* have their social problems. They may not be the same problems as in those communities plagued by gangs, drug abuse or the fear of burglary and personal violence, but they are problems nevertheless. These problems typically only occur within small pockets of the *haredi* community, but because the *haredi* community is so visible and so distinct, they can attract undue attention, far more than those which occur with regularity on an inner-city estate, or in a suburban middle-class community.

Eve Sacks is a trustee of Nahamu, a lobbying charity she helped to set up, which aims to speak out against harms systematically arising in the *haredi* community.[33] She explains that many of the behaviours they campaign against are committed through ignorance, by people who do what their leaders tell them without understanding why what they do is wrong. One of the issues they lobby on is financial crime. She calls it coerced criminality, though she suggests that I might want to call it benefit fraud. 'The reason I call it coerced criminality rather than benefit fraud is because it is presented to them as a legitimate way to get money. Because of their lack of education and the lack of other options, they are completely naive about what they are doing, and the risks. I have sympathy for the perpetrators, but not for those who put them in that position and tell them it's OK.' She says that of course those who encourage them know it is legally wrong, but they morally justify it on the grounds that there is no victim; it is government money and that they should look on it as compensation for the way that Jews have been treated in the past.

Eve says that the lack of personal choice in the lives of many *haredim* manifests itself most insidiously when it comes to forced marriages. She speaks of conversations she has had with people who tell her they feel trapped, of women who are stuck in marriages they do not have the confidence to leave, who do not have the education to earn a living in anything other than the most menial jobs, who fear they will be alienated by their friends and family should they try to get out. Women who know that, even if they were able to carve out an independent life for themselves, the community would mobilize its resources against them to prevent them from winning custody of their children or sending them to a school that would give them the skills needed to function in wider society.

The problem is greatest for women, but men can also feel trapped. The only way that a married man or woman can easily leave the *haredi* world is if their spouse leaves with them. Eve says she knows of men, including a relatively well-known *haredi* rabbi, who would like to leave but whose wives won't, and for whom getting out would inevitably lead to a lengthy custody battle over the children.

One cannot imagine an organization like Nahamu existing a generation or two ago. In the days when the community tried not to raise its head above the parapet, the idea of openly criticizing behaviours in other parts of the community would have been frowned upon. It would have been regarded as washing the communal laundry in public. That Nahamu exists is an indication of the new, more open, even self-critical, attitude in Britain's Jewish community.

Of course, it is not only in the *haredi* community that people can experience what Eve calls faith-based harms. In fact the problems can be far greater in other British minorities, particularly where young girls can be at risk of honour-based violence. Eve says she is not conducting a campaign against the *haredim* as such, and it is important for her that they are not singled out: her concern is with harm and abuse across the board.

I asked Eve what she wanted to achieve in her campaigns. She said that success for her would be for *haredi* schools to teach about the principle of consent, and for children to be taught that they have the right to marry whoever they want. And for a communal organization to help to integrate those people into the mainstream community and help them through university. 'So that a *haredi* girl or boy could say, "OK, I don't have to marry this person. And if I don't, I'll go to this organization, and I'll be looked after.' As for coerced criminality, success will come when the government massively clamps down and it's just not an attractive option any more. And that, in turn, will put pressure on them to have better education. That has happened in the *haredi* community in America. Because if you can't rely on benefits you have to get qualifications and work.'

Moshe Braun is one of those whose family did get out. His parents were part of the large Satmar hasidic sect in Stamford Hill. 'We were just regular Satmar *hasidim*, nothing really significant about us. Until I was the age of about seven or eight, when my family was involved in a quite big scandal in the community, concerning the abuse of a couple of kids at a hasidic camp. The accused was the son of a prominent rabbi in the community, and the family who accused him of abuse, who went to the police, were turned on by the community. Their house was surrounded literally by hundreds of people. They had to have police protection, and they couldn't stay in their home because it was dangerous. The father of this family was my dad's accountant. So when they had to leave their home, my dad offered to take the children into our house. And then we were pulled into this whole scandal. We had to have police protection outside our home as well. Even though we hadn't made the complaint, we were just taking the side of the family whose kids had been abused.'

Life in the Stamford Hill community became untenable for Moshe and his family. The children began receiving abuse at school, and his parents were ostracized. They stayed in the area, but the children were taken out of the ultra-religious, Yiddish-speaking schools they had been attending and sent to mainstream Jewish schools, where the tuition was in English and conformed to the national curriculum. But even there, Moshe says, there were times when he found life uncomfortable. He feels that his family's decision to remain in Stamford Hill was not a good one, that they were isolated from the community. Unlike the family who had raised the charge of abuse, who left the area, Moshe's family did not give themselves the opportunity to start again.

Such problems in the *haredi* community are distressing, but overall the community is vibrant and confident. One of its distinguishing features is its commitment to charitable giving; there are dozens of *haredi* charities and non-profit organizations. The Interlink Foundation is one of the great success stories of the *haredi* community, supporting and underpinning its charitable infrastructure. They provide strategic advice, consultancy and training, incubate start-up charities and assist their members with specialist issues such as safeguarding and policy-writing. They create partnerships between different organizations, represent their member organizations to the local authority and connect public sector bodies with community organizations. They also run training programmes for people and organizations who want to know more about the *haredi* community. Interlink's associate members include non-Jewish bodies such as the Hackney Council for Voluntary Services.

Chaya Spitz is Interlink's dynamic Chief Executive. Her own story illustrates the trajectory that the *haredi* world has taken in the past few years. Like many *haredi* girls, Chaya left school with no A-levels and went to an orthodox teachers' training college, possibly imagining that she would do what so many other young *haredi* girls do and teach for a short time before marrying and raising a family. Instead, she joined Interlink as an Information Officer and began to work her way up the organization, studying for an MBA as she progressed and stepping into the role of Chief Executive in 2010.

It was around then that Interlink started to change. It had been set up to introduce charities to the resources they needed, but it was finding that organizations outside the community, particularly the local authorities, were using it as a source of information. It was becoming more of a one-stop shop, connecting the outside world with the *haredi* community. So Interlink was restructured, turning into a membership body, which any orthodox organization in the UK could join.

I visited Interlink's offices in June 2021. It was the first face-to-face meeting I'd had with anyone since starting my research: the Covid pandemic had meant that every meeting I'd previously had was online. I happened to step into the lift at the same time as Chaya. She stopped the lift halfway up and said, 'I want to introduce you to my daughter.'

We stepped out into a brightly painted office, radiating energy and cheerfulness. 'This is Sunbeams,' said Chaya. It felt just like its name.

Sunbeams is the brainchild of Chaya's daughter, Ruchie Ostreicher. She describes their role as 'early preventative work for girls who are struggling'. It began when Ruchie was volunteering for Bikur Cholim, a *haredi* charity dedicated to the religious duty of visiting the sick. Bikur Cholim asked her to visit a young girl in a psychiatric unit who would not speak. Ruchie and her friend visited the girl regularly 'and after about five months of weekly visits, she began speaking to us. She wouldn't speak to the psychologists, she wouldn't speak to the doctors, but she spoke to us. And we were just two friends, visiting her.'

This experience inspired Ruchie to set up Sunbeams. They now work with over 100 children, each of whom comes in once a week for one-to-one support from a mentor. Sunbeams is a true community organization, a testament to the tight, self-sufficient ethos of the Strictly Orthodox world. Rather than being established by therapists and clinicians, it was founded from the ground up by a young woman who initially had no experience, but who found that she had a skill and an enthusiasm to change the lives of others. And who is trusted by her community, because of what she has shown she can do, rather than because of any academic or vocational qualifications she may have.

When we left Sunbeams and reached Interlink's offices at the top of the building, Chaya introduced me to everyone in her team and told me about the organization's origins. It was founded over 30 years ago by Esther Sterngold, whom Chaya describes as 'a magnificent woman who was very active in a charity, who found that people were asking her for lots of advice'. Esther turned to the National Council for Voluntary Organisations, who told her 'Your communal organizations are not going to come to us for support, so why don't you set up something for your own community? Model it on the Bengali associations.' And that was how it all started. The fact that the *haredi* community's premier umbrella body was founded because of advice from Britain's National Council for Voluntary Organisations and is modelled on the Bengali community undermines the myth that the *haredi* community turns a blind eye to the rest of the world.

Chaya recognizes that because Interlink is so widely connected it can be seen as representing the *haredi* community to the outside world. But she is very careful about Interlink appearing to speak for its community. The *haredi* world is very cautious, trying, as Chaya says, to maintain its way of life in the face of a rapidly changing world, with rapidly changing values. 'People are anxious and worried and because we do so much connecting, and because so much of our work is so outward-facing, people do become concerned.' Sensitivity is paramount.

Sensitivity is important. But Interlink is not a place in which people cautiously tiptoe around each other; the atmosphere is far too vibrant for that. Half an hour soaking up the energy in the Interlink offices is the perfect riposte to anyone who thinks that the strictly orthodox, *haredi* community is staid and stuffy, mired in the past and out of touch with the modern world.

Many *haredim* come from hasidic families: descendants of those who were attracted to the spiritual renaissance that swept through the Jewish communities of Russia, Poland and Ukraine in the eighteenth century. From its earliest days the hasidic world divided itself into 'courts' or sects, each headed by a rabbi, or *rebbe*, a spiritual leader who acts as a conduit for his followers, mediating between them and heaven. These days there are many hasidic sects: the largest, both globally and in the UK, is Satmar. But the one that is best known, at least by those who are not *hasidim*, is Chabad.

Chabad is unique among hasidic sects in the way it engages with the rest of the Jewish world. Most hasidic sects are inward-looking, concentrated in their own synagogues and communities. Chabad is not like that. On the contrary: openness to all Jews is an essential feature of Chabad life. Not, as many fear, because they are out to convert them to a Chabad way of life. But because they believe in the value and importance of every Jew, believe that every Jew should be embraced in love, in a refutation of the history in which Jews were hunted down and persecuted.

30 years ago very few British Jews had heard of Chabad. That it is now ubiquitous and arouses strong emotions, both in support of it and against, is an indication of both Chabad's own outreach programmes and the extent to which British Jewry has changed in that period.

Chabad is also known as Lubavitch, which causes a certain amount of confusion among those who are not familiar with the movement. The name Chabad is an acrostic made from the initial letters of the Hebrew words for wisdom, understanding and knowledge – a kabbalistic triad that reflects the mystical origins of the movement. Lubavitch is the name of the town where the grandson of the movement's founder settled, around which his followers congregated.

I spoke to Rabbi Bentzi Sudak, one of British Chabad's most articulate leaders. He told me that Chabad is passionate about encouraging Jews to have a deeper engagement with their religion, to transcend the often superficial relationship that Jewish people have with their Judaism. He gave me an example from the barmitzvah ceremony. Typically a 12-year-old boy from a mainstream family will spend the best part of a year learning to chant a passage from the Torah in the synagogue on his 13th birthday. It is a big challenge, but not one that inspires most young people, and for many boys learning their barmitzvah passage marks the end of their religious education. 'The barmitzvah is the one sure way to turn Jews off Judaism. You take a kid, he's having fun. He's playing football. You say, "Come here, you're Jewish, you're a man now." He goes, "I'm a man? I'm only 12 years old, where did my childhood go?" And you have him once a week sitting with somebody and you teach him a skill that he won't master and he'll never use. And he never wants to see the inside of a synagogue after he's finished with that.'

Bentzi's solution is to teach them, 'boys and girls alike, what it means to be a Jew, to show them its wisdom, to give them the tools to access this incredible treasure chest that they have inherited'.

Bentzi explained to me that, unlike some religions, the goal of Judaism is focused not on what happens to us in heaven or the afterlife but on the purpose for which we were sent into the world. Chabad's philosophy, he explains, is that each person is born with a specific and unique mission that God needs them to fulfil in life, that what may happen in the afterlife is merely a consequence of our actions, but not the goal. And it is about raising an awareness of one's deeper identity and unique purpose, one's eternal soul, to reach a love of every human being. 'Because the only way you can actually love someone else as yourself is if you identify with your soul more than your body.'

Chabad's philosophy is esoteric, but what makes it successful as an organization is the down-to-earth way in which the majority of their rabbis go about their work. They don't try to sell their philosophy; they are not missionaries trying to win people over to their belief system. But they are out there, trying to engage with people, being there for others, running the most successful outreach programme ever attempted in the Jewish world, a programme instituted by their late *rebbe*, Rabbi Menachem Mendel Schneerson, who regarded the need to rebuild the Jewish world in the wake of the Shoah as a religious imperative, and who sent his rabbis out across the world to fulfil the mission. Today there is scarcely a destination beyond the reach of a Chabad emissary, offering kosher meals, Passover *seders* and pastoral support to travellers who happen to be passing through. Chabad rabbis reach the places other rabbis cannot reach.

Even in Britain, where there is no shortage of rabbis of every denomination, Chabad have established their niche. They have over 100 rabbinic couples living in towns and communities across the country, establishing a presence in places with tiny Jewish populations, running prayer and study centres in areas with larger Jewish populations. They support students on campus, sometimes working for the national University Student Chaplaincy under the Chief Rabbi's auspices, sometimes working independently. A principal difference, Bentzi Sudak tells me, between Chabad rabbis working on campus or in small communities and their colleagues from other movements is their career progression. Rabbis in the other movements start their careers in a small synagogue, being promoted as they advance into larger congregations. 'The Chabad point of view is you get a space, this is your flock, and you're committed to that community. You are going to make this the best. No community is a stepping stone in your career ladder. This is your community, and your success and your growth are in the building of this community. So the rabbi in Islington is not saying, "One day I'm going to be in St John's Wood"; he's saying, "One day Islington is going to be incredible." And to do that he has to work with the local reality.'

Similarly, Bentzi tells me, each Chabad rabbi is responsible for raising the funds to run his own community. 'It's very entrepreneurial,' he says, 'there is no central fund.'

Chabad rabbis are very good at illustrating their points with stories. So when I asked Bentzi about the charge often laid at Chabad's door that they are a proselytizing organization, which wants to bring the entire Jewish world under their umbrella, he answered me with a story. It concerned the late *rebbe*, Menachem Mendel Schneerson, who, despite passing away in 1994, remains the ever-present inspiration for all Chabad followers, whose name crops up in nearly every conversation with his disciples, no matter how down-to-earth the topic.

'One of the *Rebbe*'s students got a call from his secretary. He told him that the *Rebbe* had been approached by a woman who was not a part of Chabad. She told the *Rebbe* that her son wanted to go to Yeshiva University (a modern orthodox institution in New York, not connected to Chabad). But she couldn't afford to send him there. The secretary said that the *Rebbe* wanted his student to facilitate it, to raise the money to pay the boy's fees. The only condition was that the boy was never to know where his funding came from. When the student asked why they didn't just send the boy to a Chabad institution, the secretary said, "That's not what she wants. We have to do what people want." So the student raised the money and the boy went to Yeshiva University, unaware that he was being funded by Chabad, unaware even that Chabad was playing any role in his life.

'Some years later there was a lecture at the *Rebbe*'s headquarters in Brooklyn. During the question-and-answer session afterwards, one of the audience raised his hand. It was the boy who had been funded to go to Yeshiva

University. His question: "Why do Chabad only ever take care of their own?"'

This story, Bentzi told me, illustrates the extent of the misconception that he says needs to be cleared up. He says that, if their goal was to make everybody a follower of Chabad, they have clearly failed. Not only that, he says, but their goal is not even about making everyone religious. Rather, it is to help each Jew connect and access the unique purpose for which he or she was created. Chabad in Britain, he says, is a part of the Jewish community; it is not looking to dominate the community. 'The Jewish community is like a body. And a body is healthy when it's made up of different parts. If you have two right hands, you have an unhealthy body. If you have a right hand and the left hand and they are different, that is a healthy body.'

There is an issue, though, with the Chabad philosophy of accepting and loving every Jew. The issue is the one that I discussed with Rabbi Charley Baginsky from the Liberal movement: what happens when some Jews are not accepted by others as being Jewish? Do they say, 'I love you, but not you, because I don't accept your Jewish status'?

Bentzi's answer is the only one that any rabbi anywhere on the orthodox spectrum can give. Orthodoxy holds that Jewish law is a self-supporting, wholly integrated system that derives from centuries of tradition. It can develop organically, as technological and social conditions change: responding positively, for example, to advances in medicine, addressing issues that could not have even been contemplated centuries ago. But Jewish law, according to the orthodox, cannot change just because modernity wants it to. The Progressive denominations disagree. Jewish law, they say, is sufficiently flexible to respond to changing social conditions. In biblical times Jewish status was passed down the paternal line. It meant that the children of women who had been raped by enemy soldiers were not considered Jewish. So 2,000 years ago the law was changed, so that only the children of Jewish women (or converts) were considered Jewish. Now, the progressive movements say, we live in a world characterized by mixed-faith marriages. So they will admit any child who has one Jewish parent of whatever gender.

Orthodoxy does not accept this argument. Just as with divorce, no orthodox rabbi on the planet can change the law, even if they wanted to. This is both the great strength, and the outstanding weakness, of orthodoxy: it has no central authority, no Pope, no Synod, certainly no Chief Rabbi who can resolve to change the law. So things will carry on as they always have done. Of all the religious challenges facing the Jewish world, that of who is a Jew is one of the most intractable.

The question of who is a Jew encompasses one of the great injustices in Jewish communities today. Many people who live committed and active Jewish lives, possibly even coming from families that have regarded themselves as Jewish for generations, are not accepted as Jews by orthodox communities. The reason is that they were converted to Judaism, or one of their maternal ancestors was, by a non-orthodox rabbinic court. It doesn't matter whether or not the conversion was carried out in full accordance with Jewish law; if the three presiding members of the *bet din*, the rabbinic court who oversaw the conversion, were not recognized as qualified by the orthodox rabbinate, then in their eyes the conversion is invalid.

The situation is both unjust and absurd. Unjust because ultimately it comes down to religious politics. No rabbi has the formal right to recognize or reject the authority of another. Judaism does not have a religious hierarchy as, for example,

Catholicism does. Indeed, strictly speaking, any three Jews, rabbis or not, can constitute a *bet din* for the purposes of conversion. And the system is absurd because the world is full of Jews whom the orthodox may not recognize but who are nevertheless recognized by many Jews as Jewish, and who continue to build communities and grow in numbers, irrespective of orthodox censure.

And so the question of who is a Jew is the issue that causes more heartache in the British Jewish community than any other. On one side are those who are distressed to be told that their children or grandchildren are not universally accepted as Jewish because of what seems to them to be arcane legal impediments. On the other are those for whom religious faith and law are paramount.

The tragedy is that the problem can be resolved. An attempt was made in Israel some years ago to establish a programme of conversion that would satisfy all streams. It didn't succeed, mainly for political reasons, but the protocol was established, and one day it may be revived. Relations between the different denominations in Britain are far better than they have been but still, apparently, not good enough for rabbis from both sides to put their heads together to find a solution that will gladden the hearts of the distressed in their communities, without damaging anyone's faith. There is an old saying: 'Where there is a rabbinic will, there is a way.' That applies in the British Jewish community as much as anywhere else.

4

Conformity and Dissent

As a community, British Jewry is more confident in itself than at any time in the past. But that confidence doesn't always trickle down to individuals. Many, particularly among the older generation and those whose families have been scarred by persecution, remain cautious about telling non-Jews that they are Jewish. One person told me that she felt that she lived in two different worlds. She could not do anything about the fact of her Jewishness. But she never allowed it to get in the way of her Britishness, the world in which she spent the vast majority of her time.

Some find their Jewishness embarrassing, and cringe if they see their more religious brethren dressing or behaving in a manner likely to draw attention to their faith. And some actively rail against the fact of their Jewish birth.

The notion of the self-hating Jew came into prominence in America during the 1940s and 1950s. As a term of abuse it was applied to writers like Isaac Rosenfeld, Ben Hecht and Philip Roth, who were accused of portraying anti-Semitic stereotypes in their work. The idea itself, of Jews who suffer from a somewhat indefinable syndrome known as self-hatred, goes back even further, probably to the beginning of the twentieth century, when assimilated Jewish intellectuals in Austria and Germany denounced the mannerisms of their less sophisticated co-religionists from Eastern Europe, and disassociated themselves from them. In 1930 Theodor Lessing described his journey from a repugnance at Judaism to his support of Zionism in a publication entitled *Der Jüdische Selbsthass* ('Jewish Self-Hatred'). By the 1980s the label 'self-hating Jew' had become a derogatory term used by some on the right of Israeli politics to characterize the state's Jewish opponents, and by religious critics of aggressively secular Jews. It ended up as a catch-all phrase encompassing all those who, for one reason or another, were uncomfortable with, or even embarrassed by, their Jewishness.[34]

Fewer Jews these days seem to qualify for the epithet 'self-hating'. Those to whom it was once applied are no less strident in their views, but when they criticize the Jewish world now, they are more likely to do so as confirmed, rather than reluctant, Jews. The well-publicized resignations from Judaism of the authors Will Self and then Shlomo Sand now seem even more daft than they did at the time. (Anyway, resigning from Judaism can't be done; once you are in there is no way out.) Will Self subsequently indicated that he had been reconsidering his resignation.[35]

'My dad was a self-hating Jew,' explains Georgina Bednar. 'He had a really tough relationship with Judaism. He hated it, he hated all religions. I think his father had been very scarred by the war and his experiences, and my dad too was very scarred. He was a self-hating Jew, he just hated it all. I think I'm more at peace with my Jewish identity. I guess I'm more reflective, I'm better educated than he ever was and I've had the opportunity to reflect. I feel Jewish in my bones, whereas his hatred, his rejection of the formal structures of Judaism, was a horrible kind of chasm for him.'

Coming to terms with one's Jewish identity does not necessarily involve religion. As one of the people I spoke to said: 'There is something incredibly special about being Jewish, it's an honour. We are chosen – I know you're not really supposed to say that – but I don't mean it's from God. I mean we have a special place in history, a place in the world. Different, but a burden too.' Hearing comments like that highlights the illogicality, the hubris almost, of the orthodox rabbinate's insistence that only they can decide who is a Jew.

For British Jews, she said, there's an extra dimension to that special place in history. 'I feel wholly blessed. We are the lucky Jews. Apart from war casualties and in the Channel Islands, we are the only Jewish community in Europe to have survived completely intact. Our ancestors were lucky enough to come to this bountiful, liberal, tolerant land where Jews have thrived and have been respected and safe.'

For the comedian Josh Howie the catalyst for his positive Jewish identity came from religion. Born to a Jewish mother and a non-Jewish father, he was raised as a Buddhist. He didn't have sense of a Jewish identity until he was 16, when he went on a trip to Israel. Then religion kicked in. Something appealed to him there. It's often indefinable, the thing that draws people closer to religion, and a few months later he was studying in a *yeshiva*, a school for advanced religious study, with the intention of becoming a rabbi. The rabbinic training didn't last: he was expelled from the *yeshiva* for being with a non-Jewish girl, but his Jewish identity stuck.

Nic Schlagman does not sound like a man who is conflicted by his dual British and Jewish identities. He wouldn't pass the Norman Tebbit test.[36] When I asked him whether he sees himself as a Jew who is British or as British person who is a Jew, he said he thought he was a Jew who happens to live in London. He works in the Jewish community because it feels familiar. 'I've had a slightly different experience from most of my contemporaries in that I lived abroad for half of my adult life. I was in Israel, in a country full of Jews. I relate to British Jews more easily than I relate to British people in general. I've discovered that, in general, I relate to British minorities more than I relate to the British majority.'

But that is not to say that he is uncomfortable being British. He says he chooses to work in the Jewish community in Britain because he understands how things work here. And he says that if you asked people which British minority they would choose to be born into, if they had to make such a choice, most would say they would choose to be Jews. Which sounds to me as if there is something about Nic's Britishness that complements and enhances his identity as a Jew.

One of the challenges for minorities in a society adapting to multiculturalism is finding the balance between one's own identity and that of the majority. Centuries of worldwide dispersion have led Jews to almost instinctively regard the place they happen to live as a host country. It doesn't mean they won't fully engage with every aspect of life in that country, but there is always a sense that this dwelling place too might be temporary, just as all the others have been. It is a sense of insecurity, of otherness, one that never fully departs, no matter how long one's family have been established in the land. Jews are likely to see themselves, at least at times, as guests in someone else's land, even when the citizens of that nation do not consider them so. One woman, who asked to remain anonymous, told me that she knew she has 'this ridiculous English schoolgirl accent. But over the last few years, after Corbyn became leader of the Labour Party, I began to feel like an alien in my own country, like the mask has been ripped away. And if I passed as British before, now I feel like a traveller, who has been exposed as not really belonging here.'

In her book *House of Glass*, Hadley Freeman asks whether the alternative to assimilation is self-ghettoization. 'Could there not be an option of inclusion,' she asks, 'which allows for the acceptance of a minority group's differences without this being seen as a threat to the majority?' She suggests that this question will be argued over for centuries to come.

The answer to Hadley's question may be that, when a minority community applies its values for the benefit of the majority, the question of assimilation need not be seen as a threat. Minorities can both assimilate and retain their own identity when they are confident in themselves, and confident in their place in wider society.

Jonathan Goldstein, the former Chairman of the Jewish Leadership Council, which represents Britain's communal organizations, takes a historical view: 'You can't look at Anglo Jewry today without saying that something has changed in Anglo Jewry, and that was triggered predominantly by Corbyn, by our ability to stand up and say, we will not put up with this. And to act in a way in which the historic leaders of British Jewry would not necessarily have acted.' Jews in Britain today, he says, had the confidence to do so because of the way in which the former Chief Rabbis, Immanuel Jakobovits and Jonathan Sacks, represented and established Anglo Jewry at the centre of British life, enabling the community to articulate its issues.

Both Jakobovits and his successor, Jonathan Sacks, were unusual as Chief Rabbis. Living in an age of mass communication, they were able spread their ideas beyond the boundaries of their community, in a way their predecessors were not able, and perhaps did not want, to do. They both took advantage of the opportunity, feeling it important that they presented a moral and ethical voice to the nation at large, not just to the Jewish community. But they lived at a time when divisions were opening up between the various Jewish denominations, and some were calling into question the whole institution of the Chief Rabbi. The Strictly Orthodox and Progressive communities were growing ever more strident in their insistence that the Chief Rabbi did not represent them. Unable to command the allegiance of the entire community, yet presented with a unique opportunity to make their voices heard, they relied on the force of their personalities and the connections they made.

Immanuel Jakobovits won the very public trust of Prime Minister Margaret Thatcher. She declared that she was deeply affected by his thought and his writing and wished that the church leadership would 'take a leaf' out of his book. Jakobovits in turn criticized a Church of England report that attacked Thatcher's policies. She gave him a prominence in British life that he would not otherwise have had and awarded him a peerage, making him the first Chief Rabbi to sit in the House of Lords. It was a recognition that did wonders for the emerging self-confidence of the British community, and it gave him the self-assurance to be more assertive on Jewish matters. He became a leading authority in the emerging global debates over Jewish medical ethics and was highly critical of the Israeli government's reluctance to give up occupied territories in exchange for peace.

Jonathan Sacks continued his predecessor's engagement with British society. His tenure as Chief Rabbi was marked within the community by sporadic inter-factional controversies which resulted in the first ever signing of a peace accord between the various Jewish denominations. But he had the gift of oratory and wrote prolifically; his lectures, sermons and books propelled his Jewish ethical voice into national discourse. Both Jakobovits and Sacks thrust the British Chief Rabbinate out of the cloisters and into the media spotlight, and in so doing they both played a pivotal role in enhancing the self-image of the British community.

Jonathan Goldstein quotes Sacks as saying that the British Jewish community today is the last generation that can look both left and right at the same time, left to the secular world and right to Judaism. Only time will tell whether the prophecy is correct, but the ability to look in both directions has motivated the Jewish leadership to say: 'We can hold our Jewishness as a badge of honour, and we are not going to be cowed into submission because there are people who behave in a certain way.'

There is a political consequence to Jonathan Goldstein's view that the religious leadership of the past half-century has helped British Jewry become more confident and strengthened its sense of identity. From where he sits, at the heart of the established community, the radical social action espoused by a minority of young Jews is not high on Goldstein's list of priorities. What bothers him is the recent upsurge in anti-Semitism among the extreme right and left of British politics, and among elements in the Labour Party.

The causes of anti-Semitism are complicated, but there is little doubt that, on the left, attitudes towards Israel and Zionism play a part in exacerbating anti-Jewish feeling. Leonie Fleischmann, an academic who researches anti-occupation activism in Israel, feels that media emphasis on the country has affected attitudes towards Jews. There is no logical reason why this should be so. But Israel is the world's only Jewish state, and this seems to suggest an equivalence between the ethnic group and the country. And because Israel subscribes to the principles of open, liberal democracy, it is far easier for the media to report freely from there and investigate events than it is in most conflict zones. The result is that Israel gets a disproportionate amount of media coverage, and controversial events are subject to far greater scrutiny.

As for the left's antipathy to Zionism, this is one of the great conundrums of contemporary politics. It is easy to understand why the left sympathize with the Palestinians; squeezed between the intractable self-interest of power structures on both sides, there seems to be no end to the misery endured by the Palestinian people. But classical Zionism is a socialist creed, one rooted in self-determination and anti-capitalist structures. In its heyday the Zionists' kibbutz, with its communal ownership and shared ownership of resources, was the blueprint for a successful socialist society. Rather than resorting to politics more evocative of the far right than the far left, a more imaginative left-wing intelligentsia might try to explore solutions to one of the world's most intractable conflicts by seeking common interests between the former, socialist ideals of Zionism and the geopolitics that has led to the suffering of the Palestinians.

As a Jew on the left of the Labour Party, Adrian Litvinoff is sensitive to the fragile boundary between criticism of Israel and anti-Semitism. He told me about a friend of his who raises money for humanitarian Palestinian causes. 'He started to ask me questions about Palestine. He told me I was the only person he could talk to about these things, because I was the only Jew he knew. And as we spoke about different issues I would say, "I can see where you're going with that, but if you're edging towards anti-Semitism, you've got to be careful." And he would accept that. So I got more understanding of the pro-Palestinian point of view from him, and he gained more understanding of the nuances of different Jewish perspectives. That has been a mutually beneficial relationship.'

There wasn't much overt anti-Semitism in Britain when I was growing up. We were made fun of a bit at school, but it was not hateful; it was kids' stuff, and we treated it more or less as a joke. Robert Winston told me his experiences had been pretty similar. I asked him when he thought things had changed. 'It's really interesting, isn't it? Until quite recently, it was really smart to be Jewish. The change was pre-Corbyn definitely; it wasn't the left. But until recently, being Jewish was considered rather chic and avant-garde; there was a kind of respect.

'I don't know what happened. I don't think it was Israel. There was a social change going on, a multicultural society with a large number of Muslims who were not exactly particularly well disposed towards Jews. But I don't think they started it.' He told me that he had lectured to a group of mainly religious Muslim A-level students in London's East End. He couldn't get them to answer any questions until one girl asked if he believed in creation or evolution. He told them he was Jewish and that 'we don't interpret the text literally, and the room lit up. They couldn't stop asking questions. So no, I don't know why things changed.'

Jon Boyd, the Director of the highly respected Institute for Jewish Policy Research, has a research scientist's perspective on anti-Semitism. He challenges the assumption that anti-Semitism in Britain is increasing. 'The levels of anti-Jewish sentiment that exist in this country are among the lowest in the world. That's been seen in survey after survey, conducted by us and many others. Even though there are reports every year of more and more incidents, at least part of that is because of social media. On the one hand, social media has made it easier to be anti-Semitic, easier to be racist, easier to be offensive, but it has also made it easier to see comments that might previously have been made in private, and indeed, to report them subsequently.'

Moreover, he says that when the newspapers report an increase in the number of anti-Semitic incidents, the figures are based on incidents that are reported to the police or the Community Security Trust. They are not an objective measure. Objective measures, Jon says, are based on regular national surveys of the Jewish population, when a representative sample is asked if they have experienced an incident. He says that gathering data in this way does suggest that many more incidents are happening than are being reported. But equally, it also indicates that there is little discernible change from year to year, unless a major trigger event occurs – for example a war in Gaza – in which case numbers of incidents do indeed appear to increase significantly during that period. 'But if you ask me as a social scientist, can I prove empirically that levels of anti-Semitism are rising in the UK year on year, I would have to say no. They may be, but the data do not currently exist to prove it.'

He suggests that what happened with Jeremy Corbyn was not necessarily that the actual level of anti-Semitism rose, but that there was a political change. People became very concerned about a politician becoming Prime Minister who was very critical of Israel, had relationships with Islamist extremist groups, who didn't seem to be able to see anti-Semitism even when it was in front of his face, and who wasn't willing to play ball with the community. 'And that I think engendered a huge amount of concern and anxiety. What's interesting is that since he has gone, a fair amount of that concern has dissipated – for the time being, at least.'

Whatever the causes, the recent increase in anti-Semitism in Britain did take some of the shine off the growing confidence and renewed sense of positive identity among British Jews. Sadly, it is anti-Semitism that we need to look at next.

It is impossible to discuss modern-day anti-Semitism without referring to the Holocaust, the horrific slaughter of European Jewry. Jews often refer to it as the Shoah, using a word taken from the prophet Isaiah's allusion to calamity and desolation.[37] The scale of the devastation and the numbers of lives destroyed are beyond contemplation. The innumerable tales of suffering, of six million lives snuffed out, but only after enduring torments so unimaginable that our minds recoil from them. Six million human beings, each with a life as precious to them as ours is to us.

Not every tale ended horrifically. At the age of 19 my late father-in-law, Jerzy Lando z"l, was trapped with his family in the Warsaw Ghetto, a prison city of indescribable squalor, starvation and disease. One day he dressed himself in as many layers of ragged clothing as he could lay his hands on and walked to the gates of the ghetto. The Germans were liquidating the ghetto, selecting thousands of Jews daily and shipping them to the death camps. Jerzy's father, at unknown cost, had managed to obtain a blank birth certificate for his son, with which he could construct a Polish identity. At further cost his father had bribed the owner of a Polish workshop inside the ghetto walls, whose Christian workers entered and left the compound in a tightly controlled group each day. Jerzy was able to escape the ghetto by pretending to be part of the group of workers. His father gave him a locket containing arsenic, adjuring him to use it if he had no alternative.

The Elektoralna Street gate, set in the 12-foot high walls separating the ghetto from the 'other side', was a red-and-white striped barrier and next to it stood a sentry box with a small slit of a window. The barrier was up. Several German and Polish policemen stood or strolled on the pavement, the helmeted Germans in their green uniforms, rifles over their shoulders, the Poles in navy blue, armed with truncheons.

I could hear my heart pounding against my chest while I prayed silently to God. Would any of my companions remember that I was not amongst them this morning as they were entering the ghetto? Would they give me away to the Germans? What about this leader I had met? Could I really trust him with my life? I knew that he had been paid for his services but would he be true to his word? And even if these Poles did not betray me would the sentries recognise me as a Jew?

The guide went up to one of the German policemen and presented him with his pass. The sentry examined it carefully and waved us on. He started counting. I was just passing the last of the policemen and hoping that my ordeal was over when, 'Züruck! (come back)' he yelled. As he gave me a penetrating stare I got even hotter under my extra vests and shirts. He made me unbutton my first shirt, then the next one. He looked at me again, obviously perplexed. The end has come, was my only thought. The leader turned back from the front of the column. He did not say a word but looked at the German policeman, glanced at me and tapped his forehead with his index finger, indicating the presence of an idiot. The guard must have believed him, and he waved me on.[38]

After the war Jerzy made a new life for himself in England, joining upwards of 70,000 other Jewish refugees who had arrived since the 1930s. Britain's Jews had escaped the Shoah, but it had been a close thing: there was a time when Britain stood alone and could so easily have fallen. As they absorbed the refugees into their communities, they started to hear about the horror at first hand. But only slowly: many of those who had survived the horrors of the camps were far too traumatized to speak about them. Even today there are children growing up in families where the Shoah is never discussed, so as not to distress grandparents who have never fully recovered from what they went through.

Hearing about the Shoah, being told about relatives who perished, and realizing how easily it could have been them who died, partly explains the extreme sensitivity to anti-Semitism, the fear that the same thing could happen one day in Britain. One only has to recall the outbreak of xenophobia after the Brexit referendum, the strutting of racist thugs through immigrant neighbourhoods, to appreciate that even in tolerant Britain the implausible is far closer to the surface than it might seem.

80 years after the Shoah is long enough, one might imagine, for British Jews to feel less fearful about where casual anti-Semitism might lead. Instead, their anxiety has been compounded by the ever-present threat of terrorist attack. Rooted in the Israel–Palestine conflict and exacerbated by global Islamist aggression which has singled out Jews as a

particular target, Jews the world over feel less secure than at any time since the Shoah. Guards stand outside every synagogue, every Jewish school, every communal building. Even in tolerant Britain.

Nevertheless, Ezra Margulies, who grew up in France, where anti-Semitism is also prevalent, and returns there frequently, says that the problem needs to be put into perspective. 'There was never a time when I have felt unsafe in Britain. I would feel probably feel more unsafe in Israel, or in America. England is probably one of the safest societies to be in. Yes, I probably do feel slightly more fearful these days. But there's a feeling of anxiety everywhere.'

David Newman, who grew up in Britain before moving to Israel, has a similar view. 'In 25 years I only remember one occasion when someone shouted a comment at me. And now we have security at the front of every school and synagogue. On the one hand, people are much more worried about anti-Semitism than they were in the past, and yet at one and the same time, Jews are much more outward now, you've never seen so many beards and *kippot* [skullcaps]. So it's a bit of a paradox.'

When I asked Chief Rabbi Mirvis how he thought the community had changed in the wake of Corbyn and the Labour Party's anti-Semitism crisis, he quoted something that the former Israeli ambassador Daniel Taub used to say to him: 'The good is getting better and the bad is getting worse. And that's really true. The good is getting better: Jewish education, community vitality, Jewish life, restaurants, bakeries, you know, whatever it is about us we are thriving, so many of our synagogues are amazing Jewish community centres. It's good to be Jewish. For anybody who's keen on it, it's tremendous at so many levels.

'But the bad is getting worse, that which we are worried about. I am personally an optimist. And I believe the role of a rabbi is to infuse his community with optimism, and I've always preached hope, and promise, and look at how wonderful things are. Even in the first two or so years of Corbyn my message wherever I went throughout the country was, 'We do have a problem. Anti-Semitism is something we need to be acutely aware of. But I want to tell you how amazing it is to be Jewish and British in Britain today. And the fight against anti-Semitism is being led from the government down.'

But he concedes that maintaining optimism in the face of reality was not easy. 'The closer we got to the election of December 2019, the more the reality was setting in that Corbyn was not just an aberration. He could become our Prime Minister. And that possibility existed in the minds of people until the exit polls at ten o'clock on 12 December. It made us all really worried, genuinely worried. And the sense of relief when the results were declared was palpable.'

The Jewish community's formal response to the threat of attack is adroit, professional and effective. It reflects the self-confidence with which Jews live their lives in Britain today. It wasn't always so. Jewish communal self-defence started as an ad hoc response by street fighters, who took it upon themselves to face down trouble. When the Jews and dockworkers fought Oswald Mosley's fascists in Cable Street in 1936, it was in the face of objections from the Board of Deputies. It has been suggested that the Board had infiltrated Mosley's organization and wanted to keep its powder dry. But many Jews reviled the Board's apparent reluctance to fight; it looked a lot more like cowardice than tactics.

Jews learned much more about fighting during the Second World War, when, like everyone else, their young men were conscripted into service on the front line. When the war was over, and Mosley tried to revive fascism in Britain, 43 Jewish ex-servicemen met one evening at the Maccabi Sports Club and vowed to stop him once and for all. When he and his fascists next held a rally in London's Ridley Road, a street market in the heart of Hackney's Jewish community, there were 43 street fighters waiting for him.

The 43 Group, as they were known, were controversial. They were not angels, and they had some very disreputable personalities within their ranks – but not as disreputable as Mosley. They were chaotic and undisciplined in their tactics, hurling smoke bombs and fireworks, physically attacking fascist ringleaders and their henchmen. Unsurprisingly, their methods did not please the sober leadership of British Jewry. But they won the support, and the financial backing, of a good proportion of the Jewish community. The 43 served as a model for later anti-fascist street fighters, like the 62 Group, who battled against Colin Jordan's National Socialists in the early 1960s.

The Community Security Trust (CST) is the sophisticated and much admired successor to the disorderly street-fighting gangs as well as to the staid Community Security Organisation that used to be run by the Board of Deputies. CST was established in 1994, in the wake of car bomb attacks, first against the Israeli Embassy and then, a few hours later, at the offices of the Joint Israel Appeal in Finchley. Five days earlier a bomb at a Jewish communal building in Argentina had killed 85 people and injured hundreds. It was apparent that the nature of the threat against Jewish communities worldwide needed a more coordinated response in Britain than either the Board of Deputies or the street-fighting gangs were able to provide.

For Mark Gardner, Chief Executive of the CST, the Argentina bomb explains why organizations like his do their work. He explains that the impact of any terrorist attack is bad enough, but an attack against a minority community not only damages the community's sense of self-confidence but also damages the willingness of the majority of the population to have the community in their midst.

As befits a man who spends his days strategically tackling hatred, Gardner is sober and realistic about the nature of anti-Semitism. Softly spoken and thoughtful, he pointed out to me that the fact that someone says something which sounds anti-Semitic does not mean that person is an anti-Semite. He quoted a poll that CST had carried out in conjunction with Jewish Policy Research. About 3 per cent of those who responded answered questions about anti-Semitism in a way that might lead them to be considered anti-Semites. Widening the criteria a little resulted in 13 per cent of respondents potentially being anti-Semitic. But when the criteria were widened to include everyone who said something that a Jew, on hearing it, *might perceive* as anti-Semitic, then the number of respondents rises to one third. 'That kind of explains,' he says 'why Jews encounter anti-Semitism more often than they perhaps encounter anti-Semites.'

I asked Mark if he had a view on why anti-Semitism seems to be such an enduring and ineradicable form of hatred. He said that he didn't think his organization had an official opinion but, in his analysis, anti-Semitism has been hard-wired into society for centuries. 'You're not going to get rid of it just because the Holocaust made it unacceptable for a while. I feel the same about the Black Lives Matter movement. When I go to America and I see the condition of black people there, it just feels like the racism is so hard-wired into their society.

It's far less obvious when you talk about Jews in modern-day Britain. But for the best part of 2,000 years society accepted a belief system in which the Jews killed the son of God, and were evil enough and powerful enough and conspiratorial enough to have done so. And then we wonder why anti-Semitism looks the way that it does.'

CST is regarded as a model of excellence in the way it protects the lives and interests of the Jewish community. Its public face is its network of volunteers who stand outside synagogues when services are in progress. Unarmed and often middle-aged, they are of course little protection against a terrorist attack, but that is not their role. They are a preliminary line of defence. As Mark Gardner explains, people who belong to a synagogue community will recognize things that the local police or security firm are likely to miss. They are the ones who will spot the stranger who walks by once too often, or who looks at the building in a different way from everyone else. The job of the security volunteers is not to finger oddballs or to harass unfortunates but just to be alert, to identify potential trouble as far away from the community as possible.

The hardest part of a security volunteer's job is usually on the two occasions each year, on New Year and Yom Kippur, when synagogues tend to be full and there is no room for anyone who is not a member. There is a joke about a security volunteer who had a confrontation on Yom Kippur with someone who said he needed to deliver an urgent message to his father in the synagogue. The volunteer wouldn't let him in and the confrontation grew heated. Eventually the security volunteer backed down. 'OK, you can go in,' he said, 'but don't let me catch you praying.'

The volunteers are CST's public face, but behind them is a sophisticated intelligence-gathering, hate-crime monitoring and government liaison operation. They work closely with police forces and local authorities. The threats these days are not just physical. Mark maintains that cyber terrorism is a rapidly expanding threat that demands to be addressed with urgency. 'Cyber warfare is a reality. And it is conducted by state actors and non-state actors, and by common criminals as well.'

Saddled with the unfortunate distinction of protecting the community that has been threatened longer than any other in Britain, CST has vast experience and shares it widely. They helped establish the Muslim anti-hate initiative Tell Mama, and they continue to advise faith groups who are fearful of attack from extremists of every shape and colour: fascists, Nazis, Islamophobes and jihadis, to name but a few. They run a training programme called SAFE, Security Advice For Everyone, which is run by a dedicated team and is open to all faith and minority communities.

Mark stresses that CST's work has a benefit that is far greater than its immediate impact on the street. 'The Jewish community has developed a unique way of working with the police that essentially delineates responsibilities. They fully understand that, rather than us being some weird, Dad's Army, vigilante operation, we can do things that they don't want to be doing. Things which have a really good impact on our communal well-being, and on the rest of wider society as well.'

In December 2020 Professor David Feldman, Director of the Birkbeck Institute for the Study of Antisemitism at the University of London, published an article in the *Guardian* newspaper. He argued that the working definition of anti-Semitism, as formulated by the International Holocaust Remembrance Alliance, was not viable and that the British government's proposal to force universities to adopt it would not help to protect Jewish students. The article was immediately attacked by others working in the field of anti-Semitism for providing encouragement to those who denigrate Jews. The attack on the article was itself condemned by several leading academics. If Jews cannot agree about what anti-Semitism is, or how to confront it, what chance is there that anyone else can?[39]

A few months after David Feldman's article an international group of 200 academics published the Jerusalem Declaration on Antisemitism, an alternative definition that was designed 'as a substitute for the IHRA Definition [...] to overcome the shortcomings of the IHRA Definition'. Predictably the Declaration was given short shrift in Britain by the IHRA's supporters, who accused it variously of having been written by out-of-touch academics, of setting back the fight against anti-Semitism and, incoherently, of trying to prove the signatories' hatred of Donald Trump and Benjamin Netanyahu.[40]

The IHRA 'working definition' of anti-Semitism, a 38-word attempt to put to bed a question that seems so simple but will just not go away, has become linked in the eyes of many to issues of free speech and Palestinian solidarity.

In 2018 the Palestinian Return Centre asked the human rights barrister Geoffrey Robertson to write a legal opinion on the impact on free speech of the government's acceptance of the IHRA definition. He concluded that the definition 'is likely in practice to chill free speech, by raising expectations of pro-Israeli groups that they can successfully object to legitimate criticism and correspondingly arouse fears in NGOs and student bodies that they will have events banned or else have to incur considerable expense to protect themselves by legal action'. He declared that the IHRA definition is 'imprecise, confusing and open to misinterpretation and even manipulation'.[41]

A letter in the *Guardian*, signed by several prominent British lawyers, argued that the IHRA definition went against the Universal Declaration of Human Rights, which states that 'everyone has the right to freedom of expression; this right includes freedom to hold opinions without interference'. The government's attempt to oblige universities to accept the IHRA definition of anti-Semitism, they said, curtailed debate and contravened Britain's Human Rights Act.[42]

In his article, Feldman made similar points to those advanced by Robertson. He argued that imposing the definition on universities was unworkable in practice, that it privileged Jews over other groups and divided minorities against each other. It is not true, he argued, that adopting the working definition provides a straightforward way for universities to demonstrate that they do not tolerate anti-Semitism. Nor does it prove that those universities which fail to adopt it are willing to tolerate anti-Semitism. The definition, which is so woolly in its formulation that it needed from the outset to be illustrated by examples, was originally intended to be used by data collectors, to help them monitor anti-Semitism. It was not intended as the final word on what does and what does not constitute hatred of Jews. Feldman's article reinforced for me a comment that Leonie Fleischmann made in our conversation a few weeks earlier. She had said that incorporating Israel in definitions of anti-Semitism had complicated matters, making it harder to distinguish anti-Jewish hatred from opposition to Israeli policies. She says that her university has not seen much anti-Semitism, but that when it does occur, it revolves around Israel. 'When the Palestinian Society has anti-apartheid week, it's not pleasant for Jewish students.'

Other voices took an even stronger line than David Feldman. An article in the online Jewish medium *Vashti* argued that the IHRA definition deliberately censors Palestinians. Somewhat disingenuously, the author presented examples of how the definition has been used to ban events held under 'Israeli Apartheid Week' and to condemn the Boycott, Divestment and Sanctions campaign against Israel.[43]

The *Vashti* article might have been more convincing if the author had chosen better examples. The IHRA definition distinguishes between legitimate criticism of Israel, which is acceptable, and illegitimate criticism, which is not. The article takes it for granted that both Israeli Apartheid Week and the BDS movement are legitimate criticisms. Many would disagree. They may think it a bit far-fetched for critics of Israel to protest that the IHRA is being used as a political tool by their opponents, when they themselves advocate political tactics like sanctions and use emotive terms such as 'apartheid'. Ultimately, it's the dog-whistle politics of some on the far left who appear unable to distinguish between robust opposition to the discriminatory policies of far-right Israeli politicians and anti-Jewish racism which make barely adequate tools like the IHRA definition necessary.

Does Britain need a Holocaust memorial? The question is pertinent because plans are afoot to build one in Victoria Tower Gardens, adjoining the Houses of Parliament. At the time of writing, the proposal has failed to obtain planning consent, but there are plans to override this. The cost is estimated at around £100 million, meaning, if previous landmark projects are anything to go by, that it would probably cost at least twice that amount.

As always, Britain's Jews are divided. Many support the project; others do not. It's not a question of confidence: the debate is not, as it once might have been, between those in the community who think Jews should keep quiet and those who don't. There is hardly a Jew in the world who thinks that the Holocaust is something they should keep quiet about. Anyway the proposed Holocaust memorial is not a scheme put forward by the Jewish community; this is a project emanating from the highest ranks of government.

Vivian Wineman, a past President of the Board of Deputies, remembers when the former Prime Minister David Cameron proposed it. 'It wasn't a Jewish initiative; this was something that Cameron offered us. He came out with it at a dinner of the Holocaust Education Trust in 2013. And he'd only thought about it briefly; he certainly announced it to a quite unprepared audience.'

It's not the first time that a Holocaust-related issue has split the Jewish community. Philip Rubenstein was the Director of the All-Party Parliamentary War Crimes Group during the 1980s, when the MP Greville Janner was spearheading a campaign for a bill to prosecute ex-Nazi war criminals. The campaign came on the back of a letter that the Nazi-hunting Simon Wiesenthal Centre had written to Prime Minister Margaret Thatcher in 1986, alerting her to the presence of 17 Nazi war criminals who were believed to be living undisturbed in Britain. According to Philip, 'The campaign purely was run from Parliament. And we attracted lots of very respectable, non-Jewish MPs, so that it wouldn't be seen as a Jewish campaign, it would be seen as a wider issue of justice. The press, though, weren't having any of it – they typically wrote it up as a Jewish campaign, as something fundamentally of Jewish interest. But it had that aura of non-Jewish respectability, which was what I think made it successful.'

Philip draws a comparison between that time and now. He remembers that when the news of the campaign emerged, the community was divided between those who were 'pretty gung-ho, and angry that nothing had previously been done about it' and 'a lot of Board of Deputies types who were pretty horrified by it'. He says he received a lot of phone calls from people worried that the campaign would be counterproductive and lead to anti-Semitism. The community did get behind the campaign eventually, but not until they saw that it was succeeding, and that Margaret Thatcher supported it. Then it became safe.

He compares the experience of that campaign with the present day, with the 'Enough is Enough' demonstration, 'with everyone on the streets at Westminster. The Jewish communal reaction to Corbyn was very different.'

Philip attributes this change in attitude to the confidence of his generation in their Jewishness. 'We are much more comfortable in our skin. We were born in this country – my parents were too – but a lot of that generation still had the sense of being very grateful for being here, and not stirring the pot. And we also grew up in an era of identity politics. When I was a student, Gay Pride was starting. And black students were becoming much more active. We were all more comfortable with our identities.

The other contrast between then and now, he says, is the composition of the Tory Party, and the community's political shift from the left wing to the right. 'In many ways it is the classic movement of an immigrant community, that as they gain more wealth and affluence, they tend to move more to the right.' But he thinks something else has gone on as well.

'As a small community, it's natural to go to whoever welcomes you more into their home. And I think that until Thatcher the Tory Party was a deeply inimical place for Jews. I remember a lot of the people who were on the Tory benches. Really vile Little Englanders: racist, anti-Semitic, homophobic and yet tolerated. People might have thought of them as a little stuck in the mud, but they were absolutely tolerated. And now in the Tory Party you only have to tweet the wrong words and it's a major issue! So I think the Tory Party has become a more comfortable place for Jews.'

It's not surprising that there are disagreements over the planned Holocaust memorial. There were similar divisions in 2001, when the government instituted an annual Holocaust Memorial Day. Then, Rabbi Dr Charles Middleburgh told the BBC's *Newsnight* programme that establishing a memorial day for a catastrophe of such significance and scale risked fossilizing it; Holocaust Memorial Day would in time become like Trafalgar Day, just another national commemoration which very few people were even aware of. Others argued that they could not see the point in establishing a secular commemoration; there was already a Shoah Day in the Jewish calendar, and if the government really wanted to honour Holocaust victims they should participate in that, rather than setting aside another day. But these were minority views; by and large, the Jewish community got behind Holocaust Memorial Day, taking part in national and communal commemorations.

And Holocaust Memorial Day has not diminished Shoah Day, which falls shortly after the Passover holiday and a week before Israel Independence Day. Recently, the American tradition of lighting a yellow candle to commemorate Shoah Day has taken root in Britain. The practice was first introduced in Britain in 2018, and tens of thousands of people now light candles each year in an initiative fronted by the sports, health and well-being charity Maccabi GB.

The opponents of the Holocaust memorial do not argue against it on the usual grounds of design, location and cost. One of the main criticisms is that, if it is built, the memorial would potentially be a security risk, a magnet for attack by terrorists and hate groups. It does seem a bit odd to erect a memorial to the victims of the worst excesses of human behaviour, only to have the memorial itself subjected to rigorous security and under permanent guard.

One prominent Holocaust educator told me that she considered the memorial to be a vanity project, encouraged by senior figures in the Tory Party because 'they think we are rich, and it will flood money into the Tory Party'. She told me that the few remaining Holocaust survivors in Britain are divided over whether the memorial is needed. In her view, the money being spent on the memorial would be far better spent on education, trying to ensure that nothing like the Holocaust could ever happen again.

After the campaign for the War Crimes Bill, Philip Rubenstein was appointed to be Director of the Holocaust Education Trust. He says he hasn't got a strong opinion either way about the Holocaust memorial. But the present-day leadership of the Trust are in no doubt. They believe that the memorial, positioned alongside Parliament, 'will send a clear signal for generations to come of the important place the Holocaust has in our nation's history and memory'. Marie van der Zyl, President of the Board of Deputies, wrote in *The Times* that the centre 'will give a voice to those who cannot speak out about what they endured. The diminishing band of survivors have themselves said how important it is to have a memorial on a specific and important site.'[44]

Baroness Ruth Deech led the opposition to the memorial. Her father fled the Nazis, and she lost several members of her family in Shoah extermination camps. In a speech she gave in Oxford she pointed out there are already five major memorials to the Holocaust in Britain, and a host of smaller ones. Overall the plan shies away from the real causes of Jew hatred. It was meant, according to David Cameron and other politicians who have espoused the cause, to be a statement of British values. In fact, this national ideology is what has been grafted on to Holocaust memorials around the world. They are 'increasingly used to promote a self-congratulatory and sometimes self-exculpatory image of the government that erects them'.[45]

Beth Shalom, or the House of Peace, is one of the five holocaust memorials that Ruth Deech referred to. It was set up by brothers James and Stephen Smith and their mother, Marina, after a visit to Yad Vashem, the institute in Israel that commemorates the victims of the Shoah. Located in rural Nottinghamshire, a world away from the high-profile site of the proposed Westminster memorial, Beth Shalom has run Holocaust educational programmes from its museum and visitor centre for over 20 years.

When Beth Shalom first opened, they invited Holocaust survivors to come to share their stories with visiting schoolchildren. But they knew that the opportunity was limited. Their Chairman Henry Grunwald told me: 'The numbers were dwindling. People died or were too infirm to be able to come. So we developed something in conjunction with the Shoah Foundation called the Forever Project. It took a long time and was very expensive. We recorded ten of our survivors in very high technology, telling their story and answering up to 1,300 or 1,400 questions. The beauty of the

Forever Project is its interactive technology. When it's shown on a screen up at the Centre, we can ask a question of the image, and the image answers.'

Projects like that don't come cheap. Beth Shalom's success is supported by many partners who recognize the imperative of sustaining the memory of the Holocaust, in the fragile hope of trying to build a better world. But charitable funds are not inexhaustible. There is little evidence to demonstrate that the Westminster Holocaust Memorial was so indispensable that it was worth the risk of diverting funds from other Holocaust projects. Several people that I spoke to, all too discreet to allow me to quote them by name, have described it as a vanity project. They have a point.

The argument will continue to rage until the memorial is built – as it almost certainly will be. And the real question is, just how much attention would anyone pay to the memorial then? Many countries have a Holocaust memorial; some countries have several. How would Britain's latest memorial differ from any other, either in the message it delivers or in the impact it has?

5

Community and Cohesion

British Jews are good at organizing themselves, and good at creating organizations. What they are less good at is closing down organizations that no longer have a purpose. The communal infrastructure is littered with the remains of superannuated institutions that really should have been got rid of long ago. Some do manage to reinvent themselves, shake off the legacy of their glory days and set off in new directions. Mostly, though, they struggle on, doing what they always did. Even though the need is no longer there, or at least it's not as pressing as it once was.

Everyone I discussed this with agreed that there are far too many organizations in the Jewish community. *The Jewish Charity Guide* lists 520, although, bizarrely, several have Israeli telephone numbers and are not registered with the Charity Commission, the statutory body that regulates the sector nationally. But even if we exclude the apparently Israeli organizations on the list, it still leaves an awful lot of British Jewish charities. And then there are all the communal and commercial organizations that are not constituted or registered as charities: the synagogues, clubs, many of the youth organizations, media, shops, restaurants, caterers and so on. There is no doubt that a considerable amount of consolidation would be in the communal interest.

British Jewry has been criticized for having no strategic plan, no coordinated vision of where the community is heading, of what it needs and how it will achieve it. Maybe it doesn't need one; it has muddled by quite well for over 300 years. But this lack of strategy worries Lionel Salama. A communications and marketing professional who has been involved in many of the community's major fundraising initiatives for over 40 years, he is deeply concerned about the lack of strategic planning in the Jewish community. He quotes a recent national study on funding in faith communities that estimates the Jewish community's total annual budget, from both government and charitable sources, to be in the region of £1 billion. No business, he says, would operate on such a budget without forward planning. He says he has started to speak to major donors and communal leaders to map the structure of the community, to see where the money is being spent, to work out where there can be consolidation and to try to draw up a vision and plan for British Jewry in 2030. To try to see how the community's disparate interests, synagogues, welfare and education can all be drawn together into a unified, coordinated whole.

Fundraising is a major component of his strategic outlook. He says that one major donor told him that 98 per cent of the money comes from 2 per cent of the families in the Jewish community. That represents about 1,000 families, none of which can be certain that their philanthropic traditions will carry over into subsequent generations. Salama maintains that the Jewish community has rested on its laurels for the past quarter of a century. It now needs to start thinking seriously about its ongoing financial viability.

Jonathan Boyd, who runs the Institute for Jewish Policy Research, has a more nuanced view. Because it looks at the community's data and carries out research projects on behalf of individual organizations and groups, JPR has a keen interest in the question of strategy and long-term planning. But Jonathan says that when he works with organizations he tries not to take a top-down approach; he avoids making grand recommendations about the direction communities should go in. He says he is more interested in working individually with organizations, discussing with them what the data imply for them individually, and for their future planning. 'Because you can look at exactly the same set of data with a *haredi* organization or with, say, Reform Judaism, and they mean very different things and have very different implications.'

And there are competing interests when it comes to communal strategy. Clearly, there is a benefit in better coordination between different groups and interests: economically it makes far more sense and it enables resources to be shared more efficiently. But that is not the whole picture. 'The other side is, that many people's Jewish identities are tied up in their particular organizations or initiatives. When people set up a new organization, or a new website, or a new programme or a new initiative, that is how they are expressing their Jewish identity; it is a project at the heart of their Jewishness. So if you shut those types of ventures down, you're potentially impeding people's capacity to express their Jewishness. So there's a balance to be struck between encouraging people to do their own thing and go off in their own direction, expressing their Judaism in a way that's meaningful to them, and keeping an eye on the overall structure because every single one of these things needs to be funded somehow.'

The Anglo-Jewish Association is one of those communal organizations which has successfully managed to reinvent itself after losing its original purpose. The charity no longer has the profile or reputation that it once had, but at least it still does worthy things. It was set up in 1871 by those who saw themselves as the Jewish aristocracy, leveraging the influence of the British Empire to protect Jewish rights and interests in countries where they suffered discrimination. When the Empire went into decline and the Jewish world suffered the convulsions of the twentieth century, the Anglo-Jewish Association's founding mission diminished. It is still peripherally involved in diplomacy – it is a founder member of the Claims Conference, the international body that works for the restitution of Jewish assets stolen during the Holocaust – but its main work today is in providing and facilitating grants to university students. The AJA has created a role for itself in a world very different from that in which it was originally founded. But its pedigree means that it is still regarded by those in the know as a venerable institution, even if most British Jews have never heard of it.

The Board of Deputies seems to have adjusted less well to the changing times. Purporting to represent the entire Jewish community, an impossible task at the best of times, it was seen for most of its history as the voice of the entrenched communal establishment. Subject to periodic calls for reform, it has been dismissed as ineffectual and fossilized, as slow to react to changes in Jewish communal life and as out of touch with the opinions of younger generations. More recently it has been accused of being too partisan in its support for Israel, of not representing the full spectrum of British Jewish opinion on the intractable Middle Eastern conflict.[46] But there may be sunny uplands ahead. The Board of Deputies may be changing. Its new Chief Executive, Michael Wegier, says that he is approaching his job determined that the Board represents the Jewish community to wider society in the best possible way.

The Board's origins go back to 1760. During the nineteenth century it led the struggle for political and civil rights for Jews in Britain, and it collaborated with the Anglo-Jewish Association to ameliorate the conditions of Jews in oppressive regimes overseas. The Board played an essential role in ensuring that the immigrant Jewish community successfully integrated into wider society during the nineteenth and twentieth centuries. There is no shortage of opportunity for it to play a similarly pivotal role in the twenty-first century and beyond.

The Board describes itself as the only democratically elected, cross-communal, representative body in the Jewish community: three portentous claims, each of which needs to be nuanced somewhat. The Board consists of deputies representing the various organizations, charities and synagogues in the Jewish community. It says it can be thought of as a Jewish parliament, with its deputies as the MPs. Unlike the real Parliament, however, or even a local council, its members do not represent the interests of individuals. They cannot. The Board represents organizations not individuals. Many Jews are affiliated to more than one organization or synagogue and are therefore, presumably, represented by more than one deputy, while many other Jews belong to no communal organization and are not represented on the Board at all. Worse still, many deputies are not elected but are merely appointed by their organization, which has had to cast around to find someone willing to take on the job. Often, the only opinions that deputies represent are their own or, at best, those of the committee that appointed them. So the Board can't really be compared to a Parliament, whose members are elected by the population at large on the basis of their policies and the strength of their campaigns. And of course, unlike a Parliament, the Board is not a legislative body. Its decisions and resolutions frequently have little or no practical consequence.

It does not need to be so; there are other models for representing a community, based on individual membership. They do create a greater administrative and financial burden, but the upside of creating a membership model for the Jewish community as a whole is that it may draw in people who are currently not members of a synagogue or communal organization, and are therefore not represented by the Board at all.

Nor is the Board fully cross-communal. It doesn't represent unaffiliated individual Jews, nor does it represent organizations that have not affiliated to it. Neither does it represent the *haredim*, who withdrew from the Board in 1971. Although that too may be changing, as it has recently welcomed its first representative in half a century from a *haredi* synagogue. Nor does it encompass every Jewish organization. As I was writing this book, the Jewish Council for Racial Equality was denied membership of the Board, apparently, according to newspaper reports, because some deputies believed that they 'gave help and comfort to the enemies of Israel' and had not accepted the IHRA definition of anti-Semitism.[47] If a Jewish organization that stands up for racial equality cannot be admitted to the Board because some of the deputies don't agree with its stance on Middle Eastern politics, just how cross-communal can the Board be said to be?

Nevertheless, as Michael Wegier told me, the Board is the first port of call for anyone seeking to understand the Jewish community's interests and concerns, whether that be the government, the media or the public at large. 'If you are involved in government, civil society and inter-faith matters, you've likely heard of the Board because we engage with them all the time. We regularly meet with ministers, opposition, civil society and inter-faith leaders across the country. It is almost impossible to be a senior person in British public life, and not to have a relationship with the Board of Deputies.'

It sounds impressive on an institutional level, but as far as the average member of the Jewish community is concerned, the real strength of the Board in our information age is likely to be what it accomplishes on a practical level, through the projects it runs. One such initiative is the EcoSynagogue project, which Michael told me 'Encourages synagogues to become carbon neutral. Looking at the heating, the design, the seating of a synagogue, all those areas where energy is consumed. And on a practical level, how to cater events in an environmentally friendly manner with locally resourced foods and so on.'

Apart from the intrinsic value of making synagogue buildings and activities carbon neutral, the EcoSynagogue project has another great advantage. Since its participating synagogues come from across the religious spectrum, it is truly cross-communal. For a British religious community that is characterized by lack of dialogue between its different religious factions, this is a tremendous step forward. It might even be more significant than the changes wrought by the Covid pandemic, where religious denominations found themselves almost corralled into mutual cooperation by government and local authorities. Whether or not to join EcoSynagogue is up to individual communities; it is not mandated by religious affiliation. As such, it is all the more to be welcomed.

Many community organizations struggle to enthuse young people and get them to become involved with their work. The Board probably faces this challenge more than most; it is hard to get young people to join when so many deputies are getting on in age, and its lengthy meetings have been described by many who have sat through them as little more than a talking shop. When I raised this with Michael Wegier, he told me that, because of Covid, many of these perceptions no longer apply. 'Zoom has been an absolute blessing, because we've had really good attendance. We are moving to a hybrid model, part Zoom, part face-to-face, and I think this will invigorate the debates. And we now have huge numbers of young people on the Board. The Board has people from teens to their eighties.'

Vivian Wineman, who was President of the Board between 2009 and 2015, confirmed this: 'When I was a student, the Board of Deputies seemed irrelevant. The President came and spoke to us at university and the whole thing seemed ridiculous. Why should one go to an organization like that? But as you get older, you see the important things it does.' Vivian used his presidency to try to increase the Board's youthful appeal, doubling the number of representatives from the Union of Jewish Students and encouraging representation from younger, more alternative communities that lie outside the mainstream. He recognizes that young people have got other things to do apart from take part in the Board, but he is optimistic that those who are not interested today will, as he did, eventually recognize the benefits of being involved.

Vivian was President when Yachad, a dovish Zionist movement which supports the Israeli peace lobby, applied to join the Board. Although it is a moderate voice, Yachad is viewed with a certain amount of suspicion by some on the right. Vivian told the *Jewish Chronicle* that he regarded Yachad as an important part of the Zionist movement and that he was proud to have them involved. But he struggled to get their application approved because of objections from their detractors. Twice he decided to postpone the vote to approve their membership because he was uncertain of winning a majority. They were finally admitted at the third attempt.

Vivian deemed Yachad's membership essential. Not only because excluding them on the basis of their political views would have undermined the Board's claim to be representative of the entire community. But also because they speak for a large segment of today's young Jews. When it became clear that their request to join the Board was contentious, more than 70 former leaders of youth and student organizations sent a letter in support of Yachad's application. Refusing to admit them would have severely undermined the Board's efforts to broaden its appeal to younger people.

But for all the changes that seem to be taking place at the Board, it still has an image problem. Its public profile is not what it once was, and until recently it seemed to operate largely behind closed doors. Most members of the Jewish community pay it scant attention and have little idea of what it does. It does circulate a communal briefing, but often this is little more than a list of the many meetings that its officers and staff have had since the previous briefing. It says little or nothing about what happened in those meetings (although since Michael Wegier has been in charge the briefings have become more informative). A look at the Board's website leaves us none the wiser. There are copies of statements put out by the Board, usually in response to political events in

Britain or Israel, to national social crises or to developments affecting Jews elsewhere in the world. But it gives very little information about its actual activities and says nothing about the topics discussed at its plenary meetings, although it does show recordings of the Zoom meetings it held during the pandemic. When the Board was riven in 2021 by a major constitutional dispute which led to the first electoral challenge to the organization's incumbent President for nearly 60 years, instead of presenting the issues to the community and encouraging debate, the website remained silent.

Michael told me this is changing. He said that they have just hired their first digital communications specialist. 'I hope if you follow us on Twitter, Facebook or Instagram, you should start seeing more of us. We recently produced two films which you can see on the website or on YouTube, about the Board's work. I think they are really effective. And we've had great feedback on them. But this is an ongoing journey. I think we probably weren't doing as good a job as we could, on explaining who we are to the world. We've just invested in that; it was one of the first things I did here when I joined. Hopefully, we'll see the fruits.' He says he has a small, enthusiastic team of 14 staff, 'who are brilliant. I've got three or four people who are my age, and quite a few in their twenties or early thirties. And they are utterly dedicated, Jewish career professionals. They staff our divisions, they work with deputies and they do the work behind the scenes. It's a privilege to work with them.'

The Board of Deputies' 200-year hegemony as the presumed representative congress for the Jewish community came to a sudden end in 2003 with the creation of the Jewish Leadership Council. The event had long been mooted; it had been apparent for many years that the larger Jewish charities and their major donors had their own direct channels to the nation's corridors of power and that the Board no longer played its traditional role as the sole liaison between the Jewish community and government.

The American Jewish community has never had an equivalent to the Board of Deputies, but they do have the Conference of Presidents of Major American Jewish Organizations, which represents the collective interests of those organizations doing most of the work in the community and of the donors who funded them. Many of the backers and leaders of the British community believed that something similar should exist here. It would not be democratic, but nobody was agitating for democracy in British Jewry, and it would be representative, inasmuch as all the active players would be involved.

Jonathan Goldstein, the former chair of the Jewish Leadership Council, articulates it well: 'You look across our community and you ask who has really made a difference to the lives of the people in the community over the course of the last 30 to 40 years. It's been the boards and trustees of the major charities, of the synagogues, of the cultural organizations. These are the essential elements that make up a community and make the difference to people's lives. And those people, making the difference, got more and more frustrated that they had no voice in the representative body. And the leaders of those organizations were saying, "What we actually need is to bring ourselves together, because we have a great power here for the community. Because this is really where business gets done. This is where communal change occurs."'

The story is told of former Prime Minister David Cameron, who asked one of his advisers, a Jew, how Jews seemed to be so well informed, how they so often seemed to be ahead of the news. 'They hear things in synagogue', the adviser replied.

'That would suit me,' said the Prime Minister, 'how would I go about hearing things in synagogue?' 'Put on a dark suit,' came the reply, 'and a black trilby. Go into the synagogue, put on a prayer shawl and sit down. After a few minutes, lean across to your neighbour and ask him "*nu, voss naiyes?* [So, what's new?]*". So Cameron did just that. He put on a dark suit, a black trilby and a prayer shawl, leaned across to his neighbour and asked '*nu, voss naiyes?* 'Shhh', said his neighbour urgently. 'Cameron's coming.'

Many people were unhappy when the JLC was set up. The idea that the community would be run by an unelected body did not always go down well – even though, as Jonathan Goldstein explained, the very fact that they were heading up the major organizations meant that they were already effectively running it. And the creation of the JLC was not a putsch; it was not an attempt to divest the Board of Deputies of its status. Henry Grunwald, who was President of the Board at the time, was instrumental in the JLC's creation. He says that his predecessors at the Board had not got on well with the movers and shakers in the community, the donors and communal leaders who kept the community afloat. Neither had there been any community-wide strategic thinking. Whenever the community was beset by a crisis – a war in the Middle East, an outbreak of anti-Semitism, an economic downturn affecting the charities or any of the other periodic issues that surfaced – a few of the heavy hitters would get together informally, decide what to do and get on with it. Without any reference to the Board.

This was the way things had been done for years, but both the major organizations and their donors were becoming dissatisfied with the reactive nature of communal decision-making. There needed to be a more strategic set-up, and the

President of the Board of Deputies, Henry Grunwald, was one of those who first grasped the nettle. 'So we had talks, and we decided that the way forward was to create a formal organization, an open organization, which at the time we limited to the lay chairs of the national Jewish organizations. And we were very small to begin with, with a few individuals who were there because they were necessary, they had reach, they had ability, they could help us. And the JLC has grown from that. And I think it's incredibly worthwhile.'

Vivian Wineman, who was President of the Board after Henry, remembers there was friction after the JLC was set up. 'The JLC is meant to be there to facilitate its members; it's a coordinating umbrella body, it's not supposed to compete with its members. And that didn't go down well because the Board is a member of the JLC. So the JLC is there to help the Board achieve its objectives. The tensions were grave. My successor as President attacked the JLC at a Board meeting. And there was a lot of resentment, and the jealousy could be very difficult.'

Historically the Board of Deputies was the liaison body between the Jewish community and the government. They would meet with the Prime Minister and senior politicians regularly. But because the Jewish Leadership Council includes people from senior leadership positions in industry and commerce they have considerable influence in national institutions and with the government. 'The JLC always has very good access. The Board still has that access, they do get to meet the Prime Minister regularly and they would do even if there weren't a JLC. But when I was President of the Board,' says Vivian, 'and even with Henry before me, when we went to the Prime Minister it was as part of the JLC delegation.'

It was not just the Board of Deputies which found the establishment of the JLC difficult. The Movement for Reform

Judaism didn't like it. They had to make someone redundant just so they could pay the JLC's membership fees. But they felt obliged to join because the United Synagogue had. And if the country's largest religious umbrella body had joined, then the second-largest couldn't afford to be left out in the cold.

Lira Winston z"l told me that the Leadership Council had made a tremendous, positive difference to the organizational efficiency of the Jewish community. Her first job in the Jewish community had been when she was asked to help to set up the cross-communal educational body Jewish Continuity. For her it was a baptism of fire, because the creation of Jewish Continuity led to a tremendous communal row. It had been intended as a resource for the whole community, but it didn't get buy-in across the religious spectrum: the non-orthodox synagogues complained that they were being marginalized. She said there was no strategic thinking in the community at that time. But the environment is very different today. 'I think what the Jewish Leadership Council has succeeded in doing is bringing everybody around the table. You have a very different conversation if you have the chairs of the organizations sitting together.'

Lord Michael Levy, who has experience of facilitating meetings between government and the communal leadership, feels that the existence of both the Board and the JLC leads to confusion and conflict. He says that the community cannot have two representative bodies; it sends the wrong message to wider society and leaves government uncertain as to who they should be speaking to. 'In an ideal situation, the two should be merged. And the best people should be doing what they need to do.'

Sometimes it takes a crisis to bring people together. When the argument over anti-Semitism in Corbyn's Labour Party reached a climax, the JLC worked together with the Board of Deputies and the Community Security Trust to organize a demonstration outside Parliament. It wasn't easy to get everyone on board for such a public display of Jewish outrage; opposition came from senior voices both in the community and in the political establishment. But the groundswell of opinion was in favour, and the Enough is Enough demonstration is now regarded as a turning point in the community's willingness to stand up for itself, to step out of its comfort zone and to put its collective head firmly above the parapet.

Jonathan Goldstein still recalls the moment he realized they had made the right decision. 'Half an hour before the demonstration was due to start we went into Parliament to deliver a letter to the chair of the Parliamentary Labour Party. When we went inside, there were only a handful of demonstrators in Parliament Square, and I was worried that we were about to make fools of ourselves. And when we came out of Parliament half an hour later, there were two and a half thousand people there!'

Russell Conn speaks for many people when he praises the JLC. As President of Manchester's Representative Council, he attends JLC meetings. He's been involved in Jewish community activities for many years, which is another way of saying that he has sat in on many chaotic meetings that start and finish late, where people ramble on and nothing ever gets decided. Russell is hugely impressed by the way the JLC conducts its meetings: 'It's very slick. It starts at five, it finishes at seven, and it doesn't run over. Each topic is timetabled and finishes on time. Everything is structured.' It sounds a lot like a board meeting in the real world.

Russell thinks that it was the Covid pandemic that finally demonstrated the importance and strength of the

JLC. Unhampered by an inflexible constitution, and driven by successful business people who are used to making complex decisions, they were able to take action quickly. They successfully conducted an emergency appeal for the community's three largest care charities, Jewish Care, Nightingale Hammerson and The Fed, to help mitigate the pandemic's drain on their resources. They set up a fund with the employment support body Work Avenue to assist those whose earnings had been impacted by the crisis. And they created a portal to support, guide and assist those individuals and organizations struggling to adapt to the realities of the pandemic.

Like many people, Russell's view of the JLC has changed. His organization, the Manchester Rep Council, has now entered into a formal partnership with it, with Mark Adlestone OBE DL, a JCL trustee, taking over as the Rep Council chair. Mark Levy, the JLC's regional manager was seconded as the Rep Council's CEO, the first time in the organization's history that they have had a professional Chief Executive. Russell says it will transform the organization. And it couldn't have happened without the JLC. 'If you had asked me a few years ago,' he says, 'I would have opposed the formation of the JLC. But having been involved, and seeing how they work, I can understand why Henry Grunwald did what he did. He took a lot of criticism, but I think he was much more far-sighted than people gave him credit for at the time.'

The JLC is an energetic organization, and it runs its projects with gusto. It runs a leadership training division and a network to support youth leaders and those working in informal education. It employs regional managers to work with the communities in Manchester, Scotland and

Birmingham. And it even runs activities with the Board of Deputies. Despite the apparent disparity between the drive and energy levels of the two organizations, they now manage to get on with each other tolerably well. Of course, there is still occasional rivalry between them, but that is not unhealthy, and it generally manifests itself as little more than a clash of personalities. And they run PaJeS, the highly successful Partnerships for Jewish Schools, of which we will hear more shortly. It delivers strategic support, advice and training to the community's burgeoning education sector.

The London Jewish Forum is one of the projects that the JLC runs with the Board of Deputies. It was set up at a time when the community had difficulties with the then mayor, Ken Livingstone, so that London's Jewish community could liaise directly with his office. One might wonder why the Board of Deputies didn't take on this role themselves, representing a community confidently prepared to stand up for itself. But that is to misunderstand the nature of the Jewish communal infrastructure. Why manage with one organization when two can get together to create a third?

According to the London Jewish Forum website, it has a dozen trustees and 25 people on its steering group. That sounds like a lot of chiefs for an organization with only one employee, the Forum's Director, Daniel Kosky. One of its trustees quoted to me the observation of Rabbi Jonathan Sacks that the Jewish community has never been short of leaders, only of followers.

Fortunately it seems that Daniel Kosky can do the job more than adequately, unfettered by his many superiors. He is one of the new generation of Jewish leaders who, having worked their way up through the ranks of the youth groups or the student unions, decided to begin their professional careers working in the Jewish community. Their elders, the professionals who run the community bodies today, hope that they will stay, that they won't be tempted away by more lucrative or more emotionally rewarding opportunities. Anxious to get their succession planning right, the experienced professionals trust that their new recruits will not become too disillusioned by the thankless task of working in a community where everybody else knows how to do their job better than they do, and nobody is afraid to tell them so.

The London Jewish Forum liaises with local government in almost every area in which the capital's Jews have an interest. They operate as a bridge, connecting the organizations working in education, security and social action with the officials and politicians whose decisions impact on funding and policy. At election times the Forum writes manifestos outlining the Jewish issues they would like the mayoral candidates to address, and they run hustings where candidates can campaign to the Jewish community at election time.

As the Director of the London Jewish Forum, Daniel is more aware than most of the specific issues faced by London's Jews, particularly those who are younger. They are not dissimilar to the issues that all Londoners face, but being Jewish adds another dimension. As an example, Daniel gives the cost of housing in the capital. 'This is particularly relevant for observant Jews because they want to live in places where there's a strong Jewish infrastructure. But unfortunately, in many cases, young Jews are being priced out of these areas because of the cost of housing. They are being pushed out, which has an impact on their ability to live the religious life they want.'

Britain has been aware for years that it has a national crisis over the care of the elderly. It's worse for the Jews. (When was it ever not?) The London Jewish population is one third older than the national average, and as Daniel says, 'We are facing the hard edge of an ageing population. And we have specialist care homes, which are incredibly important to our community. But they often struggle to get the same levels of funding as general care homes, because they bring together people from different local authorities, and there's a general issue about local authorities not necessarily paying what they should for the care of the elderly. Also the provision that is needed for Jewish care homes, like kosher food, results in costs that are higher than the average. It's a continuing challenge, and my colleagues at the JLC do an incredible amount of work on ensuring that our care homes get the funding they need.'

Our conversation turned, as conversations about Jewish affairs often do these days, to the question of anti-Semitism and the recent problems in the Labour Party. Daniel says he was amazed by how united the community became when the crisis first emerged. He pointed out that in the 2005 election the estimate was that about 60 per cent of the Jewish community voted for Labour. At the 2019 election the estimate had dropped to 7 per cent. 'I saw people who are probably in the category of disconnected Jews, people for whom being Jewish was right at the back of their identity, who were pleading to their friends to recognize what was going on in the party. For some people, the anti-Semitism crisis actually brought their Judaism back into their lives because they felt that their identity was being undermined.'

I asked him if his organization had any contact with those Jews on the left who did not consider that the Labour Party had been anti-Semitic, who believed that the benefits of a Corbyn-led government would outweigh the disadvantages. He said that their views were atypical, that they only represented a small percentage of the community. It is a common view, but it is not necessarily correct. Seven per cent of a community is not an insignificant number. And the figure of seven per cent who voted Labour does not include those many Jews who are so disconnected that the community doesn't even know they are out there. There is an assumption among those who are more engaged in communal life that all Jews opposed Corbyn. It is not the case. Not everyone thought he was anti-Semitic, or at least they didn't believe it was anything to worry about. There may have been serious anti-Semites in the Labour Party; they don't believe that Corbyn was among them.

Daniel was kept particularly busy during the Covid pandemic, liaising between health officials, politicians and London's synagogues. As he did so, he became aware of a phenomenon which, although unlikely to raise eyebrows among people who don't know the Jewish community, is quite refreshing to those who do.

It is a fact of Jewish life that the Strictly Orthodox communities keep themselves apart from the other religious groupings. They tend not to participate in communal organizations like the Board of Deputies or the JLC, and they rarely engage with other sectors of the community. A Strictly Orthodox rabbi, unless he happened to be a maverick in his community, would never engage in a public theological discussion with someone from the religiously progressive wing. Indeed they are likely to assert that progressive Jews do not really practise Judaism at all. The *haredi* communities withdrew from the Board of Deputies in 1971, after the Board amended a clause in its constitution to allow it to be guided by Reform and Liberal religious authorities on matters that concerned them. And yet, during the pandemic, when

Daniel began organizing conference calls between the various synagogue communities and the statutory authorities, he was delighted to find that *haredi* leaders were joining in and engaging in dialogue quite happily with Liberal and Reform rabbis. As Daniel says, it's a real change. It's just a shame that it needed a pandemic to make it happen.

There are signs that cross-communal goodwill is here to stay. There was a fear that, once the pandemic was forgotten, the Strictly Orthodox communities would once again withdraw from communal engagement. There is no indication of that. On the contrary, the discussions I have heard with leaders from across the religious spectrum is that they now acknowledge that their common interests outweigh their religious differences, that they all belong to the same community.

Russell Conn, President of the Jewish Representative Council in Manchester, noticed something similar. When the pandemic first struck, his Council, together with the regional director of the JLC and the Community Security Trust, set up a strategic group to coordinate the community's response and to begin to plan for the community's eventual recovery. From the outset they brought in members of Manchester's large *haredi* community. 'Covid gave us an opportunity to engage with a new ultra-orthodox generation who are much more adept at dealing with the wider community. And the engagement, the collaboration and the cooperation that we have enjoyed throughout the last 12 months have been, to use this overused word, unprecedented. Really, absolutely exceptional.'

The Strictly Orthodox community's involvement with Manchester's strategic group led to another bonus too. Manchester's Jewish community spans several local authorities. In order to plan ahead successfully, to ensure a robust communal recovery from the pandemic, the strategic group needed to engage with them all. To negotiate with each local authority separately would have been unproductive. So they set up a subcommittee on which the strategic group joined with representatives from all the local authorities. It led to far greater cooperation not just between the councils and the Jewish community but also between the various local councils themselves.

Russell illustrates the achievement by giving me a theoretical example of a child suffering from a mental health issue. The youngster may have gone to school in, say, Salford but lived in Bury. Previously each council would look to the other to take responsibility for the child's mental health. By bringing the councils together on its subcommittee, the strategic group encouraged them to share information and responsibility. Russell is certain that the existence of the strategic group has marked a change in the way that the local authorities collaborate. It's good for local government, and it's good for the Jewish community. 'What happens now is that the strategic group, along with the JLC and the Rep Council, have become the go-to place for interaction between Manchester's Jewish community and the wider community. This is what we wanted for decades.'

Ever since the state of Israel was founded in 1948 British Jews have been among its most visible supporters. A 2010 survey of British Jews reported that 82 per cent of respondents considered that Israel played a central or important role in their Jewish identity. Additionally, 95 per cent of them had visited the country and 87 per cent believed that Jews had a responsibility for ensuring Israel's survival. Yet, despite this overwhelming apparent support for Israel, only 72 per cent regarded themselves as Zionists.

It is Zionism, more than any other cause, that shapes the communal identity of British Jewry. Vivian Wineman says that emotionally it is a more important issue than Judaism: 'One of the left-wing Jewish organizations had their annual dinner on *Kol Nidrei* night [the Yom Kippur fast], and it didn't get any publicity at all – I only knew about it because I saw it in *Vashti*. But Jewdas had a Passover *seder*, and because they had Corbyn there, the outcry was deafening. If someone stood up at the Board of Deputies and said, "I think that the Torah was written some time during the Babylonian exile and that Judaism is rubbish and God doesn't exist," people would just shrug. But if somebody was to stand up and say, "The state of Israel has no right to exist," then they would say that he should not be a member of the Board.' The struggle he had to get the members of the Board to approve Yachad's application for membership bears out his point. It is Zionism, rather than Judaism, that binds the British community together, though in recent years the fear of anti-Semitism has probably outrun them both.

Zionism is not easy to define these days. When British Jews are asked whether they consider themselves to be Zionist, many will struggle to answer, not because they are uncertain about their attitude to Israel but because Zionism is no longer a word that they use very often, or a category that they think much about. The term 'Zionism' was once unambiguous: it meant the indisputable right of Jews to self-determination in their own sovereign homeland, in the biblical land of Israel. When the Zionist dream was realized with the founding of the state of Israel, the word 'Zionism' became more nuanced. It meant support for the continuing existence and development of the new nation, but opinions differed over whether that implied uncritical support of whichever government happened to be in power. Gradually, even that notion began to lose its potency. And then the word 'Zionism' became appropriated by Israel's political opponents as a derogatory label, implying a form of contemporary colonialism, symbolizing Western hegemony and the oppression of the dispossessed. 'Zionism' became a loaded word; it was far easier to say 'I support Israel's right to exist' than to say 'I am a Zionist'. But when asked outright whether they consider themselves to be Zionist, most people are likely to concur. For to say 'no' implies that they agree with those who use 'Zionism' as a term of abuse, who oppose the existence of the state of Israel.

For all the uncertainty over what Zionism means, Britain's Jewish community is institutionally Zionist. The Zionist Federation is the umbrella body that represents the Zionist movement in the UK. Founded in 1899, it is an affiliate of the World Zionist Organization, the body founded by Theodor Herzl to strive for the establishment of a Jewish homeland. The Zionist Federation represents both communal bodies and members who have signed up individually.

The Zionist Federation's membership has decreased quite dramatically over the past few years. In 2010 it had a membership of 120 organizations, a number that has shrunk today to a little over 30. It also claims to have 50,000 affiliate members, though it is not clear whether these are members of its affiliated organizations or whether they have joined in their own right. Somewhat inexplicably, despite the rapid decrease in the number of its organizational members, the number of affiliated members seems to have remained the same since 2010.

The shrinking of the Zionist Federation may have something to do with the political rows it has become embroiled in. They refused membership to Yachad, the same left-leaning, pro-Israel organization that had trouble joining the Board of Deputies. There was a suspicion that the Zionist Federation had excluded Yachad because of their criticism of Israel's government and their support for the two-state peace solution. However, the ZF's Chairman denied that this was the reason. Writing to Yachad, he said, 'There were no grounds for rejection, it simply went to vote, and the vote went against you.' But in 2020 a group of ZF's affiliated organizations wrote an open letter to the same Chairman condemning comments he had made supporting Israel's planned annexation of parts of the West Bank. They wrote that 'The Zionist Federation does not have a mandate to formulate policy positions in response to events taking place in Israel or the wider Middle East, or to make statements on behalf of the organizations it claims to represent.'

A few months later the groups who had written the open letter successfully submitted a motion to the organization's national council, prohibiting statements of a political nature without prior approval. Its opponents called it a 'gagging motion'. The *Jewish Chronicle* said it understood that left-wing groups were becoming increasingly influential in the ZF. It pointed to the fact that those who had submitted the 'gagging motion' had also made gains in the elections to the ZF's national council. Sources had told them, said the *JC*, 'that disunity among the "right" had allowed a unified group of "progressive" candidates to make gains'. The mood does not seem to be happy at the Zionist Federation.

Things are somewhat happier at the United Jewish Israel Appeal, even though it has lost its dominance as the largest charity in the British Jewish community. Formed as the Joint Palestine Appeal in 1947, just before the state of Israel was founded, the UJIA raised money at a time when that money was really needed. In 1973, after its supporters had argued for 25 years about its name, it became the Joint Israel Appeal.

In the 1990s, with Israel now a self-sufficient state with a growing economy and less need for charitable donations from overseas, the JIA found itself as an organization somewhat in need of a purpose. Unwilling to close down – few Jewish charities voluntarily give up the ghost – it bailed itself out by stepping into one of the periodic rows that British Jewry loves so much. The row was over Jewish Continuity, a new communal, educational initiative which had fallen foul of the religious community's fractious politics. Jewish Continuity had been set up to fund educational programmes aimed at ensuring the continuing existence of Judaism – 3,500 years of unbroken history apparently not being enough of a guarantee. It was a well-meaning project but a little too naive in assuming it could raise and disburse funds for educational programmes across the entire religious community. As soon as it made its first grants, the non-orthodox bodies complained, saying that the money was too heavily weighted towards orthodox projects. Then the orthodox weighed in, saying they could not participate if the non-orthodox were involved. The underlying problem was that it had been set up under the auspices of Chief Rabbi Jonathan Sacks, who, while wishing to speak for the entire community, only represented one wing of orthodoxy. The Jewish Continuity furore was just one of several disputes that plagued the religious communities at the time.

Fortunately for itself and Jewish Continuity, the JIA came to the rescue. It absorbed Jewish Continuity, beefed up its own involvement in education and turned itself into a charity aiming to strengthen the connection of British Jews to Israel. It changed its name again. It is now called the United Jewish

Israel Appeal. It sponsors social and educational projects among peripheral communities in Israel and is the main funder of the various Jewish youth groups in Britain. Among other things, they facilitate programmes for youth groups to take post-GCSE students on summer-long tours of Israel and offer a range of modular gap year programmes in Israel to older students, most of which include work experience opportunities in the country.

Although it is a quarter of a century since the merger with Jewish Continuity, the UJIA's mission still seems to be a little fuzzy in the minds of most people I have spoken to. But it stands out in one regard: it is currently the only major Jewish organization to have both a woman chief executive and chair. And Louise Jacobs, the chair, is in no doubt about the organization's importance in connecting the British community with Israel at a time when the attitudes of many Jews have changed, when many young people question why a relationship with Israel is a necessary part of their Jewish identity. 'We're not political, we've never been political. We want people to experience Israel, on their own terms. Our job is not to tell you how wonderful and how fantastic Israel is. Young people should make up their own minds what type of relationship they have with Israel. But if you look at the story of the Jews, there's no doubt that Israel plays a part in it.'

Louise is one of the new generation of communal leaders. She is certain that secular Jews in Britain are fully part of the Jewish community, and she says that, as such, she has a responsibility to give back to the Jewish community. But that doesn't mean exclusively focusing on Jewish causes. 'I'm involved with a children's hospice. I've done some work for Save the Children and for the Prince's Trust. Yes, I give more of my time to Jewish causes. But I still think we have responsibility to give back to non-Jewish causes. I think this is a really important part of being Jewish and living in Great Britain.'

Because Louise and her contemporaries are so much more confident about their identity as Jews, they don't suffer from the same sense of being outsiders as earlier generations did. She says that for many years, when she was working in the City, she felt more uncomfortable about being the only woman in her company than the only Jew. When she took over as Chair of UJIA, she stepped into a role that had been occupied over previous years by a succession of powerful men. And while it hasn't always been easy, she says she has not experienced anything other than total respect from her colleagues. But men and women do think differently. 'I may be the one to raise something that feels a little bit more touchy-feely. They can be much more hard-nosed about things. I think you need a combination of the two styles.'

It's important that other women follow Louise's lead and move into senior lay leadership roles in the community. British Jewry is certainly changing, but it still feels too male, with everything that entails. There are many women in senior professional roles as Chief Executives of Jewish organizations, but so far there are very few women Chairs.

Hearing Louise speak about the challenges of being a woman leader in the Jewish community sounds familiar: they are not so different from the challenges that women faced when they started to move into senior roles in the business community. Trustee meetings that take place at five or six o'clock in the evening, when many women would prefer to be at home with their families. Decisions taken on commercial grounds, an arena in which women who have not had a business career have little experience. And, of course, male-dominated conversations. But Louise hopes other women will follow her lead. 'One thing that will make a difference is if younger women see that women bring a different perspective, and that their arguments are as valued and as reasoned as everybody else's. Sometimes you've just got to take that leap and think, "I'm doing the best that I can and no one else has stepped up to do this. I probably won't get it perfect, but I will get it as good as anybody else, male or female. So I'll give it a go." You've just got to take the plunge and have the confidence in your own abilities.'

The Anglo-Israel Association sounds as if it is yet another institution set up by British Jews to connect the community in one way or another to Israel. But it is not. Zionism is not just for Jews. The Anglo-Israel Association was set up in 1949 by General Sir Wyndham Deedes, a social activist and ardent Zionist, who was a profoundly committed Christian. Deedes had served as General Secretary to the British High Commissioner in Palestine in the 1920s and, on retiring from the army, had devoted himself to voluntary social work in London's East End. He became Chairman of the London Council of Social Service. He founded the AIA because he thought that it should not be for Jews alone to support the state of Israel.

Richard Bolchover is the Deputy Chairman of the AIA. He told me that the organization was set up by Deedes and a number of prominent non-Jewish Zionists shortly after Israel was declared as an independent state. They were excited by the new nation's potential and wanted to develop its relationship with Britain. There are a few Jewish members of the AIA, but it is mainly a non-Jewish organization, with some very prominent and well-connected individuals among its membership.

Richard, who is one of the few Jews on the AIA's executive, told me that they operate with the explicit cooperation of both governments and their embassies, 'bringing together top people in any field where we think Israel is making a contribution that will be of interest to its English counterparts. It could be architecture, it could be oncology; we may bring over the Israeli Supreme Court, or Israeli generals, to meet their counterparts here.' He told me that health professionals from both countries are working together, because the way Israel runs its health service has become of great interest to the British.

Before Covid the Anglo-Israel Association aimed to run two major events each year, one in Israel and one in the UK, taking key experts from one country to the other. 'It's just a way of bringing together experts from the two countries in the hope that those connections will go on to spark more cooperation and understanding, and also just to benefit the general relationship between the two countries.'

And yet, despite its standing within the circles of influences, the AIA is largely unknown within the British Jewish community. Richard says that, even when the Association sends out press releases about major events, they get very little coverage in the Jewish media. 'And that's obviously because they think that it's not Jewish, as indeed it isn't. But I would say that it is relevant to the Jewish community, because I think Israel is very relevant. The Jews that do come to our dinners, particularly the first time they come, are always very struck. Usually, they're very heartened. They expect to walk into a room where they will know, or recognize, 97 per cent of the people. And they don't. They see all these non-Jews who love Israel.'

There are very few organizations in the world like the Anglo-Israel Association. Many nations have bilateral commercial links, to promote trade and business, but few organizations exist solely for ideological reasons, simply to strengthen relationships between two countries. The support of prominent non-Jews for the idea of Israel is a powerful rebuttal to those who see Zionism as Jewish colonialism. 'And I think the non-Jews who are involved in the AIA think that most anti-Zionism is anti-Semitism, and certainly they're well aware that Israel is not treated in the same way as other countries. They believe that is because Israel is the Jewish state in the Holy Land.'

Jonathan Boyd is a man with his finger on the pulse of the community. As Director of the Institute for Jewish Policy Research, he is the go-to authority for all information on communal attitudes, demography and trends. He writes a regular column for the *Jewish Chronicle* called 'The View from the Data'.

JPR's role is to generate data to support community planning in the UK and across Europe, trying, as Jonathan puts it, to be as responsive as possible to the questions and concerns that exist in the community. They conduct their own surveys but also make use of the considerable amount of data in the public domain. They did a lot of work during the Covid pandemic on the impact of the virus on people's jobs, their income, physical and mental health and on their Jewish lifestyles, actively producing relevant, up-to-date information. They publish their reports and discuss their findings communally. Jonathan says he spends much of his time presenting data to different organizations, to help them make use of it.

JPR started life in New York, in 1941, as the Institute of Jewish Affairs, a project of the World Jewish Congress, which is a sort of global Board of Deputies, with a similarly high self-regard and low relevance in the minds of most people. The Institute of Jewish Affairs broke away from the World Jewish Congress in 1966 and moved to the UK. 30 years later it changed its name to the Institute of Jewish Policy Research, gave up its traditional role as an academic research unit and refashioned itself as a think tank concentrating on policy issues, producing a small number of weighty reports each year. Under Jonathan's leadership it has moved towards producing smaller, more frequent reports, responding to the demands of our information age by keeping as up-to-date as possible. They are a small but growing team of 11, most of whom work for JPR part-time.

Jonathan Boyd has been the head of JPR since 2009. He says that one of the most visible changes in the Jewish community in that time has been the growth of the Strictly Orthodox, or *haredi*, community, chiefly because of their large families. Projections are that by 2030 half of all Jewish births in Britain will be into *haredi* homes, progressively making the community more and more Strictly Orthodox. This will have major implications, affecting the way British Jews are regarded by the public at large and changing the way their interests will be represented to government and policymakers. The periodic tensions between the Board of Deputies and the Jewish Leadership Council may become of no consequence not because the two organizations will have resolved their differences but because the *haredim* may one day comprise the majority of the community, and as things stand they are not represented on either organization.

But that hasn't happened yet. The change that is having the most noticeable effect on the demography of the community today is secularization. In the USA, where the mainstream community is largely Reform or Conservative, the synagogues are more open to mixed-faith couples. American Jews with partners who are not Jewish find it relatively easy to stay connected to the community. In Britain, however, for family or historic reasons, many non-observant people remain affiliated to orthodox synagogues. And orthodox synagogues do not have strategies for retaining intermarried congregants. So there is little incentive for intermarried people to involve themselves with their synagogue.

Nor do the cultural aspects of Judaism offer them much incentive. In previous generations people connected with other Jews socially and culturally, or through their support for Israel. But those ties are weaker now. In Britain it is easy for Jews who have little interest in their identity to drift away from the community altogether. The result is that those who remain connected are those who are more engaged and usually more observant, while those on the margins distance themselves even further.

The Liberal and Reform movements do try to engage some of those who are drifting away, but the likelihood is that the community as a whole will continue to become polarized between the marginally engaged, on one side, and the *haredim*, for whom faith is the entirety of their lives, on the other. Meanwhile, unless the centrist synagogues find new ways of stimulating their increasingly disengaged membership, the traditional middle-of-the-road centre of British Jewry will continue to weaken and shrink. Of course, it is not a one-way process: many rabbis will point to the successful educational and social programmes that they run in their synagogues. But they are swimming against the tide. What little religious fervour there is, outside of the committed orthodox and *haredi* communities, is among small circles of younger Jews who are experimenting with new ways of expressing their Judaism.

Of course, projections don't always come true. The *haredi* community may not continue to grow at the same rate, and even if they do, there are many other considerations that may impact on the community's demographic profile in coming years. Social factors may impel the disengaged to take a greater interest in their roots and their identity, perhaps, as in the USA, leading them to find a way of expressing their Jewishness in a manner that they find personally meaningful. Alternatively, economic pressures may oblige the *haredim* to come out of their self-imposed ghettos and play a fuller role in the life of the mainstream community, thereby strengthening the centre.

Jonathan Boyd thinks it essential for the long-term sustainability of the Jewish community that the *haredi* community works harder at accommodating some of the norms of contemporary British society while simultaneously maintaining its own particular Jewish lifestyle. The wider Jewish community, he says, does not feel comfortable being identified with a group that is perceived to be separatist, however self-sufficient, and as detaching itself from society at large. Not that they are all separatists by any means. Jonathan says that the work he has done with the *haredi* community indicates that they are often keen to have research done, that they really want to know what's going on within their community, but they are sometimes wary about having the results of the research publicized because it feels exposing, even voyeuristic.

The *haredi* influence on British Jewry is tied up with the vexed question of Jewish religious particularity: the idea of a community that is concerned only with its own distinctiveness and centrality in a world that celebrates diversity and difference. Judaism is universalist in outlook, but issues like anti-Semitism and the tensions in the Middle East have encouraged introspection and self-concern to dominate much of the conversation in the British religious community. As someone who is conscious of trends, Jonathan flags religious particularism as an issue worth keeping an eye on.

We discussed some of the other issues that he feels are coming to the fore in twenty-first-century British Jewry. There is the perennial question of how to sustain a consequential and enriching sense of Jewish identity as society changes. How, in other words, to ensure a positive feeling about one's Jewishness, to guarantee that being a Jew adds value to one's personal sense of self-worth. Today's young Jews are far more confident about their identity than their parents and grandparents, but there is no knowing if they will transmit that confidence to their children. For many people in the late twentieth century it was the creation of Israel, the first Jewish state for two millennia, and its struggle for survival, that made them proud to be Jewish. Far more so, for example, than their religion or culture. But support for Israel is not as all-encompassing as it once was. Teachers, rabbis, educators and youth workers whose work includes fostering a sense of Jewish identity need to be mindful of the impact on Jewish identity of changing social and political attitudes, and to develop appropriate responses.

There is something else to be learned from the difference between the religious make-up of the British and American communities, from the dominance of the progressive denominations in the USA. Boyd describes a study which noted that when Americans spoke about their Jewishness they used the word 'comfortable'; their Judaism had to feel comfortable to them. In contrast, a similar study in the UK found that the equivalent word for British Jews was 'proper'; Judaism had to be done properly. He says that distinction is quite important, 'in that the community here is fundamentally more conservative, more traditional, more British, in the sense of there being proper, authentic ways of doing things. Whereas in America, the sense is that Judaism has to be meaningful; it has to be comfortable.'

Jon's comment reminded me of what Rabbi Zarum of the London School of Jewish Studies told me, that his college aims to 'voice a reason where Judaism has more meaning today than it ever did'. In other words, it seems that for Judaism in contemporary Britain to flourish, the old British sense that things have to be done properly needs to be augmented with the newer American emphasis on comfort and meaningfulness.

American Jewry seems able to accommodate many different nuances and approaches to being Jewish, the key determinant being whether it feels meaningful on an individual level. In Britain, however, the emphasis on doing things properly suggests that nominal affiliation to a not too demanding form of orthodoxy will continue to be the default approach for those who want a religious component in their lives.

6

Not Just London

Jews have lived in Manchester since the end of the eighteenth century. They came for the cotton trade, and as Manchester grew to become the industry's global centre, the Jewish community grew with it. Manchester is the second-largest Jewish community in Great Britain, with a population of around 30,000.

Around one third of the Manchester community is Strictly Orthodox. That is about twice the national average; overall the *haredi* community account for around 15 per cent of Britain's Jews, a figure that is expected to increase rapidly over the next few years owing to their large family sizes. Manchester's Strictly Orthodox community lives in a small enclave centred on Broughton Park in Salford, although as their numbers grow they are gradually moving beyond their heartland into areas where the Jewish population has traditionally been more mainstream.

The Manchester Jewish community was always perceived as being somewhat more observant than its London counterpart. And there were always some who were Strictly Orthodox. But not as many as today. The expansion of the *haredi* community in Manchester is a new phenomenon, and the unbounded ghetto in which the *haredim* live used to be occupied by the community at large, by traditional Jews who bore both their Judaism and their Englishness in equal measure. I know this because my grandparents lived there. They were typical Jews of the mildly orthodox variety. They didn't have a *haredi* bone in their bodies.

One reason why many *haredi* Jews moved to Manchester was that they couldn't afford to live in London any longer. House prices were rising, their families were growing and Manchester offered a cheap alternative, a community where the religious infrastructure was already in place, where it was possible to live a life of religious devotion without worrying quite as much about how to pay the bills.

Concentrated in such a small area, and constituting such a large proportion of Manchester's Jews, it is no wonder that the Strictly Orthodox community exerts a far greater influence over religious life in the city than it does in London. It can feel as though there is a sort of sanctity to certain parts of Manchester, that one is touched by holiness just walking its streets. Until we remember that this is just another damp and cold English city, and that what happens in its *haredi* community is no different from anywhere else in the country. *Haredim* may strive for holiness, but they are people like the rest of us; their lives are beset by the same difficulties and failings as everyone else, and their communities are susceptible to the same social problems that can be found in neighbourhoods everywhere. Jews, as the old saying goes, are just like everyone else, only more so.

Haredim aside, the majority of Manchester's Jews live in the suburbs to the north of Broughton Park, in a strip along the A56 from Prestwich to Bury. And there is another much smaller community, numbering perhaps no more than

1,000 Jews, in the south of the city. The south Manchester community has always regarded itself as somewhat distinct from the enclaves in the north. Russell Conn, President of the Manchester Rep Council, who lives in the north, says that there is something of a different mentality between the two communities. 'The southern area is more leafy, there's more space. It is not as jammed together. Whereas we live cheek and jowl in this area.'

It's much easier to live Jewishly in the north of Manchester than in the south. There are kosher butchers, delis and restaurants galore. There are none in south Manchester. 'We have the infrastructure which they don't have in the south,' says Russell Conn. 'There are only five synagogues in the whole of south Manchester. Up here in the north there are new ones every day; even the Council doesn't know how many there are.'

In fact, the Representative Council's website lists about 50 synagogues in the Greater Manchester area. That doesn't include the dozens of small *shtiebels*, often just a room in someone's house, where small groups of the Strictly Orthodox gather to pray.

There are around 20 Jewish schools in Manchester, all in the north of the city. Most are small and serve the *haredi* community. None comes close to the educational standard set by Manchester's King David schools, the city's flagship institutions, which offer everything from nursery to sixth-form education. King David High School, one of the top-performing schools in the country, is rated as outstanding both by Ofsted, and by Pikuach, the Jewish community's inspectorate for religious education. Uniquely, as an option to its main high school, parents who want their children to receive an intensive religious education on top of the standard curriculum can enrol them in one of the school's two single-sex divisions.

When Ofsted visited the school in 2019, they found that the school day for pupils in the single-sex divisions was longer than in the main school. They accused the school of breaching the Equality Act and downgraded it from 'Outstanding' to 'Inadequate'. The school responded vigorously, applying for a judicial review of the ruling. Three months later Ofsted admitted that they had been wrong, reinstated the schools 'Outstanding' rating and were ordered to pay the school's legal fees, in the region of £80,000.

In 1867 the town's leading Jewish citizens set up the Board of Guardians for the Relief of the Jewish Poor of Manchester, to provide bread, meat and coal to the needy. As the community grew and the needs of the needy became more complex, the Board of Guardians took on a social work mandate. In the 1960s it changed its name to Manchester Jewish Social Services and employed its first social worker. And then a few years ago it merged with Heathlands Village, Manchester's oldest Jewish residential care home. The new organization was renamed again, as the Federation of Jewish Services. Universally known as 'the Fed', it now provides a full spectrum of residential, nursing, dementia and end-of-life care services, offers independent living facilities for those who don't need residential care and runs an on-site children's centre and a mental health drop-in. It also functions as a community hub, hosting other organizations on its premises.

Mark Cunningham, the Chief Executive, has been there for 24 years; he says he came as a student and loved it so much he has been there ever since. He says that, one way or another, the Fed provides support to one in every eight Jewish homes in Manchester. And that doesn't include the extra support they provided during the Covid pandemic, which, as in all care homes across the country, was devastating for the Fed's staff, residents and families. Mark told me that within a six-week period they lost 20 people to Covid, predominantly over the age of 85.

Mark chairs the National Association of Jewish Homes. He told me that the challenges that Jewish social care providers grapple with across the country are little different from those faced in any similar organization. People are living longer, with more complex conditions, and there is never enough money or support from local authorities and government. And yet people still expect their local authorities to provide what he calls a National Social Care Service, sending in home carers 'to come and do high-level dusting and things like that. It just is not there.'

The challenges facing the Fed and the other social care agencies are becoming ever more complicated and the need for additional financial and practical resources ever more urgent. But the Jewish agencies have one inestimable advantage. It is the volunteering ethos of which the Manchester Jewish community is rightly proud. Volunteering is a cultural Jewish trait, and although it seems to have gone into decline in many places, in Manchester the Jewish voluntary spirit remains strong. Mark says that the Jewish community is lucky 'because we have a real depth when it comes to volunteering. It doesn't exist to the same extent in the wider community. We have 355 staff and around 500 volunteers, so we really punch above our weight when it comes to volunteering. That is absolutely our jewel in the crown.'

Money is always an issue in the care sector. The funding that local authorities contribute towards the care of their residents is never adequate for the standard of care that charitable homes wish to provide. So Jewish care charities rely heavily on donations from their local communities, and it is here that the Fed is at a noticeable disadvantage. London charities have a far larger donor base and can raise greater sums. This might suggest that it would be in the Fed's interest to merge with the much larger, London-based Jewish Care, an option that is discussed from time to time. But it is at this point that the inequalities in the British housing market come into play.

The basic principle for all Jewish care charities is that nobody is refused support on financial grounds. Equally, though, if care home residents can afford to contribute to the costs of their care, it is expected that they will do so. They often do this by selling homes they are unlikely ever to return to, or releasing equity from them in other ways. But since house prices in London are far higher than in Manchester, a merger of the Fed and Jewish Care would mean that care home residents in London who release equity from their houses would effectively be subsidizing those in Manchester. And while this may be a communal ambition worth striving for, it doesn't seem to be an idea that has much support at the moment.

And yet, while London may be unwilling to subsidize Manchester, it doesn't stop several London charities from running fundraising initiatives in Manchester. Of course, those charities would argue that they are national organizations, benefiting the Manchester community as much as London. But from a Manchester perspective, they are still taking money out of the city. It doesn't affect the Fed so much: during the Covid crisis they worked in partnership with the London charities to raise money for distribution nationally. But from the perspective of one of the small Manchester charities, watching London charities hold a fundraising dinner on their turf might not be the most encouraging of experiences.

With such a large Jewish community it is not surprising that Manchester sees its fair share of anti-Semitic incidents, typically from small-minded racists hurling abuse across the street or as they drive past. Although the *haredim* are the most visible of Manchester Jews, Russell Conn says that anti-Semitic abuse is not restricted to them alone. 'It's not just reserved for the ultra orthodox because they're more identifiable. I think anyone going out dressed smartly, say on a shabbat or a festival, could be fair game. Most of the abusers are weak, they don't come up to you, although there was an incident, about a year or so ago, when a youngster was physically attacked. It's always beneath the surface. So much so that CST to their credit have been beefing up the security of most of the major synagogues. In my synagogue we are in the process of having new fencing installed, paid for almost solely by CST.'

In addition to the Community Security Trust, who have a regional office in Manchester, the neighbourhood watch group Shomrim operates patrols in Salford and Prestwich. Shomrim, which was originally set up to protect *haredi* neighbourhoods in New York, is staffed mainly, but not exclusively, by members of the Strictly Orthodox community. They work closely with local police, alerting them to suspicious activity or sharing information they have received. They are similar in some ways to the private security firms that now operate in upmarket locations across the UK. But, being community-based, they have far better local knowledge than the private contractors. And they differ from CST. Their president, Rabbi Herschel Gluck, explains that, unlike CST, who monitor the entire hate crime spectrum and develop strategic and tactical responses accordingly, Shomrim's focus is on what is actually happening at any moment in the streets they patrol. He says they are on the lookout for criminal activity anywhere in their area, whoever it is directed against. They try to protect their entire local community, not just its Jewish members.

Although CST and Shomrim are both concerned with the security of the community, there is little contact between them. It distresses Rabbi Gluck. He says he can't explain why his overtures to CST are rarely reciprocated. Since CST and Shomrim are, in his words, 'completely different animals', he says he finds the lack of a relationship between the two organizations deeply problematic.

Ask any London or Manchester Jew how many small Jewish communities there are in Britain and they may hesitate for a moment before guessing at maybe six or seven. If they have friends or family who live in a small community they may increase their guess to ten or 12. In fact, according to Ed Horwich, who runs the Jewish Small Communities Network there are over 100 groups that self-identify as small communities – 55,000 people altogether. That is almost one fifth of the total number of people in Britain who declared themselves Jewish in the 2011 census.

Nevertheless, Jews tend to live together in large clusters. One fifth of the population may live outside London and Manchester, the main centres of Jewish life, but another fifth live in the London borough of Barnet, the country's most Jewishly saturated local authority. And of the 55,000 who live in small communities, over 20,000 live in just seven: Leeds, Gateshead, Brighton, Glasgow, Southend, Birmingham and Liverpool. Of those, Ed Horwich says that Birmingham and Liverpool are not really small communities yet; they affiliate to the Network because they are shrinking and want to plan for the future by drawing on the experiences of those communities that are small. The remainder, those who are not in the towns Ed has enumerated, are scattered around the country, sometimes in pockets that number no more than a handful.

There is no doubt that numerically Britain's Jewish population has gravitated over the past hundred years towards the large centres of London and Manchester. In the 1920s the Jewish population of Leeds was 25,000; now it is fewer than 7,000. Liverpool shrank from 8,000 in 1914 to 2,000 today. Yet there are more small communities today than ever before, even in places where Jews traditionally had never lived. There are Jews living in every one of the 348 local authority areas in England and Wales.[48]

Jewish life in a small community is very different from that in the big centres, but not necessarily in terms of commitment: Ed Horwich believes that most small community members aspire to live as full and as rich a Jewish life as is practical, given where they live. The few Jews in a small community are far more visible than they would be in London or Manchester and those who associate with the local Jewish community are more likely to be called upon for their knowledge of Judaism than their co-religionists in the cities. Schools may want someone to come and speak about Judaism; hospitals may need to know how to cater for a Jewish patient; social work departments may be looking for someone to help out a Jewish client in crisis. Jews in small communities cannot easily hide away.

Being a Jew in a small provincial town can bring other challenges too. Adrian Litvinoff is one of a handful of Jews in Leamington Spa. He told me about a woman he knew who would make remarks to him about being Jewish, implying there was something slightly exotic about him, something a bit different and strange. 'There are these little currents,' he said. But he doesn't regard it as anti-Semitism. It is just that some people, from certain backgrounds, are uncertain how to react the first time they encounter someone who is Jewish.

Adrian says he has encountered very little overt anti-Semitism in Leamington Spa. But he did when he worked in Warwick some years earlier. He was working for the county educational authority. 'There was a staff magazine. And in one of the Christmas issues some guy who fancied himself as a bit of a comedian wrote a number of anecdotes about the year. Some of these were actually quite offensive. In one, he used the word *yid* about something that had been going on in Israel. He wrote something like "See what the yids have been up to", or something like that. So I wrote a letter to the editor, saying the word "yid" is always offensive. And a senior manager came up to me and said, "I'm really glad you wrote that letter. I'm Welsh. And I'm always being sniped at for being Welsh."'

Living a full Jewish life is not as easy in remote locations as it is in the big centres. So much of Jewish life seems to revolve around food, and it is obviously harder to get hold of Jewish food in a small town where there is little commercial incentive for the local delicatessen to stock it. Of course, the problem not insuperable – online shopping has made everything so much easier – but it is still far more hassle to plan ahead, order online and wait, probably a little longer than usual, for a delivery than it is to nip down to the local kosher baker or butcher whenever it is convenient. In some ways the most difficult foods to obtain are not the religiously mandated things like kosher meat and *kiddush* wine for a Friday evening, which many people are not too bothered about. The problems come when they want the occasional festive foods, the cultural foods, like *hamantaschen*, the small, glazed tricorn pastries filled with dates or poppy seeds that are traditionally eaten at the carnival festival of Purim. Or *schmaltz* herring, the fatty, brine-pickled fish that is a perfect accompaniment to a glass of whisky after a hard shabbat morning's prayer in synagogue. Such things are hard to get on a typical supermarket delivery, and, depending on where one lives, sourcing a kosher delicatessen that will deliver dependably and economically is not always easy.

Synagogues can also be a source of problems for small communities. When only a few people are willing to commit to regular synagogue attendance, the question of what style of service to conduct can become divisive. Living Jewishly in a small community is likely to demand a quite high level of compromise. Although Strictly Orthodox Jews are very rare in small communities, the nominally orthodox, those who are familiar with the traditional synagogue service even if they don't maintain a rigorously religious life, will typically not enjoy a Reform or Liberal service, where a greater number of prayers are in English and may be accompanied by music. Conversely, Reform and Liberal Jews will not enjoy the longer, Hebrew-intensive orthodox rite. Ultimately the choice of service style is likely to depend on the tastes and skills of those able to lead a service, who know the tunes, can read the Hebrew and are familiar with the rituals and procedures.

When Ed Horwich started working with small communities, he says he regularly heard people say that the small communities look to the large communities for support. 'It's not the case,' he says, 'the large communities have no interest in supporting small communities. There is a twinning scheme which has been running for some years; there are some twinning things going on, but not a lot. Twinning schemes between small and large come and go, and some communities have enjoyed the benefit for a long time, but there's not many of them.' Ed told me that the once much larger but now small community in Southport has twinned with Bowdon in south Manchester, largely because former Southport residents now live in Bowdon.

Covid helped the small communities. Suddenly every Jewish area became an 'isolated' or 'remote' community, its residents cut off by lockdown from the synagogue, from their usual shops, from meeting over a coffee … 'just like being the only Jew in the village'. Ed told me about his encounters with London-based community organizations and agencies. Before the pandemic nearly all would confine themselves to supporting people who could walk through their door. Video conferencing or 'virtual meetings' were not something they would contemplate. Lockdown has changed that attitude, has opened up the possibilities and most organizations now will have a method of reaching you remotely. But there is still a way to go in understanding the out-of-London perspective. Ed says that bringing that understanding to the table is one of the things for which the Small Communities Network advocates.

Perhaps the biggest problems a small community faces are those of leadership and finance. Synagogues need to be cleaned and maintained; services need to be scheduled and planned; a family may be arranging a wedding or a barmitzvah and want to know that the synagogue can cater for their needs. Local schools might want to bring a class for a guided tour of the synagogue; a sick person may need visiting; someone may pass away and need to be buried. Money needs to be found for major repairs, or for new books or to support a needy local family. 'Who is going to do it?' and 'How will we pay for it?' are recurring themes in small communities. Particularly since the members of small communities tend to be disproportionately the elderly.

For many years small communities struggled by on their own. Occasionally one of the central religious bodies would send someone from London to help take a service or conduct a funeral. But the day-to-day burden of running the community fell on a small number of people, often just one or two communally minded souls. I lived for some years in Exeter, a town with a beautiful eighteenth-century synagogue but a community that we assumed was tiny. Three of us ran the community; we would have happily involved others, but nobody else wanted to join in. We knew how slim our chances were of finding anyone else to help, because the community was so small.

We knew how small it was because the services we held were orthodox, which meant we needed a minimum of ten men to conduct them properly. Most of the time we just about got our ten, but rarely more than that, and we hoped that nobody would die or leave, because then we could no longer hold services. Until one day we held a Hanukkah party, an event with no religious component, no prayers or anything that might threaten the peace of a secular mind. We got the local radio station to announce the party – and 100 people turned up. All Jews, the vast majority of whom had no connection at all with the community, because they weren't religious and had never required a synagogue, never needed to organize a wedding, barmitzvah or burial.

But even without the Hanukkah party it is likely that many of those with whom we'd had no previous contact would have got in touch one day. We would regularly receive phone calls from people who'd had no contact with a Jewish community for decades but who said that, now they were in their old age, they thought they should get in touch again. What they were really saying was that they wanted to make sure that, when the time came, they would receive a Jewish funeral. As Ed Horwich says, at some point most people do engage, even if it's at the point of death.

Ed set up the Jewish Small Communities Network project in 2003 as a simple self-help website. The demands on it grew, and by 2016 it had turned into a registered charity. His organization has made the task of running a small community much easier. He holds regular meetings of leaders from small communities, usually online, and runs professional development and leadership training programmes for them. He explains that most small community leaders did not start out with any ambition to take on the role; they just fell into it because there was nobody else who would do the job.

They may have known nothing when they took on the job of running the community. But after a while they become the go-to person for everything. And everybody tells them, 'You're the expert, you carry on.' And they carry on until they leave or die, at which point the next person takes over and starts from scratch again. The community's success then depends on their personal interests, ability, knowledge and stamina. But it can be a lonely job. Ed says that when the Small Communities Network offers them the opportunity to be trained in leadership skills and to be given access to resources, they tend to jump at it. Leadership is the key issue for every small community. Some communities will say, 'We're very happy, we've sorted things out for ourselves. Don't worry about us.' But the reality is that they all need help to some degree.

British Jews are frequently lumped together under the heading 'Anglo Jewry'. It is a designation that seems to disregard the Jews of Ireland and Wales, and overlooks the unique customs of the small, and shrinking, Scottish Jewish community. No other Jewish community in the world has its own bagpipe band, and no Jews, other than those from Scotland, eat haggis and drink Irn-Bru on Burns night, when the country celebrates the life of the poet Robbie Burns.

The first Jews began to trickle into Scotland around 300 years ago, and started arriving in substantial numbers around the mid-nineteenth century. That is, unless you are persuaded by the arguments set out in the book *When Scotland Was Jewish*. Published in 2007, it claims to establish, through DNA evidence and archaeology, that rather than Scotland being a Celtic culture, its history from the twelfth century onwards shows that 'much of her population, including several national heroes, villains, rulers, nobles, traders, merchants, bishops, guild members, burgesses, and ministers were of Jewish descent'. It doesn't really matter if the thesis is right or not; it makes a change to come across a pseudo-history that is philo-Semitic, rather than anti-Semitic.[49]

Many of the nineteenth-century Jews who first settled in Scotland arrived en route from Eastern Europe to America. They'd booked passages with shipping companies who transported them by way of Scotland. Those who were already travel-weary by the time they reached Scotland opted to remain, rather than undertaking the lengthy Atlantic crossing. Others had no choice; they were obliged to remain in Glasgow until they were able to meet American health requirements.

The number of Jews in Scotland peaked at around 20,000 before the Second World War. It has fallen to a little more than 6,000 today, but the community continues to organize itself with a vigour that belies its numbers. The Scottish Council of Jewish Communities, the umbrella body that represents Scotland's Jews, has a website which, according to Ephraim Borowski, the Council's director, contains between

13,500 and 14,000 pages. That's over two website pages for every Jew. Borowski challenges the figures. He agrees with the figure of 13,500 web pages. But he is dismissive of the census figures that place the Jewish population at 6,000. The census figures, he says, are not reliable.

He points out that in the 2001 census two questions on religion were asked in Scotland. One was 'What religion do you belong to?' The other was 'What religion were you brought up in?' Since the questions were voluntary, many people didn't answer them at all. Of those who did, different totals were scored for each question, largely because Jews don't need to 'belong' to anything to be Jewish. Only one religion question was asked in the 2011 census, but taking into account the results of the previous census, Borowski calculates that Scotland's Jewish population today could be anywhere between 9,000 and 10,000. That's scarcely one web page per Jew.[50]

Borowski points out that many Jews were reluctant to answer the voluntary census questions about religion because of their memories of the Holocaust. The leaders of the Strictly Orthodox communities in London and Manchester, whose memories run deep, were particularly anxious that their members should avoid the question. 'They shot themselves in the foot,' Borowski says, 'when they told everybody not to answer the religion question. They didn't answer the question then suddenly discovered there was no money for schools.' By refusing to answer the religion question they had made themselves invisible as Jews and excluded their communities from the government's school funding calculations.

The largest Jewish community in Scotland has always been in Glasgow. There was a time when its tenements were packed with Jews. Some, like the former market trader Sir Isaac Wolfson, clawed their way out of the slums to wealth and fame.

Others, like my grandfather Johnny, clawed their way only as far as the First World War trenches, where he was gassed; he spent the rest of his life struggling to breathe properly.

Glasgow's synagogues are poorly attended now. There are more ghosts than worshippers, and ghosts don't count in the *minyan*, the quorum necessary for public prayer. The decline in numbers is partly attributable to assimilation – large numbers of people who see no reason to connect with the Jewish community – and partly to an exodus of younger people, lured by economic opportunities elsewhere or by the appeal of London and Manchester as vibrant centres of Jewish life. They leave behind them the elderly and the ageing. The synagogues struggle on, sometimes banding together for religious services.

The community has declined, but the care services that were set up when it was larger and stronger continue to function, Glasgow has a full spectrum of Jewish care services including residential homes, a day centre, meals on wheels services and specialist support and facilities for the elderly, the vulnerable and those with special needs.

Ephraim Borowski is not optimistic about the ability of the community's care homes and sheltered housing to retain their Jewish identity. They are vulnerable to economic pressures. 'People might not go synagogue, but when the time comes, if they need to go into a retirement home they want it to be one with a Jewish atmosphere. And that's a very big issue because of the pressure on public funds; if somebody dies the charity that runs the place can't afford to keep the bed empty so they'll take the next person who wants to come in, and you can't then ship them out again because someone Jewish wants it.'

One of the most poignant illustrations of the Glasgow community's decline is the story of the Queen's Park

Synagogue windows. In 1987 the synagogue commissioned the artist John K. Clark to design a set of 22 stained-glass windows depicting the Jewish festivals. The project was to be the community's contribution to Glasgow's year as European City of Culture in 1990. Striking both for their use of colour and for their abstract symbolism, the windows were described as the defining commission of Clark's career, one that he described as 'the most incredible project to make'. Sadly, just 12 years later, the Queen's Park Synagogue closed down and the windows were relocated to the Giffnock synagogue, Glasgow's largest. Clark said that he was devastated when the synagogue closed. 'I've never had a relationship like that with a building where I've created art. It felt like the building was mine. It was such a wrench.' The story of the Queen's Park windows shows just how quickly communities can fall into decline as populations dwindle and move away.[51]

Other than Glasgow, there are Jewish communities in Edinburgh, Aberdeen and Tayside, and there are informal Jewish networks in other areas. According to the census, Jews live in every one of Scotland's 32 council areas. Edinburgh is the largest community outside of Glasgow. It has suffered from the same decline in numbers, owing to the same assimilatory pressures and the exodus of those looking for a more vibrant Jewish life elsewhere.

Tayside and Fife is the new name for the Dundee community. After struggling for several years to maintain their synagogue in Dundee, paying out far more in maintenance than any benefit they received from the five or six times a year they used the building, they came to accept that the nearby St Andrews University, with its many Jewish American students, was a far more promising location. The message was driven home one Yom Kippur, the day when synagogues expect their highest attendance of the year. Only six people attended services in Dundee, while 50 did at the University. So now the community have relocated to the University campus, where they are able to use a room in the Chaplaincy Centre for their services. They have sold their old Dundee synagogue building, and instead of a drain on their financial resources they now have money in the bank.

Ephraim Borowski, who was awarded an MBE in 2008 for his work on behalf of the Scottish community, believes that the decline in the Jewish population of Scotland may have stabilized. People do move to Scotland, usually as part of their work. He gives the example of an Israeli whose IT company wanted a UK office. London was too expensive, so the Israeli and his family settled in Glasgow and they are now active in the community. And they are not the only ones. Young families come to Scotland. Perhaps not many, but the trickle is steady. And Ephraim is optimistic about the impact the changing political climate may have. Should Scotland opt one day for independence and seek to enter the EU, it should create job opportunities. Particularly in the financial and legal sectors, areas in which Jews are disproportionately represented. 'So would that drive a population shift? Well, one can hope so.'

Birmingham's story is not unlike Glasgow's: an old community that has shrunk in size, many of its members now elderly, its synagogues empty or shut down altogether. But that is where the similarity ends. Whereas most Jews in Glasgow were born in the city, many in Birmingham come from elsewhere. According to the community's website, there are around 2,000 Jews in Birmingham and the West Midlands. The 2011 national census puts the figure at 4,500. Part of the discrepancy is because of the 1,000 Jewish students at

Birmingham University, one of the largest Jewish student populations in the country. And although the students, being a transient population, do not see themselves as part of the local community, the fact that they are there helps the community to tick over. Having four or five students turn up at the orthodox Central Synagogue during term time makes the difference between holding a service and not holding one.

The students tend not to stay in Birmingham once their courses end. And nor do many of the various families who pass through from time to time, the academics and doctors who may take jobs in the town for a few years before moving on. But the Birmingham community has managed to establish relationships with those Israelis who have come to live in the area. Marion Kinshuck, who has lived in Birmingham for 30 years – but who says that since she was not born there she can never be counted as a true Jewish Brummie – explains that the city's two previous rabbis were Israelis who connected socially with other Israelis, and brought them into the community.

There is one Liberal synagogue in Birmingham, two orthodox synagogues and a third a few miles away in Solihull. The two Birmingham synagogues, Central and Singers Hill, are just one mile apart, and as the community dwindled, plans were made for the two to merge. When the proposals were put to a vote of the membership of the Singers Hill in 2004, they were rejected by a 0.4 per cent margin. Unhappy with the result, the synagogue's management brought the proposal back to the membership for a second time, and saw their plans rejected by a bigger majority.

Singers Hill Synagogue was built in 1856. It is Britain's earliest surviving 'cathedral' synagogue – a quasi-architectural term that indicates scale, grandeur and prestige, rather than any sort of religious superiority. By the time the proposed merger with the Central Synagogue fell through, the once sumptuous building was looking tired and shabby, its neoclassical interior infested with wet and dry rot. The congregation obtained a grant from English Heritage to eliminate the rot and raised additional funds to repair the stonework and windows. When the restoration was complete, English Heritage designated the building as the 'most improved place of worship in the West Midlands'. The congregation was proud of the results, but its membership was still declining. The merger plan was dead in the water, and the newly renovated building would always require ongoing maintenance. Then the management had a brainwave. Located in the centre of the city, the synagogue has a large car park that was rarely used. So they rented out parking spaces to the city's workers and shoppers and created a revenue for themselves of around £100,000 a year.

Then they had another idea. Unlike Manchester and London, there was no burial scheme for members of Birmingham's synagogues to pay into, to cover the cost of their eventual funeral. Singers Hill, which maintains the city's Jewish cemeteries, would simply charge families for funerals when the time came to bury their loved ones. In the wake of the failed merger, the Singers Hill executive decided to charge their own members less for burial, and to charge everyone else more.

The immediate result was that many of the Central Synagogue's elderly members transferred their membership to Singers Hill, potentially saving their families some money one day. And of course, once Singers Hill decided to up the burial fees for Central Synagogue members, a massive row broke out between the two congregations. The Central started looking around for other solutions. They entered into discussions with the United Synagogue, the centrist-orthodox umbrella body in London to which over 60 congregations belong. At the time the United Synagogue was looking to expand beyond its traditional London base. It had already incorporated the Sheffield synagogue into its portfolio, and Birmingham's Central Synagogue was exactly the sort of congregation it was looking to absorb.

In 2016 the membership of the Central Synagogue voted by an overwhelming margin to join the United Synagogue. The synagogue's assets were transferred to the United Synagogue (it serves as much as a property company as a religious organization), the members of the congregation were given access to the United Synagogue's burial scheme, the US took on responsibility for organizing work permits should the congregation wish to recruit a rabbi from Israel or elsewhere and the chairman of the synagogue looked forward to long-term security for the community.

The president of Singers Hill, perhaps slightly miffed that they were losing burial revenue from Central members, hoped that the two congregations could 'still keep together as a community'. Central and Singers Hill may be separate synagogues, but the members all know each other: the Birmingham community is too small to be divided. And the Central provides services that benefit Singers Hill members as well, such as the *mikveh* – the ritual bath – and the deli. Open three days a week, it is the only kosher food shop in the city. But although all the members of the Birmingham community are able to use the deli, the Singers Hill and Solihull synagogues themselves do not. At the time of writing, if you were to buy food at the deli on behalf of Singers Hill, the chances are you wouldn't be reimbursed.[52]

The King David Primary School has been part of the city's Jewish life since 1843. Originally known as the Hebrew

National School, its foundation stone was laid by Queen Victoria's Jewish knight and personal friend Sir Moses Montefiore. Of course, the community is no longer large enough to fill all the places in the school – there just aren't enough Jewish kids in Birmingham. So these days King David is a multicultural school, but one with a clearly defined Jewish ethos.

It is not the only Jewish school in the country which only has a minority of Jewish pupils, but it is certainly unusual in that the vast majority of the staff, who are not Jewish, provide a Jewishly orientated education to children of all backgrounds, the vast majority of whom are Muslim. There are also children from the evangelical Christian community, who choose to send their children to a Jewish school where they will get a grounding in the Hebrew Bible. And it works well. Some of the parents of non-Jewish children attended the school themselves when they were kids. The school celebrates all the Jewish festivals, closes early on Friday afternoons for shabbat, teaches the children to read Hebrew, organizes trips to the Israel Dance Festival in London and celebrates Israel Independence Day.

It's important to be optimistic about the future when living in a community that has seen better days. Marion Kinshuck thinks that is one of the reasons the United Synagogue welcomed the Central into its fold. 'They can see there is potential. If London's house prices continue to rise, then people will move to Birmingham. It's just a natural progression, people tend to move north, and HS2 is coming eventually. And then if people continue to commute, then they see that this is potentially somewhere that could grow.' But she is realistic. The community's age profile is old. If it's going to grow, it had better hurry up.

Brighton is another Jewish community with declining numbers and synagogues that just can't bring themselves to merge, no matter how sensible that appears to be. But, unlike some other small communities, it has ambition: they are building a new community centre, with a nursery, housing and a deli, that they hope will be the JW3 of the South Coast, acting as a catalyst for the revival of Jewish life in the town.

Brighton has the largest Jewish population of any Sussex town, but it is far from being the only place in the county where Jews live. Jews are ubiquitous across the county. Arundel, Littlehampton, Worthing, Eastbourne, Lewes – name a Sussex town and the chances are there will be dozens of Jews, perhaps even a couple of hundred, living there. Most of them tend to be retirees, who may have retained synagogue membership in their former city in order not to lose their rights as members of a burial scheme, but otherwise had no qualms about leaving their Jewish community for a quiet life in the country. Few of them intended to look for a Jewish community near their new homes. But it is hard to shake off an identity which thrives on connecting with others like oneself, with other people who don't quite fully fit into rural Britain, people with the same cultural DNA, other Jews.

Nick Beck runs the Sussex Jewish Outreach Group, which aims to connect Jews across the South Coast. He started it because he was worried by the prevalence of assimilation in the area. He knows from his own family's experience just how easy it is for people to marry outside the Jewish community and drift away. When he started the group in 2016, he had few contacts outside Brighton and no idea how many people were out there. So he used the telephone directory to identify people with surnames that sounded Jewish: Cohen, Levy, Rose, Gold, etc. He ended up with 170 potential contacts. He invited them to a Passover *seder* meal, and about 20 people turned up.

Once the group was established they began to hold monthly services. The Quakers have always been willing to accommodate other faith groups, so he hired rooms in their Meeting Houses and put on monthly services, on a Friday evening or Saturday morning. He was not trying to proselytize or make anyone religious; the services were mainly an opportunity for a social gathering. He laid on lunches or dinners as an additional incentive and expanded his list to about 100 households. And he started travelling around the local schools with an exhibition about Jewish life. It helped to expand his network.

No Jewish community is complete without an argument, and sure enough, not long after the Outreach Group was started they had their first row. There's an old Jewish joke about a man who is stranded on a desert island. He has nowhere to pray, so he builds himself a synagogue. Then he builds another. When he is finally rescued they ask why he had two synagogues. 'That's my synagogue,' he says, pointing to one of them. 'And that', he says, pointing to the other, 'is the one I refuse to go to.' A similar story could have been told about the Outreach Group. A couple who lived in one of the towns on the South Coast ran a small group for Jewish families. They'd have an annual garden party and ran one or two events linked to the Jewish festivals. When the Outreach Group started up they contacted Nick, told him they were getting too old to carry on running their group and asked him to take over. So Nick began holding monthly services in the town, to which 25 or 30 people would turn up. Then the couple who had handed over the running of their group to Nick decided to take it back. They accused him of muscling in. Nick says that the whole thing became very politicized. He shrugs. 'We are our own worst enemies.'

Running a small community can involve a lot of work, and it can be tremendously frustrating. But it can also have its rewards. Nick tells the story of an Iranian teenager, aged about 16, who contacted him a few years ago. His mother was Jewish, but his father was a militant Islamist. His father wanted him to go and fight for the Islamist cause in Syria, but the young man refused. He wanted to live a Jewish life, something his father would not countenance. So he escaped from Iran, running away with money given to him by his grandfather and mother. He went first to Canada, but the father tracked him down and threatened to kill him. He fled to England. He landed at Gatwick and was resettled as a refugee in Worthing. While he was there, he heard about the Sussex Outreach Group and wrote to Nick. Nick introduced him to a rabbi in Brighton, who took him under his wing, taught him about Judaism, encouraged his religious observance and found him a family with whom he could live. Over the next couple of years he became increasingly religious, until he ended up living in a Strictly Orthodox community in London.

He rang Nick recently and told him he was becoming disillusioned with the Strictly Orthodox lifestyle. He'd decided that Nick's type of Judaism was more fun and that he was drifting back towards a less intense form of Jewish life. Which just goes to show that religious journeys are not always one-way. And that, for all the aggravation that running a small Jewish community can bring, sometimes the rewards make it all feel worthwhile.

7

Giving and Caring

British Jewry is more confident than at any time in its history. Confident enough to hold public celebrations and erect swanky buildings. But traditional Jewish values demand more than pageantry and panache. Throughout their history Jewish communities have made it a priority to support those in need, the sick, the aged and the poor. Most of the time they did not have the economic or sociopolitical freedom to support anyone other than the vulnerable and needy within their own ranks. But today Jewish organizations are looking beyond their own. As volunteering and social action have moved more firmly onto centre stage in British national life, many young Jews are creating projects that reflect Jewish values, for the benefit of society at large. These young Jews are not missionaries or zealots; they aren't trying to sell Judaism, and most of them are not even religious. They are simply drawing on the value culture they were brought up with, because they find it worthwhile and it resonates with the zeitgeist.

The phrase 'Jewish values' is rather overused. I used it twice in the previous paragraph alone. It falls into the same category of hackneyed, throwaway lines as the hard-to-conceptualize

'Judaeo-Christian tradition', a historically meaningless trope that seems mainly to be used to aggrandize Western neo-conservative values over any others.[53] But although the phrase 'Jewish values' is overused, the idea that there are values which are exclusively Jewish is not quite so vague. It does have some grounding in reality.

All modern liberal societies share the same basic set of values. They include the eradication of poverty, the value of education, support for the vulnerable, access to healthcare and so on. All Jewish values fall into these and similar categories. The things that set so-called Jewish values apart are often quite nuanced, the result of the different ways in which Jews relate to their communities.

The underlying Jewish value principle is the concept of *tzedakah*. Often translated as 'charity', the Hebrew word more accurately translates as 'virtuousness', or 'righteousness'. Whereas charity benefits the recipients, *tzedakah* benefits everyone: the giver, the receiver and indeed wider society. *Tzedakah* assumes that everyone is part of a community, that we all have a responsibility to each other.

But community is a difficult thing to define, particularly in modern cities. Many people belong to several communities; some belong to none. When Jews support or are activists for causes in wider society, the reciprocity of *tzedakah* doesn't always apply. Rather, this new sort of Jewish activism has recently acquired its own name. They call it *tikkun olam*. It means 'repair of the world'. It is a more evocative idea than *tzedakah* and has a nice ring to it. 'Repairing the world' sounds a lot grander than a word that translates as 'righteousness' or some other similarly obscure idea.

For many people, *tikkun olam* is what Judaism is all about. Yet, in its current incarnation of setting the world to rights through social and environmental action, it is a very recent Jewish activity, one that was unheard of even half a century ago. The phrase itself, *tikkun olam*, has been around since at least the third century CE. It was originally used in a legal context to protect social harmony.[54] Later, the kabbalists, the Jewish mystics, used it to describe the process of restoring creation to its pristine, primordial state. But today it involves neither law nor mystical invocation. Contemporary *tikkun olam* is wholly practical; it refers to activities leading to a decent society and a sustainable environment.

Nic Schlagman runs social action programmes within the framework of the West London Synagogue, Britain's oldest Reform community. He works on projects supporting vulnerable people in Central London: the destitute, the homeless, asylum seekers and refugees. Nic points out that Jewish values mandate these activities, obliging Jews to seek out and support vulnerable people.

Nic sees the synagogue's direct involvement in social action as an indication of how Jewish identity has evolved. West London Synagogue's members have always fulfilled the obligation of *tzedakah* by donating money to worthy causes. Then a new rabbi joined the synagogue, who encouraged them not just to give money but to involve themselves more fully with the causes they donated to. They began donating time as well as money, with those who had time to spare involving themselves more directly in delivering the projects the synagogue supported.

And Nic sees a further evolution taking place. Rather than just giving money and time to paper over the fissures in society, the synagogue is now trying to address some of the structural issues that lead to deprivation. 'Ten years into our scheme there were still 50 or so families coming along who had turned up at the beginning. Our volunteers began saying: "Look, we've given them a meal and clothes and helped them in a small way for the past ten years, but why on earth are they still here ten years later?" And then we began to think about what's really going on and we realized that we are a Central London synagogue with MPs and peers and people who have the ear of power among our members. We realized that we have a different responsibility, that we can be more effective in other ways. So alongside our direct work with our beneficiaries, we are now starting to campaign and lobby, to try to make a difference structurally.'

Nic sees this move towards giving time as well as money as an indication of how the Jewish community has changed during his lifetime, of its increased self-confidence. Of course, volunteering has always been an important part of Jewish life for those who have time to give, but traditionally most Jewish volunteers gave their time to the community. Nic thinks it has become much more prevalent for Jewish charitable projects to engage with both Jewish and non-Jewish beneficiaries. 'Which I guess comes with a stronger sense of civic responsibility, or that the Jewish community feels a greater sense of privilege today than in the past.'

One way of repairing the world is by building bridges between different ethnic and religious communities, particularly between those which have a history of tension and conflict. Multi-faith dialogue has been around for a long time, but until very recently its focus was on encouraging religious tolerance rather than on healing social and political divisions between communities. The London theatre company MUJU was one of the first initiatives to widen the discourse, bringing young Muslims and Jews together through drama and comedy, to address the tensions caused by the Israel–Palestine conflict.

Georgina Bednar joined MUJU in her twenties. She eventually took on the role of the company's Jewish co-artistic director, working alongside her Muslim counterpart, Salman Siddiqui. She told me just how big the challenge was. 'It was a massive learning curve; I was 25 and running a company taking Muslim and Jewish young people from the ages of 20 to 30 through a theatre process to make something together, celebrating our collaboration and not focusing on our differences. It felt incredibly important at that time, the Gaza Strip was blowing up every five minutes, and it seemed like we were the only people offering anything constructive in the arts space. Our real success was bringing family audiences into the same space together, so that a Muslim mum and a Jewish mum would be sitting together in the audience, each feeling as proud as the other, watching their kids on stage.'

Social and political activism is part of a long-standing Jewish radical tradition. It stretches back to the early days of Jewish emancipation in the eighteenth century. Unlike old-school radicals, like the fiercely secular Jewish Labour Bund in pre-revolutionary Russia, today's activist Jews, who are a tiny minority of the Jewish population, are far more likely to root their activism in their Jewish heritage and to use creative techniques rather than socialist ideology to achieve their aims. They may seek to identify as Jews even when they belong to organizations where ethnic or religious identity is unimportant. XR Jews, a 200-strong group within the environmental activist movement Extinction Rebellion (XR), describe themselves as a faith-based community who consider non-violent civil disobedience to be a religious duty. They argue that their actions in defence of the environment are rooted in the Jewish value that prioritizes the saving of life over everything else. Georgina Bednar describes the artists, performers, creatives and even non-conformist rabbis who make up XR Jews as the people she should have been hanging out with when she was growing up in middle-class north-west London's Jewish community, an area from which she fled by going to university in Edinburgh. Radical Jewish activists rarely fit neatly into the more conservative, mainstream Jewish community.

Other activists see an association with the established community as a politically astute means of furthering their aims. Amos Schonfield is one. He founded and runs Our Second Home, an organization dedicated to the welfare of the many refugees who have found their ways to Britain's shores in recent years. He is also a member of the Board of Deputies, representing Masorti Judaism.

Schonfield comes from a distinguished lineage: his grandfather Rabbi Dr Solomon Schonfeld was an extraordinary man, one of the lesser-known, non-combatant heroes of the Second World War. Relying largely on force of personality and a refusal ever to be rebuffed, Schonfeld personally rescued thousands of Jews from Europe. He obtained visas and identity papers to get people out of danger by cajoling, browbeating and begging civil servants and officials. He persuaded donors both large and small to provide him with the funds to ransom and liberate as many people as he could and sought out homes in Britain for *Kindertransport* children.

Many Jewish families took refugee children into their homes and raised them as their own. But not enough. It remains one of the most egregious stains on the reputation of British Jewry that so many Jewish refugee children were dispatched to families outside the community, who knew nothing of

Judaism. They saved their lives and provided them with good and loving homes. But they inadvertently deprived them of their heritage and diminished the possibility that one day they might reconnect with family members who had survived.

When the war was over, Solomon Schonfeld was one of the first to reach the liberated Belsen concentration camp, helping to resettle the survivors. His grandson Amos's work captures fewer headlines but is no less essential.

Our Second Home resulted from a conversation that Amos had with his mother. It was during the refugee crisis that dominated the news in 2015 and 2016. Amos, who was then the National Director of the Jewish youth movement Noam, was wondering what he could do to assist the many refugees and asylum seekers arriving in Britain. His mother suggested that he should take some of the creative techniques used by the vibrant Jewish youth movements and incorporate them into a programme that would assist young refugees.

The various Jewish youth movements all tend to run on fairly similar lines. They meet weekly with a residential summer camp as the highlight of their year. Our Second Home took the summer camp model and adapted it to the needs of 14- to 18-year-old refugees, young people who are often in Britain on their own, isolated, living in refugee centres or foster homes. Unable to speak English, with few or no friends or family, they have little opportunity to develop socially. Through its summer camps Our Second Home offers them the chance to step away from the pressures and uncertainties of their day-to-day life.

Although their main purpose is to give refugee kids a holiday, the camps are activity-centred, with creative and vocational workshops, informal education, sports and games. They are not an end in themselves, but are designed as an entry point into a more ambitious programme, also based on the Jewish youth movement model. The youth movements are led by their own graduates: young people who were trained to be future leaders, without their even realizing it, as part of their regular club activities. The refugee summer camps have a similar aim. When the attendees outgrow the camps, they are encouraged to join Our Second Home's leadership scheme, which trains them to become camp leaders themselves when they are old enough, and ultimately to transport their leadership skills into their chosen vocations or careers.

Using residential camps to help young people to establish themselves is a model that Jewish communities have employed successfully for decades. During the 1930s and 1940s the Zionist movement Mizrachi set up kibbutz farms in the English countryside, to help young Jewish refugees from Europe rebuild their lives in a structured and supportive environment. Today the youth movements have reversed the aim: rather than helping young Jews to feel more British, they take British kids and help them to feel more Jewish. But the process is the same, and Our Second Home helps young refugees to acclimatize to British life in much the same way as the Jewish youth groups strengthen the identity of their young people.

One of the key principles of Judaism is that everyone should give one tenth of their income to charity. This applies even to the poorest people; it doesn't matter how destitute they are, there is always someone who is worse off.

In his code of Jewish law, the medieval philosopher Maimonides set out eight levels of charity, the highest of which is to help a poor person to become self-sufficient by setting them up in a trade, or through a loan or partnership. The lowest of the eight levels is to donate money, but to do it with bad grace, to give sulkily. It may count as charity, but since giving to the poor is a religious obligation, money should be donated gladly. Indeed, a donor should thank the recipient for giving them the chance to fulfil a religious duty.

Maimonides ruled that charity begins at home, that the priority is to support the poor of one's own community. And for centuries this principle was followed: Jews concentrated on supporting their own. They almost certainly would have done so even without Maimonides. Throughout most of history many Jews lived from hand to mouth, and there was always someone in the local town or village who needed help. And there were the destitute communities in Israel who relied for a great extent on the largesse of their brethren overseas. Even today Jews across the world donate to Israeli charities, although Israel is now a mature and self-sufficient economy.

A question that is both new and unique to British Jewry is what it means to be one of the oldest-established and most secure Jewish communities in the world. The question could not have been asked before 1939; until the destruction of Eastern European Jewry, the British community was relatively unimportant in the Jewish universe. Whatever influence it had was due to Britannia's power on the global stage, but within the Jewish world itself British Jewry was relatively insignificant, in terms of size, leadership and attitudes. That all changed after the Shoah. And today, with many communities in Europe dwindling, struggling to survive, the British community is uniquely positioned to support them and work with them.

But the evidence suggests that, far from playing an active role on the world stage, the British Jewish community is becoming more self-absorbed, happy to leave the diaspora for American Jews to take care of. British Jews are interested in what happens in Israel, but rarely pay much attention to what is going on in the rest of the Jewish world. Even though, as Rabbi Herschel Gluck, one of the community's best-connected religious leaders, notes, Commonwealth communities, particularly in South Africa, Australia and New Zealand, still look in some ways to Britain for leadership. The Chief Rabbi is not just the religious authority for many orthodox congregations in Britain. His title is Chief Rabbi of the United Hebrew Congregations of the Commonwealth.

Impoverished Jews in Europe rarely impinge on the consciousness of most British Jews, who when thinking of supporting Jews overseas still tend to think of Israel. But there are initiatives in the religious and charitable sectors that do focus on Europe, particularly in the old Jewish homelands of Eastern Europe. And yet, even that is changing. Many of those communities are ageing and diminishing to such an extent that there is already little left to support. Some of British Jewry's charities, such as World Jewish Relief which has been supporting Jewish communities in Europe for years, and the far newer Tzedek, are turning their attention elsewhere, beyond the Jewish world.

In 1933 the Central British Fund for German Jewry was set up by a group of wealthy, communally minded donors, to rescue Jews from Nazi persecution. The fund was instrumental in organizing the *Kindertransport*, sharing in the diplomatic, financial and logistical responsibilities of extracting around 10,000 Jewish children from Germany and bringing them by boat and train to the UK. After the war the fund widened its focus, helping to evacuate Jews who were being expelled from their homelands, supporting them as they built new lives for themselves in the UK.

The focus of the Central British Fund's work changed again in the 1990s as it became clear that a humanitarian crisis was evolving among elderly Jews, most of them Holocaust survivors, who were living alone or in fractured communities behind the Iron Curtain. Many were in poor health, desperately poor and with no families or friends to look after them. The organization raised funds to provide them with basic survival needs, with food, medicines, healthcare and home repairs. They put programmes in place to help them to deal with issues of mental health, loneliness and dementia.

With the change of focus came a change of name. The Central British Fund became World Jewish Relief. And as the number of surviving Jews in Eastern Europe diminished, and the world seemed to lurch from one humanitarian crisis to another, the organization expanded the scope of its operations, adding a global dimension to its ongoing work in Eastern Europe.

Today World Jewish Relief conducts emergency fundraising appeals in response to humanitarian crises across the globe. The name World Jewish Relief belies its Britishness. They are an outstanding example of how Britain's Jewish community has widened its focus beyond its borders. They partner with NGOs and local agencies to distribute food, medicines and basic necessities to those affected by natural disasters or wars. They ran an emergency appeal following the 2010 hurricane in Haiti, raising over £500,000 to provide mobile healthcare clinics, water tanks and basic survival needs. They work alongside government and other agencies to support refugees, helping them to find work and resettle. When thousands fled Syria during the civil war, WJR raised funds to provide food and medical care in the refugee camps in Greece, opened a legal resource office for unaccompanied child refugees in Athens, set up welfare programmes for refugee women and established educational provision for their children. Then, when the

British government committed to allowing 20,000 refugees to settle in the UK, World Jewish Relief set up a training and employment programme, working with employers and other refugee charities to help the new arrivals from Syria to learn English, find jobs and settle successfully into their new lives. Today, World Jewish Relief is leading the Jewish community's response to the humanitarian crisis caused by the invasion of Ukraine, raising funds, working with partners on the ground in the war-torn cities, and helping refugees.

World Jewish Relief is a very different organization today from when it was a volunteer-run effort to rescue as many Jews as possible from Germany. Yet all its work is directly related to the Jewish refugee experience. Many Jewish families have a refugee background and an emotional affinity with those undergoing the same experience today. And the British Jewish community has had practical experience since the 1930s of absorbing Jewish refugees and helping them to resettle. When I spoke to Henry Grunwald, World Jewish Relief's President, he quoted the organization's Chief Executive, Paul Anticoni: 'We helped refugees in the 1930s because *they* were Jewish, and we help refugees today because *we* are Jewish.'

One project in particular relates directly to the organization's work in the wake of the Holocaust. World Jewish Relief works in Rwanda, a country where there are no Jews but which, in 1994, suffered its own traumatic holocaust, in which 800,000 people died. Nobody escaped untouched by the horror, and the nation was afflicted in ways reminiscent of the suffering that survivors of the Shoah went through. Drawing on its experience of working with genocide survivors, World Jewish Relief now works with young Rwandans who were orphaned by the country's holocaust, teaching them the skills that will enable them to work in small scale, commercial farming enterprises. The goal is to help them to earn a sustainable income, sufficient to feed themselves and their families, and have enough left over to enable them to send their children to school. Comic Relief gave them a grant of £365,000 to cover the costs of the project.

Then in 2020 the UK government gave them a grant of £500,000 towards a project helping vulnerable young Rwandans into work. The project helps them to develop the technical skills necessary to get a job, and provides soft skills training to develop their confidence and give them a better understanding of business and markets. The government grant covers three-quarters of the cost of the project, with World Jewish Relief contributing the rest.

With an income in excess of £6 million and a permanent staff of over 30, World Jewish Relief is one of the more substantial charities in the Jewish community. They raised £1.3 million at one dinner alone, when Prince Charles was the guest of honour. And it is in no danger of turning away from its Jewish roots; notwithstanding its involvement with global humanitarian work, its main focus remains on work with Jewish communities.

Tzedek is an international development charity that works to relieve poverty in some of the most destitute regions of the world. Unlike World Jewish Relief, whose international programmes grew logically out of their early work rescuing the victims of Nazi genocide, Tzedek's *raison d'être* is the biblical imperative, 'justice, justice you shall pursue'.[55] Tzedek was inspired by Band Aid, the rock music industry's fundraising movement founded by Bob Geldof in 1984 in response to the famine in Ethiopia. It appealed initially to those with a slightly alternative or left-of-centre point of view, who felt that the Jewish community was a little too inward-looking. The word Tzedek means 'justice' or 'righteousness' in Hebrew.

Founded in 1990, Tzedek has an annual budget of a little less than £500,000. It sends volunteers overseas to work with local NGOs and community-based organizations, currently in Ghana and India, helping those in extreme poverty to build a better future for themselves. Depending on the needs of each group they work with, they may help create savings schemes for village women, provide access to microcredit or run skills training programmes that show their beneficiaries how to set up and run sustainable craft-based businesses or empower them to become involved in the political and developmental needs of their local communities.

And while their most urgent work is directed at improving the lives of those in extreme poverty, Tzedek's volunteers are also encouraged to see themselves as beneficiaries. Tzedek recruits its volunteers by emphasizing the opportunities their projects offer for personal growth, the chance to act on their Jewish values and, most alluringly, to participate in *tikkun olam*, that multivalent phrase which has come to signify Jews putting the world to rights.

Tzedek and World Jewish Relief are examples of how attitudes are changing within the British Jewish community. A generation ago a Jewish charity working to alleviate poverty outside the Jewish world would have been deemed unnecessary. Why, it may have been asked, would Jews need to have their own charity to support this type of work when they could donate to any one of the dozens of secular organizations working in the field of international aid?

But as attitudes have changed, the idea has taken root that it is safe for Jews to be outward-facing and to participate in social responsibility projects under their own banners. In his book *The People and the Books*, Adam Kirsch remarks that the first-century CE aphorism, 'When I am for myself what am I?' is understood differently today. Ascribed to the rabbinic sage Hillel, it used to be understood as referring to our responsibilities to God. Today it is more likely to be interpreted as a call to social justice.

This change in attitudes has helped Tzedek to move from the fringes of the community into the mainstream. Just how central it is to the community's new outlook can be appreciated from its participation in the Ben Azzai scheme, an initiative set up by Chief Rabbi Ephraim Mirvis, after he and his wife Valerie had paid a pastoral visit to India in 2014. They visited 19 Jewish communities in five cities, and the slums of Kolkata and Mumbai. 'Anybody who's been there knows just how awful such places are. It's not just how people live, it's how it is possible that people allow people to live such a life. We were highly inspired by seeing some projects there funded by Jewish individuals and organizations and we returned back to London, determined to do something.' They started the Ben Azzai programme, to provide opportunities for Jewish students to learn about the problems of the developing world, taking them on what is described as an immersive educational trip to aid projects run by Tzedek and its partners. Not, says Rabbi Mirvis, as poverty tourists but to learn about challenges, about sustainability, about what we can do to change things for the better for others. The idea is to create a network of student ambassadors to promote the centrality of social responsibility to Jewish life, and to encourage others to become involved.

When I asked Rabbi Mirvis what he would like his Chief Rabbinate remembered for, he said he hoped it would be for his contribution to the religious imperative of responsibility to others. 'A key platform of my Chief Rabbinate has been social responsibility beyond the Jewish community. We have a responsibility towards every human being created in the image of God. At a practical level. We are good Jews when we are good citizens. We've only got one life. We are privileged to be Jews, to be responsible to ourselves, to our families, to our communities, our country, to the world. We have a responsibility towards every human being created in the image of God.'

'It's an incredible organization, frankly, the facilities are quite stunning. It's considered a leader not just in the Jewish community but a leader in wider society in what it does. It is often used as a role model.' So says Michael Levy, Lord Levy, who has successively been Chairman, President and now Life President of Jewish Care. He has been involved with the charity for over 30 years, since the Jewish Welfare Board and the Jewish Blind Society merged in 1990 to create Jewish Care, long recognized as British Jewry's flagship charity, a model of excellence in the care sector.

It was my mother, Joan Freedman, who first encouraged Michael to devote his tremendous energy and skills to the charity. They met when she was Vice-Chairman of the Jewish Welfare Board and he joined the executive committee, shortly before the merger. 'Joan was amazing,' he says. 'The facilities today were her dream and ambition. They are quite stunning. If she could see them now, I'm sure she'd cry.'

Jewish Care is far and away the largest charity in the British Jewish community, employing well over 1,000 people and attracting 3,000 volunteers. It runs care homes, day centres, dementia, bereavement and mental health services across London and the south-east of England, touching the lives of 10,000 people each week. Jewish Care's budget is similar to that of a local authority's department of social services.

But what makes Jewish Care stand out is not just its size or the scope of its work. It is a flagship by virtue of its good governance and the way it is run. Its Chief Executive, Daniel Carmel-Brown, says that as far as the local authorities and central government are concerned, Jewish Care is the go-to organization for social care and welfare in the Jewish community. 'And that gives us a lot of access to stakeholders and influencers, to talk about policy and how things develop around social care. We are also held up as a beacon of success in the wider social care sector. There has been a lot of criticism over the last few years, of care homes in particular and social care more generally, where a lot of the organizations are privately run for profit. And we, of course, are not. We are here for, and only because of, the community. So many people see us as an almost perfect example of how society should provide care for older people. Providing not just good-quality care, but engaging volunteers in the community and fundraising from the community. That's the triangle which is necessary for us to succeed.'

Jewish Care is a family. Daniel has spent most of his career there, or in one of the organizations that eventually merged into it. He started as a young volunteer at a Jewish community centre in Ilford, studied for a postgraduate degree in community education and progressed into professional youth work. He was appointed to be the manager of a Jewish Care day centre in Stepney, and was then seconded into the Head Office's fundraising team, where he stayed, eventually becoming Director of Fundraising. Ten years later he was appointed Chief Executive. His predecessor as Chief Executive had also spent his career at Jewish Care. And although the Chief Executive before him had been recruited from outside the organization, he applied for the job because his mother had been a lifelong volunteer, a senior member of the lay team. So Jewish Care has effectively had three generations of home-nurtured Chief Executives. And Daniel is not the only one who has spent his working life at Jewish Care: many of his colleagues have long associations with the charity, often starting their careers on the front line.

Arnold Wagner is a Vice-Chairman of Jewish Care. He has been on the board for a long time and has offered to step down, but they have told him 'Not quite yet'. He describes the organization as 'subscribing to and practising a strongly driven values culture'. He told me that he has been involved with many Jewish organizations, not all of which would qualify for inclusion in nominations for good governance. 'But Jewish Care is very well run. It's not overly bureaucratic, but it is well governed. And, most importantly, there is a focus on well-being and care, which is reflected in the way we treat our staff. We deliberately pay our front-line staff above the market rate. The reasoning is very simple. It boils down to this. If you truly believe that the quality of care that you give people is critical, and really believe what you say about our front-line staff being our most important asset, then you have to pay them enough to make them feel valued. If you don't, you will get what you deserve. You'll either get poor-quality people or you'll get a rapid turnover of staff, both of which affect the quality of delivery.'

As long as the money is available, paying people well is an easy way for an organization to acknowledge the value of its staff. It takes far more effort to show appreciation through practical action, to recognize people's achievements, to make it a nice place to work. Jewish Care runs events for its staff and volunteers, to recognize those who have excelled or achieved further qualifications. 'There's a constant sense of trying to do that. And I think it pays off. Of course not everybody has a great experience: having a relative in care is a stressful experience for families. But the proportion of complaints to compliments is really very low. It's just a nice place to work. When you go into a Jewish Care facility, you feel you're in the presence of people who believe in what they are doing.'

Jewish Care's size and reputation work to its advantage when it comes to fundraising. It is reaching the end of a 20-year-long modernization programme which has allowed it to upgrade or sell off its old care homes built in the 1950s and 1960s, and to build campuses housing a variety of services on one site. The investment in campuses has been substantial. Its site in Friern Barnet, with over 200 beds, is, Daniel Carmel-Brown believes, the largest in the UK. The commitment to projects of this size demonstrates the organization's confidence in the long-term future and eminence of Jewish life in Britain.

Daniel explains that they developed the campus model for two reasons: one practical, one social. Having multiple services on one site is far more efficient operationally. And campuses create community. 'Care homes today largely are for people living with some kind of memory impairment. You don't see that many people making their own choice to move into a care home. So at our new campus in Stanmore we have built a care home alongside assisted living studios and retirement living apartments. And right in the middle of it is a community day centre for those still living in their own homes. The model is one in which people can transition between different types of care, as their needs change.' His aspiration is to match the quality of care to the quality of the environment in which the care is offered. Nobody should be housed in sub-standard accommodation.

The new Stanmore development is impressive by any standard. And it's not only a testament to Jewish Care's vision and skill. The story of how the site was acquired shows what can be done when an organization is run by people who are quick-witted, agile and imaginative. By 2001 it was becoming clear that there would soon be a large, bustling Jewish community in the south Hertfordshire area. London property prices were accelerating, young couples buying their first homes were moving further and further into the suburbs, and the transport links and existing community infrastructure in south Hertfordshire made it apparent that this was an area where the size of the Jewish population was about to mushroom.

There was a care home in the area run by a Masonic lodge. It was running out of steam, struggling to keep its head above water. A member of its committee happened to mention to Michael Levy that they were about to put the home up for sale and asked if Jewish Care might be interested. Within 24 hours he had convened a board meeting and agreed to purchase the home. They knew that they were ahead of the game, that the local community didn't need a Jewish Care facility yet, but that it would do one day. Jewish Care bought the home and ran it for its existing residents, gradually converting it into a Jewish facility as vacancies occurred. Then in 2015 they obtained planning permission to redevelop the site, and the new campus was born.

Of course, there are huge problems in the social care sector. It is a heavily regulated environment, funding is complicated, people are living longer and the demand for services is increasing. And Covid had a disastrous effect. Many of the smaller care charities were unable to survive, and Jewish Care found itself having to step in to accommodate the residents of two smaller Jewish homes which were forced to close. So alongside its primary role as a major social care charity Jewish Care has, over the years, become a sort of sponge for organizations that have found it impossible to survive on their own.

Nor has Jewish Care emerged from Covid unscathed. The pandemic had a dramatic impact on occupancy in its care homes. Since each care home resident is subsidized by local authority funding, apart from the human tragedy, the effect of Covid was to hit the organization financially. They had to reorganize, and there were job losses.

The pandemic created a financial crisis for every charity in the care sector. Jewish Care and the two other large care home providers, Nightingale Hammerson and the Fed, conducted a joint appeal, hoping to raise enough to see them through a crisis that was escalating daily, and to which no end was in sight. It was agreed that 10 per cent of the funds raised were to be shared among the smaller care homes in the Jewish community, and the remainder would be split between the three larger charities proportionately. Michael Levy spearheaded the appeal to major donors, and the charities ran adverts in the Jewish press over a four-week period. On the fifth week they ran an ad thanking 'the major philanthropic foundations, trusts and those individuals in our community who have been incredibly generous and supported our appeal'. They had raised in excess of £4 million, enabling them to buy the hundreds of thousands of pieces of personal protective equipment needed to keep their staff safe.

I asked Lord Levy if the success of the joint appeal indicated that there should be consolidation in community's care sector. He was adamant that there should be. 'I would like to see a merger of our care facilities; I would much prefer to see it all under one umbrella. People will say if we merge we will raise less, but that's nonsense. They said that when we merged the Jewish Welfare Board and the Jewish Blind Society, and in actual fact we raised more because people saw the relevance of Jewish Care and what it meant. So that's how I would like to go forward.'

When the pandemic first hit, Steven Lewis was coming to the end of his term of office as Jewish Care's long-serving Chairman. Steven is a pillar of the Jewish Care family, with a connection to the organization going back many years. His uncle David Lewis was Chairman of the Jewish Blind Society when it merged with the Jewish Welfare Board to create Jewish Care, and Steven joined its board in 1990 as the Chairman of Young Jewish Care.

'I used to go to board meetings with 30 people. What a nightmare. Five or ten would be enough, never mind 30. And I took a position of keeping my mouth shut, of not being the young kid who was coming along giving it large and all the rest of it. I listened and I listened. But there were 30 people on the Board, plus all the professional staff.'

At the age of 35 – a comparatively tender age for a Jewish organization – he was asked to take up the role of Jewish Care's Deputy Chairman. 'The previous Chairman said I could do all the schmoozing, and he could get on with running the organization. So, 14 years later, when I became Chairman of Jewish Care, it wasn't a case of "Oh, surprise, surprise, it's Steven". It was "Oh, it's about bloody time", because I'd been Deputy Chairman for 14 years.'

Looking back on his time as Chairman, Steven says that his great skill was in bringing his lay leaders together as a team. 'That was the secret of what I did. When they look back at the previous Chairs of Jewish Care, people will say, "Steven was able to bring all these people together as a team." And we had a fantastic group of people. I was head of recruitment. So whenever someone said to me, "So and so's a good person,"

I'd go to see them, have a schmooze, test them out. And if I wanted them, more often than not I got them. After all, it's not for business. It's for charity at the end of the day.'

Steven is a natural fundraiser, and an avowed disciple of Lord Levy. He calls Michael a phenomenon, quite unique in the community. But when it comes to fundraising, Steven is not far behind. When Covid took its toll on the organization, Jonathan Zenios, who had been nominated to succeed him as Chairman but was not yet in post, suggested that he take over the day-to-day tasks, so as to free Steven up to concentrate on fundraising.

Steven has, of course, seen some big changes in the Jewish community in the 35 years he has been involved. Perhaps the most important, in terms of governance and management, is the new relationship between the lay and professional teams in most organizations. Trustee boards of large charities now recognize that their organizations will not flourish through benevolence alone, that a substantial charity is no different from a business and needs to be run professionally.

It wasn't always so. There was a time when working for a Jewish charity was a last resort, reserved for those who couldn't get a job elsewhere. Decisions were invariably made by the trustees, the lay board of volunteers, who fitted their charitable activities as best they could into the gaps in their daily work schedules and then told the paid staff to carry out their instructions. There was an expectation that the trustees were there to lay down the law and the staff were paid to do as they were told, even though the staff had probably been in the job far longer and were much more familiar with the day-to-day needs of their organizations.

All that has changed. Today the largest Jewish charities recruit the best talent they can, and they are stronger for it. Louise Jacobs, Chair of the major charity UJIA, is in no doubt about the quality of the chief executives running Jewish organizations these days. 'Running a big organization now is no longer seen as a second-rate job. If you are running a big charity, it's not just about doing good and nice things. You're running a business. And that's the way we run UJIA and how other communal Jewish organizations are run. These are proper jobs with decent salaries that attract the best people.'

Steven Lewis stresses that the respect that exists between the two teams cannot be underestimated. 'Every speech I ever made, I stressed the partnership between the professionals and the lay. And I think it's made us better as a result.'

Steven is proud of his Jewishness and sees his business and charitable involvements as essential to each other. But he is critical of successful people in the community whose philanthropy is not directed at Jewish causes, or whose donations are proportionately far less than they could be. 'If we don't look after our own,' he asks, 'who will?'

As my conversation with Steven wound down, he interrupted me. 'There's just one more thing I want to say. I want to tell you that Adam Science changed my life.' Adam Science was a young leader in the Jewish community who was tragically killed in a road accident in 1991. Active in many causes, he had been described in the *Jewish Chronicle* as the leader of a new generation of communal leaders.[56] After he died, his parents and friends, including Steven Lewis, set up the Adam Science Leadership Foundation. 'I think it is one of the most important things we ever did,' says Steven. 'Adam always said to me that the most important thing about Young Jewish Care was to create a forum for young Jews to meet other Jews. Because without that forum, intermarriage would ensure that we would not have the institutions and the financial support we need in the long term. When I spoke as Chairman of Jewish Care for the first time, Adam was in my speech. When I spoke for the last time as Chairman of Jewish Care, Adam was in my speech.'

Steven Lewis stepped down as Jewish Care's Chairman after nine years in the job. He knows it was time; he had done 23 years as Chairman or Deputy Chairman. And he thinks that Jonathan Zenios has a more appropriate skill set to take the organization forward at this stage. Steven was the right chairman while the focus had to be on fundraising for capital projects. But now, in the wake of Covid, the priority is to keep costs down. It is a role for which Jonathan, coming from a financial services background, is eminently suited. It gives him a perspective on the community that is more down-to-earth than that of many other communal leaders.

Jonathan served as Jewish Care's Treasurer before taking on the role of Chairman. He says that he found the job rewarding, not just because he was working for a good cause but in a personal sense as well. 'I enjoyed doing it and I learned how charities run. I found it interesting.'

Looking at the Jewish community from the perspective of a finance professional, Jonathan describes it as having a strong balance sheet but a weak income statement. 'We've got lots of properties, lots of buildings, lots of stuff. But we've got loads of charities, we've got loads of things which can't pay for themselves. I think the biggest challenge for the community is actually accepting that we need collectively to sweat our assets better.'

He's right, of course, but it's hard to imagine many organizations following his lead. The glamour and prestige of a new building are always going to be seductive: donors like to give to something they can see and perhaps attach their name to; many lay leaders like the idea of saying, 'I built that.' But when Jonathan was appointed as Chairman of Jewish Care, he says his mantra was one of separating buildings and services. 'We don't need to provide all of our services exclusively from buildings that we own. We can provide services from other people's buildings. And other people can do things in our buildings.'

He was fortunate that, when he put on the mantle of Chairman, Jewish Care was coming to the end of its lengthy building programme; he didn't need to implement his plans by wielding an axe. And the effect of Covid has been to establish new ways of working and to accelerate his decision-making. He says that Jewish Care has two jobs: to help people to live in their own homes for as long as they can and then, when they're no longer able, to provide a home for them. And those who are living at home do not need to be as reliant on day centres as they were previously; Covid has shown that there are other ways to be connected. 'I would say that is a shift which is going to continue; it means that we become much less precious about buildings.' It sounds fine, but one wonders whether elderly people living at home really do want to become less reliant on Jewish Care's buildings. For many of them, their visits to the day centre are the highlights of their week. It is true that Covid has shown us that there are other ways of being connected; the question is how popular these new ways will be.

Jonathan has devoted a significant proportion of his life to Jewish communal work. It's hard to know whether he is one of a declining breed. It certainly feels as if lay leadership in the Jewish community attracts fewer people than it did a generation or two ago. He has sat on the boards of several organizations, and then one day decided he needed a break. 'I said, "I don't want to be the guy who is always on the board, who says we shouldn't do this, or I'm worried about that, or whatever. I felt it wasn't healthy."' So he decided to step back and spend some time on the front line, volunteering for two or three years at the North London Hospice, a charity with close connections to the Jewish community.

'I decided to go to the hospice because I felt quite strongly that people who are dying are absent from society, and this is actually a big thing about Jewish Care, the idea that we need to keep people as part of a community. Until you die, you have a right to continue interacting, not to be forgotten. The hospice was the extreme version of that, because I thought that people should really feel part of a community up until the very end, and if I'm not prepared to volunteer, then should I expect other people to?'

Jonathan is deeply committed to the British Jewish community, but his commitment doesn't come through religion. Many people feel the same way, but he articulates it better than most. He is an atheist and says he has profound concerns about many of the narratives that he reads in the Bible. But it hasn't stopped him from being involved with his synagogue and being a lay mentor for his rabbi. He says he loves being Jewish just as he loves being British, and that being part of the Jewish community is an important part of his life. His commitment to Jewish Care is not just about the work it does; it also derives from his belief in the value of the community of which he is a member. 'Being part of the Jewish community is a very important part of my life; it always has been. I want to make sure that it keeps going. And I think that if we did not have Jewish Care, then we'd start to lose the idea that there's such a thing as an organized Jewish community. It's not the only institution in that regard; there are others, but it's one of the big ones.'

Neville Goldschneider has run Camp Simcha since 2005. He was working at the United Synagogue, helping local communities to manage their assets and loving his job, when he received a phone call. It came from an acquaintance, Meir Plancey, who for the past ten years or so had been running a small charity with his wife, Rachely, helping children who had cancer. They would entertain the children, try to give them a great time, take them on trips and once a year send them to a dedicated holiday camp in the Catskills, in the USA. The charity was called Camp Simcha.

Meir explained to Neville that his charity was developing rapidly. It was serving more and more families, and had now reached a size at which it needed to be run professionally. He asked Neville if he would be interested in taking on the job of Director.

Neville went to the USA to visit the camp in the Catskills and get a better understanding of what they did. He saw that the camp was not just helping children with cancer; it was working with children suffering from all sorts of serious illnesses. He came back to England and told Meir he would take the job but that they needed to widen the charity's remit to embrace all life-threatening conditions. Not only would they be able to offer support to many more children and families who needed it, but a wider remit would also make the charity more sustainable. Meir agreed. Neville took the job and he has been at Camp Simcha ever since.

Many sick children suffer from rare illnesses, and families who have a sick child may not know anyone else with the same condition. They feel they have nobody to turn to, because they have never met anyone in the same position. So an important part of Camp Simcha's early work was to make sure that the hospital staff knew about them, and could direct distressed families to them. But when Neville first tried to explain that Camp Simcha was a Jewish charity for sick children, he met resistance. Often the nurses he spoke to could not appreciate the cultural nuances; they did not understand why families might welcome support from a charity rooted within their own community. He remembers one nurse asking him if Jewish cancer was different. So they started a toy drive, delivering toys at Hanukkah to children in hospital, Jewish or not.

Today they deliver 12,000 toys a year. 'And why do we do that?' asks Neville. 'Because the nurses now say, "Oh, those Camp Simcha people, they're lovely." And why does that matter? Because we want them to care. So that when they get family Cohen or family Levy, they'll say, "There's a lovely organization, called Camp Simcha. They can do a lot for you."'

And indeed they do a lot. Not just for the patients, the children who are desperately sick, but for the whole family. Because often the whole family needs support. There can be profound emotional issues for the parents and siblings of very sick children; sometimes Camp Simcha needs to provide a greater level of support to family members than to the child themselves.

This support takes many forms. The charity has family liaison officers in London and Manchester, and dedicated volunteers in cities across the country. They work with families with a sick child suffering from one of over 50 different medical conditions. They provide counselling and therapy services, offer respite care, run family retreats and provide home tuition to those who need it. Some of their younger volunteers take on a role as big brother or sister, visiting the child in hospital, providing treats, making them feel special. As Neville says, it is the little things that count: helping with household cleaning, doing the shopping, giving advice on benefits, making sure the family gets the specialist equipment and services it needs.

Camp Simcha is unique in what it does. Yet it is not unique in being a Jewish charity that offers specialist support to a particular group of beneficiaries. The Jewish community is full of them. Everyone agrees that it would make sense from a financial, operational and logistical perspective for there to be a considerable amount of consolidation in the Jewish charitable sector, for many of the smaller charities to merge. Yet we only have to look at charities like Camp Simcha and Tzedek, and the dedicated people who devote their lives to them, to realize that charities are like people. Some are good, some not so good, but they are all unique. If there is to be consolidation, it has to be done sensitively and thoughtfully. The wrong sort of consolidation could be disastrous.

Over the past 30 or 40 years the profile of those who fund the community has changed. The old school of donors, largely self-made business people, donated money to causes that they personally favoured, either for emotional reasons or because it was likely to gain them recognition and status. They ran the community as if it was their own personal fiefdom. One of the most fascinating books on Anglo-Jewish history is the late columnist Chaim Bermant's *The Cousinhood*. It's about the wealthy, upper-class Jewish families who ran the community in the nineteenth century and well into the twentieth. They married within their social circle, hence 'the cousinhood', and did their best to keep the community on a tight rein. There were advantages to this of course; these were well-connected people with access to power and government, who were often able to get what they wanted by virtue of who they were, rather than through the merit of the particular initiative they were proposing.

But there was a downside too: the whims of a wealthy elite are no way to run a community. As Steven Lewis puts it, 'The days are gone where you can have a big chequebook, and come along and say, "Right, I'm calling the shots." It doesn't work any more. I can honestly say, in the time I've been involved with Jewish Care, I've never known anyone with a big chequebook come along and say, "This is the way it's going to work." I won't mention who, but there are a couple of donors, of whom I was asked, "What happens if they use that threat?" I'd say, "Tell them to keep their money."'

Daniel Carmel-Brown, who was Director of Fundraising at Jewish Care before becoming its Chief Executive, says that the Jewish community is blessed by having huge generosity within it. Providing me with a figure similar to the one that Lionel Salama gave me, he says that there around 1,200 families whose donations prop up the communal infrastructure. And their generosity to the community is amplified by a change in their priorities. Until the late twentieth century their philanthropic emphasis was largely focused on Israel; the dominant charities were those which raised money for Israeli projects. 'And I think what's happened over the last couple of decades is that people have recognized that, even though it's a cliché, charity does start at home. People's priorities have changed and Jewish Care, alongside others, has benefited from those changes, to a recognition of the need to invest in the future of Care in our community. Despite the fact that we've had a tricky few years around anti-Semitism, when I talk to colleagues across

Europe, when I compare our situation to what's going on elsewhere, we are very fortunate in this country.'

It has often been noted that, wherever they are in the world, Jews adopt the behaviours and attitudes of the people they live among. The same is probably true of any immigrant population, but it is more noticeable with Jews because their patterns of migration are so fluid. The past couple of decades have seen an influx of new, often quite wealthy arrivals into the country, from places like South Africa, Iraq and Russia. And there has been a culture clash between the often (but not always) understated British characteristics of the established donor community and the attitude of the newly arrived donors. Philip Rubenstein pointed out that many of the new philanthropists were a lot blunter and much more direct in their opinions. They weren't honed to English moderation. 'The establishment was happy to have their money. But the newcomers felt they were being treated with a certain amount of disdain. It was interesting to observe.'

David Latchman is the Chairman of the Wohl Foundation, one of the largest of Britain's Jewish charities. I asked him whether, in the light of Philip's comments, he thought that the new money coming into the community had changed the philanthropic landscape. He said that he thought that a more dramatic change was the way in which projects in Israel that had previously been supported by the diaspora were now being funded by wealthy Israelis. Jews have given money to relieve poverty in Israel for centuries; the tradition goes back as far as the beginning of the earliest dispersions. In the nineteenth century, as Jews fleeing persecution and prejudice made their way to Israel, the diaspora sent funds to support efforts to create a new national infrastructure. Substantial amounts of money were raised for Israel in the early days of the state, and Jewish communities across the world still raise significant sums for the country. But Israel is now a mature economy, and the tables are turning. David told me that not only are Israeli philanthropists supporting charitable projects in their own country but the Israeli government is now supporting projects in the diaspora. He said that he chairs an enterprise called Educating for Impact, which supports small communities and schools across Europe. It is funded by several diaspora charities and by the Israeli government.

David agrees that fundraising in the Jewish community has become much more professional. Good charities research what their donors are interested in, and what they have given to previously. 'Then they'll come along and say, "Look, this is where we sit; we know that you have an interest in whatever it may be, the elderly, welfare, Jews or whatever it might be. We work in that area. Could we have a meeting to see whether there's anything that fits? And if it doesn't, then thank you and goodbye.'''

As Steven Lewis had done, David confirmed that the days of the autocratic, wealthy donor have gone. The founder of the charity that he chairs operated a bit like that. If he liked somebody and they came with something that seemed reasonable, then he funded it. Today, he says, it's more targeted. The new generation of philanthropists are more hard-nosed than their parents and grandparents. They want to know about impact, about how many lives have been changed as a result of their donation, about the measurable benefits that their philanthropy has achieved. Funding these days is far less dependent on the whims of individual donors.

In addition to being a charity trustee, David Latchman is the Vice-Chancellor of London University's Birkbeck College.

He wears two hats, as both a charity supplicant and a provider. He seeks funds for Birkbeck College's activities, and with his co-trustees he evaluates projects for the Wohl Foundation to support. As a supplicant he knows only too well the hoops that charities have to jump through when applying for project funding. He told me that when the college started fundraising, he was called into a meeting with Henry Drucker, the fundraising guru who had conducted a hugely successful campaign for Oxford University. David remembers Drucker telling them that it is no good saying, 'We want to endow a chair in Italian history, and here's a rich man, let's ask him for a chair in Italian history.' Rather, they needed to understand the donor first. For example, if he had a wife who collects Japanese art, then the fundraisers have to ask themselves if they want a chair in Japanese art. And if they do, that's what to ask him for. And if they don't want a chair in Japanese art, then he is not the right donor for them.

Lord Michael Levy is probably the Jewish community's most successful fundraiser. His strength is his ability to build personal relationships and to show potential donors how much he genuinely values them. He agrees that fundraising has become a little more sophisticated, but says he still thinks that one can pull the heartstrings and make an emotional appeal. 'But a charity needs to run itself in a very professional way. That is very, very important. A large charity has to be run in terms of governance in the best possible way. All charitable foundations need that assurance. When you go to them for funding, you need to be precise on why you're going and what it means. But I think the general rule of thumb, as far as I'm concerned for any charity that I'm involved in, is that I need to look a donor in the eye and never worry that they could investigate the charity, God forbid, and find an issue.'

Of course, the personal preferences of the old school of donors have not been completely eradicated. Good trustees of charitable foundations are conscious of where their funds came from, of the work that went into building up the fortune they are now charged with making responsible use of. Typically they will aim to support projects that would have appealed to the charity's founder. David Latchman says that he and his trustees will periodically have a debate about the sort of projects they want to focus on. But in general it will be projects that interest the trustees, which were also known to be of interest to the founder. In the case of the Wohl Foundation this results in quite a broad spectrum of funding, including schools, care facilities and retirement homes.

The Pears Foundation exemplifies this new model for Jewish philanthropy. Like Jewish Care, it is a benchmark for how things can be done, when they are done well. Sir Trevor Pears, who runs the Foundation, told me he gets a lot of pleasure from philanthropy. He doesn't say this, but he exemplifies the religious stricture that charitable giving, *tzedakah* as it is called in rabbinic lingo, should be carried out cheerfully and with an open heart. One gets the sense that the Pears Foundation do their work not just because of social necessity but because they enjoy what they are doing. Their philanthropy is a choice, not just an obligation. They are not alone in this; there are many donors across the world who see their philanthropy as a vocation. But the Pears Foundation is one of the principal standard bearers for this new attitude among British Jews.

Trevor Pears is the second of three brothers. They are all involved in the Foundation as trustees, but he is the one charged with running it. The family has always been philanthropic, and after their parents passed away and the brothers took over the Foundation, Trevor says he decided to see if he could make its activities less disparate, to give it a cohesive sense of direction. 'The idea was simply to increase the scale a bit and try to make a bit of sense out of it. I was in my mid- to late thirties and I thought I'd give 10 per cent of my time to doing that. What I found four or five years later was that it wasn't 10 per cent of my time, it was 70 or 80 per cent of my work life, and an awful lot of my brain space. I realized that this was more of a calling for me. And within it all was an exploration of what it meant to me to be Jewish.'

The Jewish component of the Foundation's work suffuses everything. Not that they give exclusively to charities working in the Jewish community: they also support many non-Jewish charities, covering a very wide range of activities, everything from the Trussell Trust who run food banks across the country through charities that empower young people, like the Duke of Edinburgh's Award and the Scouts, to organizations focused on education, health and social deprivation. But when Trevor is asked what percentage of the Foundation's work goes to Jewish causes, he answers, 'every penny'. Well-directed philanthropy is a Jewish activity, no matter who the recipients are.

If you ask Trevor Pears what it means to him to be Jewish, he will tell you it is a call to action to make the world a better place. And to those who say that it is the role of Jewish philanthropists to support the Jewish community, his response is that the best way to support the Jewish community is by being outward-looking, not inward-looking. He talks about journeys, and he says that, as he went on his own personal journey into philanthropy and helping others, it opened up his own interest in his Jewishness. And the more that he expressed the fact that his work was rooted in Jewish ethics,

the more confident he grew about saying it. And then he
found that other individuals working in the areas of human
rights were whispering to him that they were Jewish too. 'And
I felt that these people should be doing things because they
are Jewish. Not despite the fact that they are Jewish.'

There is no doubt that the Jewish community in Britain has
changed substantially over the past 20 years. Sir Trevor gives
the example of a task force his Foundation set up in 2008 to
raise awareness of the issues affecting Arab citizens of Israel,
and to encourage efforts to address the problems. Many of
Britain's Jewish communal organizations signed up to it, but
with some reluctance; it was seen as an internal Israeli issue,
not something that Jews in Britain should involve themselves
in. 'Today,' he says, 'it's absolutely normal to talk about such
things. British Jewry in my opinion has matured. It has
grown-up conversations.'

He talks about the enthusiasm with which many of today's
young Jews exhibit their Jewish identity. Traditionally the
youth movements tried to shape Jewish identity by running
summer experiences and gap year programmes in Israel. But
Trevor says that, although the young people he speaks to still
find the Israel experience important, it has become incidental;
they considered going on a fact-finding mission with Tzedek
to Ghana to be just as empowering Jewishly. Today's young
Jews are more interested in the universalistic aspect of their
Jewishness than in its particularity; for them being Jewish
means engaging with the world, looking outwards, rather
than inwards. It's a point of view I encountered time and
again when speaking to people for this book.

Yet in Trevor's view the sense of change in British Jewry
is constrained by the terminology the community continues
to use about itself. He says it needs to stop calling itself

Anglo Jewry, and to start thinking in terms of British Jewry. Even though the majority of Jews in Britain live in England. '"Anglo Jewry" doesn't resonate with me, and my sense is that it doesn't with the younger generation either. It doesn't convey a sense of confidence, of being inclusive, outward-looking. It feels more divisive, less confident, more inward-looking, it belongs to the past. There is a vision that can be built around being part of British Jewry, that is harder to do as part of Anglo Jewry.'

The Pears Foundation sees its work with its recipients as a partnership. They refer to the organizations they support as their partners and they choose them through a process of examining their values and their methods of working. 'We work in a particular way with everybody, listening, engaging, trying to understand where they're at, what they're trying to do. We go with them on the journey.'

A distinguishing feature of the Pears Foundation's philanthropy is that it supports the running costs of the organizations it donates to. It is a distinguishing feature because most grant-making bodies and private donors don't like paying for overheads, for head office salaries, rent and all the things that enable organizations to stay afloat. They would rather pay for a project in which the benefit of their contribution can be easily identified, and to which they can, if they wish, attach their name. Supporting core running costs is not as glamorous or appealing as supporting a defined project.

By supporting core costs, Trevor Pears helps charities to be more direct in their fundraising. They can ask him for what they need, not for what they think he will fund. But he says that when he started working full-time in the Foundation, experienced donors that he spoke to advised him not to support core costs but to fund short-term projects instead. He was advised that long-term core funding meant that organizations would become reliant on the Foundation, and the aim instead should be to support a project and then get out. 'Success was always an exit. And I didn't mean to do things differently, but we just found that when we met an organization we liked, with people we liked, when we believed in what they were trying to do, and we had built a level of relationship and trust, then we wanted to be part of the story.' So now he tries to encourage other donors to take an interest beyond projects they can stick their name on. 'We name things occasionally. But there's a philosophy to that as well.'

Trevor told me about the Foundation's three rules of philanthropy. Number one is Isaiah Berlin's stricture that the first rule of philanthropy is to do no harm. 'It's interesting for philanthropy to start with that. It gives you a certain perspective; it slows you down and makes you think. It is easy for high-net-worth people to just wade in and tell their recipients what to do and how to do it. "Do no harm" encourages you to think a damn sight harder about what you're doing. And to realize how challenging and difficult it is to engage in what are often intractable issues, and to have a bit of humility. And frankly, it's very, very challenging. Sometimes action can cause harm, and inaction can cause harm. It's a really hard thing to think about.'

For his second rule Trevor cites two American presidents: 'Truman said this, Reagan said this: there's no limit to what you can achieve if you're not concerned who gets the credit.'

Rule number three is to give with good grace. He says it is remarkable 'how often, by the time you part with your funds, you're actually rather disliked by the recipients because you've made their life so uncomfortable. It's all about behaviour, thinking, having some humility and working with people, listening to where they're at.' Trevor adds, however, that it is also about the Foundation being appropriately listened to 'as over the years our professional team have acquired considerable relevant experience and learning too!'

Trevor Pears uses a football team metaphor to describe his vision of what British Jewry needs to do. 'We always need to be alert. We need to be safe. We need to be concerned. I do a lot of work on what you might call defensive issues for the community. But I also believe that, like a football team, you need the defence, the midfield and to be scoring goals. And I've asked people, what does it look like to score goals? What does it look like for the Jewish community to score goals? That's usually the end of the conversation, because the individuals I am speaking to do not have any language for this. They can talk about what it is like to defend the goal. But they can't talk about what it looks like to get down the other end and score. And I feel very strongly that we needed to be scoring goals as well.'

Sir Trevor's vision drives the Pears Foundation, but the substantive work of bringing its activities to fruition is carried out by a professional team, for whom he has the highest praise. Pears Foundation has multiple areas of work, but the two key members of the team who work with the British Jewish community are Shoshana Boyd Gelfand and the foundation's director, Amy Braier.

Shoshana has spent her career in Jewish community organizations. Before joining the Pears Foundation she was the Executive Director of the Movement for Reform Judaism. She was born in the USA and was ordained there as a Conservative rabbi before marrying and moving to the UK. And as an American she sees the British Jewish community very differently from others I have spoken to:

unlike most British-born Jews she is astonishingly positive about it. Where many British Jews see a community that at best muddles along, she sees energy and creativity. She lists JW3, Limmud, the peer-led youth movements and the Jewish schools as examples of a community that does things well. 'I was looking around at this community and thinking, there is a renaissance going on here. And little did I know that I would end up getting headhunted to work with one of the architects of that.'

Trevor Pears brought Shoshana into the Foundation to run JHub, an incubator for small, growing Jewish community organizations. Her role was to professionalize the start-ups, particularly in the fields of social action, a job that she was ideal for because of her knowledge of similar models in America. But she says that she didn't just want to plant American seeds. Even though some of the organizations she was incubating were based on American models, she wanted them to reflect the context of the British community. 'So I encouraged each of them to dismantle themselves, right down to their fundamental mission, and then rebuild using British assumptions.'

JHub was a new sort of initiative in British Jewry, but it wasn't driven by a desire to break the mould. 'It wasn't that we thought that things like combating anti-Semitism were not important. On the contrary, we fund the Anti-Semitism Policy Trust, we fund Holocaust education; these are important things. But we felt that needed to be balanced by a positive, outward-looking, confident Jewish life. And when we did a landscape analysis of the British Jewish community, we saw that the social action sector was woefully underfunded.'

Before Pears came along, social action organizations like Tzedek were wholly run by volunteers. They had limited budgets, and as a result their capability for getting things done was severely constrained. Had the Pears Foundation operated as a traditional Jewish community funder, they might have dispensed a few grants here and there, to help the various organizations to get started, and then left them to get on with it. Instead, Pears acted as if they were investors in a start-up, helping the organizations to build an infrastructure. They provided consultancy to help them assemble a trustee board and create a strategic plan, gave them seed funding so they could hire professional staff and furnished them with a desk or two in the JHub building, a physical space from which they could operate. Shoshana explained that this way of operating may be unique in the British Jewish community, but it is well established in the wider philanthropy space, where it is known as Funder Plus.

The Funder Plus strategy worked for the JHub organizations. But after ten years Shoshana told the trustees that she thought they should close JHub. She felt they couldn't keep spinning out new social action organizations indefinitely; the community's finite resources wouldn't be able to support them. So they closed JHub itself but continued to use the same incubation techniques with some of their non-Jewish grantees. Shoshana says that the Jewish community isn't really aware of their work with these organizations. 'But if you say the Pears name within the autism community or within Scouts or Girlguiding, they know us really well. So we started using some of the leadership development tools that we had used with the JHub organizations and sharing them more broadly with foundation grantees, and they loved it. And we learned that these were applicable more broadly.' Shoshana now furnishes all Pears Foundation grantees with the professional and leadership development programmes originally developed for the JHub organizations.

When JHub closed, Shoshana said they felt they had achieved what they wanted: the centre of gravity of the British Jewish community had shifted. Of course, it wasn't the Pears Foundation alone who shifted the community's centre of gravity: their interventions would not have succeeded had the zeitgeist not been right, had there not been people out there who were driven by the new mood in the Jewish community, the generational shift towards a greater sense of social responsibility. JHub achieved what it had set out to achieve because the mood of the Pears Foundation aligned with the mood of those who were looking to do things differently, and who were open to doing it from a Jewish perspective.

And JHub had an unexpected consequence too. Before closing it, Shoshana, whose job title is Director of Leadership and Learning, wanted to discover what they had learned over the past ten years. So she got someone to interview people from different organizations who had been part of JHub. 'One of the primary findings was that women who had returned to their careers after starting a family told us they never would have done it if JHub had not been there. They said, "I have a university degree and I knew I was competent. Then I took a break to have kids, and I just didn't have the confidence to come back in. JHub was a supportive space that held my hand and helped me to scale me up and made me feel confident. And now I'm a Chief Executive, or on a board or whatever." And I thought, that's interesting. We did not set out to do that for women. We set out to do it for everyone. And who did it attract? It ended up attracting really talented women.'

When Shoshana joined the Foundation, she didn't have a job description. Trevor told her he was hiring her for a full-time job, part of which was to run JHub, which would take up about half of her time. They would figure out what she would do the rest of the time. And they did. She says she has never been bored. She developed JDOV (a sort of TED Talks for the Jewish community), manages their international development grants and helped set up Faith in Leadership, an inter-faith leadership development programme in which rabbis, imams, priests and clergy of all denominations learn together. It took two years to develop the programme, which has now been running for a dozen years or so, first in partnership with Cambridge University and latterly with St Benet's Hall in Oxford. It's not just for clergy: lay leaders, professionals and journalists have also taken part in the programme, which has around 1,000 alumni. Having set it up, Shoshana has stepped back; she still teaches on the programme but has now moved on to other projects.

Shoshana works full-time for the Foundation, but she manages to find time to be one of the new public faces of British Jewry. She broadcasts on BBC radio, is a Research Fellow at St Benet's Hall, the Benedictine college in Oxford that runs the Faith in Leadership Programme and is a Visiting Scholar at the ecumenical study centre Sarum College. She regularly speaks at communal occasions: when I met her, she had just been asked by Jewish Care to interview the former Prime Minister Theresa May at a forthcoming charity event. She does all these things, she says, because she has a deep need for cognitive stimulation. 'I love diving into something, learning about it, and then I get a little bit bored. And I need to dive into something else. And then I love making connections between all those different things so they can learn from each other. And Trevor and the Foundation enable me to do that kind of work. I think, in a different kind of role, I would be much more constrained. I'm so lucky. I'm really, really lucky.'

Sometimes the Pears Foundation's openness leads them into unexpected places. Shoshana told me about a discussion she and Trevor had with the chief executive of a large Islamic charity. He told them about the problem his community had with young people becoming radicalized. He wondered if it might be possible to adapt the successful strategies used by the Jewish youth movement to suit the needs of his community. 'We all laughed,' says Shoshana, at the irony of Zionist youth movements helping to prevent the radicalization of Islamic young people. But the question was serious, and after a few moments' thought they came up with an answer. 'We do a lot of work with the Duke of Edinburgh's Award for young people. And we had facilitated a kosher Duke of Edinburgh scheme through the JLGB youth movement. So we ended up connecting them with that, so they could create a halal Duke of Edinburgh scheme. That is a really good example of how something that the Jewish community piloted could benefit the Islamic community.'

The Pears Foundation, of course, is not the only organization that is bringing the Jewish minority experience into wider society. The Community Security Trust advises other minorities on how to protect themselves from extremists and fanatics, and worked with the Islamic community to establish the anti-hate initiative Tell Mama. The Board of Deputies has cooperated with the Muslim Council of Great Britain over matters of shared concern and World Jewish Relief works with NGOs and government agencies on international humanitarian projects.

These are the sorts of thing that the Jewish community in Britain should be doing. It is encouraging that they are happening. We are an immigrant community with a presence in Britain dating back nearly 400 years, and we have managed, at least to some degree, to square the impossible circle of successfully integrating while keeping our own identity. Individual Jews have always played an influential role on the national stage. Many have achieved great things, and a few, like the late Rabbis Jonathan Sacks, Hugo Gryn and Lionel Blue, have made sure that authentic Jewish voices were heard on national media. But the community as a whole had always failed to make a distinctive Jewish contribution, to show that we as a collective have something to offer in national life. Perhaps it was because we were so worried about our own position that we were reluctant to do anything that had a Jewish label attached. More probably, it just never occurred to us.

Britain's Jews have much to offer as a community, particularly to more recently arrived minorities. It does feel as if, after more than 300 years, we are ready to begin. We still have much more to do.

8

Education

Education is a central pillar of Judaism, a priority that stretches all the way back to the Bible. Of course, the Bible had religious education in mind, not secular knowledge, but in biblical times they pretty much amounted to the same thing.

Chief Rabbi Mirvis describes education as 'the petrol in our tank. It is a lesson that others can derive from us. A lot of people marvel at the Jewish capacity to succeed, winning Nobel Prizes and so on. What is it? Is there something in our genes? I put it down to education and the commitment of parents to their children. The immigrant parents slaved to give their children a decent education. They never took pity on themselves; they worked exceptionally hard; they were inspired by education.' Such a deeply ingrained emphasis on education leads to a culture that values learning, ideas and books.

Jewish life in the past was not always easy, but knowledge was the one thing that could not be destroyed by hardship, persecution or displacement. Education is hard-wired into the Jewish psyche, and most parents want the best education for their kids. And for parents who value education, and who are alert to the advantages a good education can bring, what better school to send their children to than one founded on the principles they share?

In the past 30 years the number of pupils in Jewish day schools has doubled. It has increased sixfold in two generations. In the 1950s there were just 5,000 kids in Jewish schools. By 2015 there were over 30,000. There are currently 139 Jewish day schools in Britain; in the 1950s there were 26. And this is against a backdrop of a shrinking community and an overall decline in religious observance. It does seem a bit odd.

But, as Robert Winston pointed out to me, faith schools in general achieve more highly than their secular counterparts. 'Catholic schools have done far better than the secular schools, and Jewish schools have as well. Of course, the fact that a lot of the teachers are not Jewish doesn't do any harm at all.'

The explosive growth of Jewish schooling was fuelled by the zeal of the philanthropist Benjamin Perl. Encouraged by Chief Rabbi Immanuel Jakobovits and his successor, Jonathan Sacks, who regarded the building of new Jewish schools as essential for the community, Perl has raised funding for around 20 new schools since the 1990s. He sees Jewish schools 'as ways of maintaining Judaism', though in reality most parents send their kids there for the quality of education rather than because of any religious imperative.[57]

The schools that Benjamin Perl built were intended to educate children from the mainstream orthodox community, whose families wanted them to have the best of both worlds: a secular education that would equip them for life, and a religious education appropriate to their level of observance at home. But new mainstream orthodox schools are not the only institutions where pupil numbers have mushroomed.

The Strictly Orthodox have always educated their kids in their own schools. *Haredi* couples tend to marry at a much younger age and typically have many more children than the norm. Pupil numbers in *haredi* schools have risen stratospherically in past decades, and they now account for the majority of children in Jewish schools. Unless things change – which they often do – the Strictly Orthodox community is expected to outnumber all other British Jews before the end of the twenty-first century.

If Jewish parents have always wanted the best education for their kids, then the question is, why have they only recently begun turning to Jewish schools? Generations of Jewish children have been successfully educated in ordinary, mainstream British schools, and until the 1990s nobody ever thought Jewish children needed their own schools in order to get a good education. So what has changed?

PaJeS, the Partnership for Jewish Schools, was set up in 2012 by the Jewish Leadership Council in the wake of a report into Jewish education that concluded there was a need for a long-term strategy. The report came up with 23 recommendations. The late Lira Winston worked on the report under the Chairmanship of Professor Leslie Wagner. Whereas many reports come up with recommendations that nobody ever acts upon or pays attention to, Lira said that the Jewish Leadership Council did pay attention. They set up a working party, the School Strategy Implementation Group, to monitor how the recommendations were to be carried out and to agree who was doing what. 'We looked at every recommendation, and we spoke to schools, asking "Is this worth doing? How do we do that?" At the end of three years and another report, the JLC's conclusion was that a new body was needed to service and support all schools, and that's why PaJeS was set up. It was a way of acknowledging the extraordinary growth in Jewish schools and ensuring that their issues were high on the communal agenda.'

Lira Winston was PaJeS's Assistant Director. She said that no school is pressured to work with them. 'Everything we do is offered to everybody, and they may or may not participate.' She told me that PaJeS acts as the conduit between government and the schools, building on the good relations it has with the Department of Education, Ofsted and Downing Street's faith and education adviser. They intervene on behalf of schools that, for example, may have a problem with Ofsted, or a query over the delivery of an aspect of the curriculum such as Sex and Relationships Education. Sometimes schools may be at risk of being downgraded in their Ofsted inspection because they don't teach relationships in the right way. She says it is damaging for a school to fail an Ofsted inspection and anyway, failing them is no way to motivate them to become better; many schools will teach according to their own values whatever the government says. So PaJeS will step in to mediate on the school's behalf, to try to find a mutually acceptable solution.

PaJeS also acts as a coordinating body when it comes to addressing social problems. Lira described to me how they organize meetings on issues like well-being, eating disorders or drugs, to which parents from all schools are invited. 'If one school runs it, people automatically think they've got a problem. But if we run it, and it's for all parents of secondary school pupils, then it is seen as a neutral, community-wide concern.'

Rabbi Michael Pollak, who coordinated PaJeS's resources in secondary schools, doesn't beat about the bush when it comes to saying what he thinks. He describes PaJeS as 'doing some amazing things. It's got a large and very impressive staff. We do a lot of curriculum work for the schools and all the political representation for the schools to government. We raise serious money.'

Michael traces the origins of the growth in mainstream Jewish schools to the introduction of comprehensive education in the 1960s and 1970s. It left aspirational Jewish parents confused as to where their kids would receive the best education. Those who had always intended to send their kids to private schools carried on doing so. But parents who, under the old system, would have sent their children to grammar schools did not want to send them to the new comprehensives into which the grammars had been merged. They'd heard that the comprehensives were just not performing as well as the grammars had done. And at the same time they saw that the quality of education in the few Jewish schools was noticeably improving.

It was then, says Michael Pollak, that the communal leadership began to appreciate how willing parents were to send their children to Jewish schools. 'They ran an aggressive campaign to open new schools. It started towards the end of Lord Jakobovits's tenure as Chief Rabbi and was picked up by his successor, Jonathan Sacks, and by key donors, Benjamin Perl being the most prominent. By the time we got to the late 1980s, early 1990s, it was like building the M25; however many lanes were created, there was always a need for another one. Every time a school opened, everyone said, "Well, that has *got* to be one too many." And then there would be another one. So we've now got something like 50 primary schools in the country. And that's not including all the Strictly Orthodox schools.'

Jewish schools are typically built in areas with a reasonably large Jewish population. But populations tend to shift, and it can happen that a school finds that there are no longer enough Jewish children in the neighbourhood to fill its classes. Other than closing the school, which nobody wants to do, the only other remedy is to admit pupils who are not Jewish. This happened many years ago at the secondary school in Liverpool and the primary in Birmingham, both named after King David. It has happened more recently at King Solomon School in Ilford. Some may find this a matter of regret, but Michael Pollak sees it as a positive development. 'King Solomon is a really good school, and they do amazing things. Because, unlike the other Jewish schools, their pupils are a true cross-section of society. And they're performing really well. It's a great school. It's a bit weird, but roughly 200 kids in each school year are being taught Jewish values, in a secularish sort of way. And they are being taught that Israel's a great place. What's wrong with that?'

Like all faith schools in Britain, Jewish schools are eligible for state funding, subject, of course, to their meeting appropriate standards of governance and education. This has allowed them to thrive more successfully in Britain than in other countries where state support is not available. But as Rabbi Pollak acknowledges, it also throws up a challenge. Those who passionately encourage the building of new Jewish schools do so because they want pupils to have a first-class religious education. But many parents see it differently. The vast majority of children in Jewish schools are there for the quality of secular education, so that they don't have to go to comprehensives. As one parent told me: 'We were lucky, we could afford to send our children to private schools.

Otherwise, a Jewish school would have been the fall-back option.' Which is not quite what those who passionately build Jewish schools have in mind.

Kids do not go to Jewish schools because they are hungry for, or even necessarily interested in, religious studies. And because they all come from homes with different levels of religious observance, they enter the Jewish studies classroom with varying degrees of knowledge and abilities in key skills, particularly their competence in reading Hebrew. The challenge for Jewish studies teachers is to provide a relevant and meaningful religious education in the face of these constraints. For Michael, the answer lies not in the fool's errand of trying to make children religious but in putting together a programme that helps shape Jewish identity. Covering subjects like Israel, the Shoah, *tikkun olam*, volunteering and charity. Combining those topics with the GCSE in Jewish studies and the A-level in religious studies, he says, seems to work.

Rabbi Dr Andrew Davis, deputy headteacher at the 1,000-pupil Yavneh College in Borehamwood, is confident that the challenge is being successfully met. He believes that Jewish schools provide a better religious education than the old model, where children went to religion classes attached to their local synagogues and maybe attended a youth group on a Sunday afternoon as well. Obviously a lot depends on the school, but he thinks that Jewish schools are far more holistic in their education now, weaving Jewish perspectives into the whole of the curriculum. 'If you go back 20 years, the attitude in many of the Jewish schools was very much: "These lessons are Jewish Studies. Everything else is the rest of your education." One of the difficulties that schools have is that they are meant to be academic, factories if you like, delivering academia, skills and qualifications. And the Jewish studies piece doesn't really fit that route. In the majority of schools now, there's a much more holistic approach to education. They'll get a Jewish outlook, Jewish ethics and values, across their entire school educational career.'

Andrew Davis does believe that one of the motivations for parents in sending a child to a Jewish school is that they want a Jewish education for their kids, one that they themselves do not have the knowledge or resources to provide. They are not looking necessarily for a religious education but certainly one that is culturally Jewish, that allows their kids to identify with their heritage and to understand their lives in those terms. Most parents want their children to marry somebody Jewish, and education in a Jewish school is one way they believe they can influence this. In this sense, he argues, Jewish schools have taken over from the youth movements and the synagogues in shaping a sense of Jewish identity.

The undoubted educational success of Jewish schools raises a different, arguably bigger, problem. Is the Jewish community creating ghettos for itself by encouraging its kids to grow up in a Jewish bubble? These days a Jewish child, even from a non-religious home, can be educated in a Jewish nursery, a Jewish primary school and a Jewish secondary school, and then go to a university like Birmingham or Leeds, where there are large cohorts of Jewish students, with whom they will almost exclusively socialize. Almost the whole of their education will have been in a cloistered, largely Jewish environment.

Then, when they come out of university, they may get a job in a company where the majority, if not all, the staff are Jewish, maybe in a law firm or a boutique financial institution. They can go through the whole of their life without having significant contact with anyone outside their own cultural and social bubble.

Of course, the same can be said for other groups. It is a symptom of a multicultural society that has not yet solved the problems of integration. British society is still largely structured by class, and few people are comfortable with those from radically different backgrounds. But ever since the days of Jewish emancipation, beginning in the eighteenth century, Jews have thrived by maintaining a careful balance between their own culture and that of the mainstream, host society. They haven't always got it right. The nineteenth-century immigrants tried too hard to turn their children into Englishmen, and were culturally impoverished by it. Today, many Jewish families assimilate fully into the wider culture and lose almost all sense of their Jewish identity. But the current trend, in which middle-of-the-road Jews can easily spend their lives hardly interacting at all with the rest of British society, is new. And it is a trend which Andrew Davis sees as continuing, as a generational change. Today's grandparents, he says, were educated in ordinary schools, and have both Jewish and non-Jewish friends. Their children, today's parents, belong in social circles with a much higher proportion of Jews. And today's children, those educated in Jewish schools all the way through, may be even more restricted in the diversity of their contacts.

'I think we are going to see the problem in another ten years,' he says, 'when today's children start having their own kids, and they start going to Jewish primary schools.' This new generation will be the children of people who were schooled in a Jewish bubble themselves. If they are also educated exclusively within the bubble, how integrated into wider society are they likely to be?

There is also a question about how effective Jewish schools really are in developing a sense of identity. Might they just be producing children with a monochromatic circle of friends and no sense of heritage? Vivian Wineman told me that evidence from the USA, albeit a few years old, is that attendance at a Jewish school alone, in the absence of a strong sense of identity at home, does not promote Jewish commitment in later life. 'The studies that are produced in favour of Jewish education show that pupils who have primary Jewish education are more likely to marry someone Jewish than the people who don't. If they have secondary Jewish education, they are again more likely to marry in, and even more so if they have tertiary Jewish education. But if you isolate out other factors like home environment and social life, the benefits are not so great.'

So if Jewish schools are to be anything more than centres of academic excellence, secular replacements for old grammar schools, their challenge is not just to provide a Jewish education that engages the children and gives them a sense of identity but also to make sure that it is underpinned by a strong and supportive Jewish home life. Otherwise, what is the point? Jonathan Goldstein says that for him this is the community's greatest challenge. 'If we're going to have 60 to 65 per cent of our children in Jewish schooling, let's take advantage of that. Let's not waste that opportunity.'

Rabbi Michael Pollak was educated in a public school with a strong connection to the Church of England. He describes having his commitment to Judaism formed at school in a cauldron of fire: 'People thinking that we were weird. On a daily basis, we had to say, "Look, I'm sorry, I don't do that", or "I don't eat that." And you'd get a quizzical look and you'd say, "No, seriously, I'm Jewish." And so we were forever having to reflect and improve our understanding of our religion and to be able to present it to other people. And if you came through that, your Jewish commitment was pretty strong. But on the other hand, a lot of people lost their Jewish commitment along the way.'

But his son's experience was different. He went to a Jewish school and then studied at a university where there were not many Jewish students. 'He came back and said, "They're OK." I said, "Who's OK?" He said, "*goyim*". I said: "Well, when did I ever suggest that they weren't OK?" And he said: "Well you kept me away from them for 21 years. So I reasonably assumed that they're a bad lot. But they're OK."'

The purpose of Jewish schools is to engage pupils with their own culture more effectively than they might experience in a secular state or private school. The schools recognize this means their students may grow up with a skewed view of life in other communities, and that this is detrimental both to their life chances and to society as a whole. Explaining why his school has invested significant time and resources in creating a course for its pupils about world religions, Andrew Davis explains: 'We believe that it is important for our pupils to learn about the beliefs and practices of others, in order to prepare them to be knowledgeable adults in British society.'

One of the charges laid against schools in the Strictly Orthodox, or *haredi*, community is that they do not share this view, that they are not interested in producing knowledgeable, productive members of British society. Rather, so the argument goes, their concern is to produce the next generation of *haredi* Jews. Far from being concerned that their schools might create ghettos, they do everything they can to isolate their communities from the wider world.

A generation ago that charge was accurate, and there is no doubt that in some parts of the *haredi* world the attitude still persists. But it is an attitude that is becoming increasingly rare. Economic pressures, social change, the advent of the internet and the intervention of government bodies have all impacted on the way *haredi* schools are run, and on the curriculum they teach. There is still a desire in *haredi* communities to screen their children from the outside world, but that is to protect them from the perceived dangers of modern inner-city life, not to completely deny them the chance of a successful career.

I spoke to Eli Spitzer, who at the time was the headmaster of the independent Tiferes Shlomo school in London's Golders Green. The Strictly Orthodox school caters for boys aged from three to 15. In 2015, before he joined, the school was inspected by Ofsted, the government inspectorate. It was rated as Inadequate, with deficiencies in reading, writing and mathematics, and an unsatisfactory equilibrium between secular and religious studies. The report said there was a lack of balance, breadth and depth of learning. The school appointed a new, young headteacher, Eli Spitzer. It took him nearly five years to turn the school around, until in February 2020 it finally received a Good rating.

Eli grew up in a hasidic family in Stamford Hill. Like most of his peers, his first language was Yiddish; he says that he knew enough English to go shopping or to visit the doctor but that he struggled to have a meaningful conversation in it. He received a fairly typical *haredi* boy's primary education, in a school where the tuition was in Yiddish and the focus was almost exclusively on the study of Talmud and its associated commentaries and law codes. *Haredi* girls tend to have a slightly broader education: their curriculum is geared to preparing them for domestic life, motherhood and, subsidiary to these, a means of earning a living.

At the time of his barmitzvah, at the age of 13, Eli graduated to a junior *yeshiva*, where again the curriculum was textual study, with no secular education at all. Although the pupils were still of school age, the *yeshiva* was not registered as a school; like many other institutions in Stamford Hill, it operated beneath the state's radar. After a couple of years he went to a similar institution in Belgium and then returned to yet another *yeshiva* in London, where he remained until the age of 18.

By the age of 15 Eli was very conscious of his lack of English, his 'major literary deficit' as he puts it. It jarred with his home upbringing; he and his siblings had always been encouraged to achieve highly, yet he felt his lack of English held him back. He began listening to radio programmes under the duvet at night, to hear English spoken fluently. When he should have been asleep, he would phone in to chat shows using a false name, to give himself a chance to speak in English. He began to read English literature prolifically while keeping up his religious studies. He married and joined a *kolel*, an institution for advanced Talmudic students.

When a school in Stamford Hill offered him a teaching job, his father encouraged him to accept it. Within two years he had been appointed as the school's head of secular studies. The job probably sounds more prestigious than it actually was: secular studies was of limited importance to the school. The fact that Eli didn't have any teaching qualifications didn't matter to them; they were in no legal position to appeal to a qualified teacher. But the job gave him a taste for education. 'I saw it as an opportunity to learn a lot and to get some practical experience, to be put in a leadership position at the age of 23. Even though it was a dysfunctional school by any standards, I was still in charge of a department with 15 people answering to me, trying to transform it. I knew that I would be extremely limited in what I could do. But at the same time, I could learn a lot.'

It was then that Eli decided he needed qualifications. He took his GCSEs, something he had not been given the opportunity to do as a teenager. He studied on a community programme to gain Qualified Teacher Learning and Skills status and finally enrolled at the Institute of Education at University College London, to sit for the National Professional Qualification for Headship.

Eli Spitzer realizes that what he did in overcoming his deficiency in English is not something that most young *haredi* men are able to do. He knows he was more determined, perhaps more confident, than most of his peers. And he sees this as one of the major flaws of the *haredi* community. 'I'm becoming more convinced with every latest development in the mainstream world that the benefits of the social cohesion that exists in the *haredi* community and the support networks it offers to its members far outweigh the drawbacks of a poor education. However, I don't think that the only way for this sort of social innovation to survive is by having its members grow up to be illiterate. There's no need for that.'

He describes the deficiencies in secular *haredi* education as a 'dignity gap'. He argues that the primary purpose of education is not necessarily economic advancement. Poverty is rife in the *haredi* community but not always because of lack of income. Although there is little data to prove his point, he argues that most *haredi* families have a reasonable income; they may not be university-educated professionals but they are economically active, working particularly in property or in small businesses, roles for which a sophisticated level of education is not necessary. The reason he claims there is poverty in the *haredi* community is the large number of children in each family, the consequent size of house they need and the requirement to live in closely defined neighbourhoods like Stamford Hill, where the cost of housing may be high. 'I think, and this is from my own experience, knowing hundreds of people in the *haredi* community, that if you were to look objectively at the average household income in the *haredi* community, it would probably be above average. And at the same time, relative poverty is probably also higher, because £50,000 a year might be a very comfortable income for a family with 1.8 children and a pet, but it doesn't quite cut it for someone with eight children to feed, having to pay school fees at private institutions and so on.'

Good education for the *haredi* community is not, according to Eli, an economic necessity. Rather, it is a question of dignity, of a feeling that is growing particularly among younger *haredim* that they cannot take part in the conversations going on in the world. The internet, of course, and the advent of social media, have been seminal in bringing about this change. When the internet first emerged, the *haredi* rabbis discouraged their communities from using it; they said it would pollute their minds and expose their children to lewdness. They forbade the use of smartphones. But during the Covid crisis, when everything went online, the internet became essential for shopping and communication. Digital media are infiltrating the *haredi* world, and young *haredim* who are unable to read, write or converse in English find themselves profoundly disadvantaged.

The *haredi* rabbis fear that by accessing the internet, young impressionable *haredim* may easily be seduced away from their communities to the glittering world beckoning to them from the screens of their phones and computers. But this is why, Spitzer maintains, young *haredim* need a good, formal secular education, to enable them to discriminate between the worthwhile and the vacuous, to allow them to take advantage of the opportunities that the internet offers them, opportunities that will come their way whether their rabbis like it or not. He compares the situation today to that in nineteenth-century Germany, when the orthodox world felt threatened by rising populist Jewish movements, particularly Reform and, to a lesser extent, Hasidism. The solution of orthodox leaders was to use education as a bulwark against populism. 'They understood very early on that if they wanted to win against the Reform, they had to bridge that dignity gap. They could not allow their members to be tempted over to the Reform world, not because of theological arguments, but simply because Reform gave a better account of themselves.' In other words, he implies, for *haredi* Judaism to survive it has to confront the world by speaking its language, not by retreating into intellectual isolation and obscurity.

Listening to Eli Spitzer, I couldn't help comparing his fears with those of the non-*haredi* community. Non-*haredi* Jews, mainstream Jews for want of a better word, are disturbed by the demographic evidence which suggests that the *haredim* will soon constitute the majority of the British Jewish community. Conversely, from a *haredi* perspective, Eli worries that the tight social fabric of the *haredi* world may rupture, that *haredi* Judaism itself may be under threat, because it is unable to respond satisfactorily to modernity.

Eli Spitzer's arguments are persuasive. It seems that many young *haredim* agree with him. Some leave the *haredi* community, but most remain, because the social structure is so supportive and inviting. But the very same social structure impedes the opening up of education for *haredi* children. In their closed world the newspapers never print photos of women, devote as much space to visiting rabbinic dignitaries as they do to national and international news and publish religious exhortation alongside political observations on their opinion pages. They create an illusion that everything is safe and straightforward in the *haredi* domain – which to some degree it is – and that it is better to look inwards than to pay any attention to the world beyond their boundaries.

The determined, the insightful and the ambitious, like Eli Spitzer, will always recognize that things are not so simple, that there are great advantages to be had from the right sort of exposure to modernity. And that conversely, without a sustained effort to acknowledge the perils of modernity, their world is in danger of succumbing to the unsavoury influences gathering at its gates. There is no guarantee that others, less insightful, will share Eli's vision.

It is those less insightful *haredim* who worry Eve Sacks. She has been lobbying for years against illegal, unregulated *haredi* schools that only teach religious texts and that offer virtually no education in maths, English or any of the subjects that all children need to learn if they are to make their way in the world. The existence of these schools is well known, but she is concerned that the authorities haven't been able to close them down even when they know about them. Because of a legal loophole, which regards the institutions not as schools but as clubs, it is the parents, rather than the schools, who are culpable in law for not educating their children. Even when the authorities do manage to shut down a school due to its inadequacy, another opens in its place. Without stronger powers and proper alternatives, she says, the authorities are fighting a losing battle. Close down one school, and another will pop up elsewhere.

Eve's aspiration is for *haredi* children to get GCSEs and A-levels, 'to give them more autonomy in adulthood'. She sees two possible ways that the government can achieve this: either by setting up a voluntary aided school to cater for those currently in unregistered schools or by closing all the inadequate private schools and only allowing those that have good standards to remain open.

Eve grew up in a modern orthodox home in Glasgow but had some *haredi* friends. But she grew increasingly alarmed with what she came to see as a highly controlled environment, one that may appear ideal on the surface but which she feels does more harm than good. She saw that boys in the unregulated schools were receiving no secular education, and she says that even the girls, who are taught enough to earn a living, can be 'functionally illiterate and innumerate. They have any career aspirations completely stripped away from them, and they have no chance to go to university. And they are forced into arranged marriages.' And, she continues, there are knock-on effects. The parents were educated in similar schools, and know nothing about the modern world. They don't know, for example, that corporal punishment is forbidden, or that parents are not to hit their children. So a process that starts with bad education can lead to abuse, both physical and sexual. The women don't understand the concept of consent, and the men believe they have a right. And Eve's point is that this is not because they are bad people but because of ignorance owing to an insular lifestyle and a lack of contact with the outside world.

Chaya Spitz strongly disagrees with Eve's assessment. Chaya is the Chief Executive of two Strictly Orthodox Stamford

Hill organizations: Interlink, the umbrella organization and resourcing body for *haredi* charities, and the Agudas Israel Housing Association, which runs care homes and supported housing for their community. Chaya argues that although the *haredi* world is very conservative, and does lag behind developments in the wider world, it does follow trends. And she says it is following the same trajectory in education as other conservative faith communities; there are clear signs of a trend within the *haredi* community towards a statutorily acceptable level of secular education.

She accepts that there are some schools, the Talmud Torah schools, as they are known, that only offer a small amount of secular education, and receive 'Inadequate' ratings from Ofsted. Part of their challenge is that they were never set up as schools in the conventional sense. They are intended as elementary religious institutions, preparing their brightest graduates for advanced study in *yeshiva*, rabbinic college. But they are now receiving far greater scrutiny from government, and Chaya told me that there is real movement to improve the extent and quality of the secular education they deliver. 'There's a huge amount of work going into that. I think it's going to be slow, but there is clear movement. As for the girls' schools and the more open boys' schools, they are certainly offering far more secular education than in the past.'

Chaya told me that when she went to school, nobody studied for A-levels; it just wasn't an option. 'Now there's no such thing as girls' schools not offering A-levels. I think the bit that Eve is worried about is what happens after Talmud Torahs finish, at the age of 13 or 14.' That is when the boys coming out of Talmud Torah go to a junior *yeshiva*, where they receive no secular education at all. She says that she used to be 'much more hardcore about this. When I was younger, I used to think that these boys were hard done by, and there's something wrong here. Now, I've become much more relaxed.'

She is more relaxed, she says, because her own sons have been through the system and have come out successfully. 'They're fabulous. They've got careers themselves, they're happy, they're successful. It's good. They've got good lives.'

Religious politics are rarely far from the surface in Jewish communal life, and in the British community they are more often than not tied to questions of authority. This is rarely more pertinent than in the question of admission to Jewish schools. Many Jewish schools in Britain accept the Chief Rabbi as their religious authority. They accept that his office has the last word on who is Jewish and therefore eligible for admission to the schools under his aegis.

Britain's oldest Jewish school is JFS, the Jews' Free School. Established in 1732 to educate the community's orphans, it was once the largest school in the world, with 4,000 immigrant children on its books. Its East End building was destroyed in the Second World War, and when the school reopened in north London in 1958, owing to some complicated and arcane politics, it found itself under the religious authority of the Chief Rabbi. Only those children who were regarded as Jewish by the orthodox authorities, in the person of the Chief Rabbi, could be admitted to the school.

In 2007 JFS found itself at the centre of a legal action that challenged this admissions policy. A boy whose mother had converted to Judaism under the non-orthodox Masorti movement applied for a place at the school. The school refused to admit him because his mother's conversion was not recognized by the orthodox authorities. The family went to court. They lost on the first hearing but appealed against the judgement, and the dispute ended up as the first case to be heard by the newly established Supreme Court, the highest court in the land. There the judges ruled by a majority of five to four that the admissions policy was discriminatory because it relied on the Jewish ethnicity of a child's mother to determine whether the child was eligible for entry. Even though there was no suggestion of racism, the policy fell under the category of racial discrimination.

Many in the Jewish community were distressed by the ruling. Before the Supreme Court's ruling, all parents had to do to get their child into a Jewish school was to show that they were Jewish. Now, in order to comply with the law, they had to produce evidence that they actually practised the Jewish religion. One of the dissenting judges in the Supreme Court described this as 'a non-Jewish definition of who is Jewish' requiring 'a focus (as Christianity does) on outward acts of religious practice and declarations of faith'.[58]

As a result of this case, admission to Jewish schools is no longer based on whether a child was born to a Jewish mother but on the parents' ability to demonstrate their commitment to their Jewish faith, an improbable notion, almost impossible to regulate. While this resolves the injustice of children being excluded from a school because their mother was converted by a rabbinic court not recognized by the orthodox, it fundamentally changes the idea of Jewishness. For religion is only one aspect of Judaism, and one is no less Jewish, and certainly no less worthy, even if one has never entered a synagogue.

Nevertheless, that is what the law demands, and to qualify for admission to Jewish schools these days children are obliged to rack up points to demonstrate their religious observance. Points can be obtained in different ways, depending on the school, but for those under the auspices of the United

Synagogue, kids need to obtain a Certificate of Religious Practice by attending synagogue services, taking part in a Jewish educational activity or having their parents volunteer for a Jewish organization. The only exception to this is for Free Schools, which are obliged by law to only allocate half their intake to those who meet the faith criteria. The remainder of places are awarded using standard admission criteria such as the family home's proximity to the school. So it is still possible, under the Free School system, for a Jewish child who has not racked up the points and does not meet the orthodox criteria to attend an orthodox school.

Perhaps the oddest consequence of the arrangement devised by the Supreme Court is that a child who is not Jewish can go to a Jewish school simply by wandering into synagogues, attending services and gathering the required number of points. Apocryphal evidence suggests that in areas where the secular state schools are below standard, several non-Jewish families have adopted this tactic. It's not a bad thing. Perhaps it's the best antidote to ghettoization.

The IHRA definition may be inadequate, but one of the top priorities of the Union of Jewish Students is to get it adopted by all universities and higher education institutions. When I spoke to James Harris, midway through his year as President of the UJS, he told me that they had recently submitted a Freedom of Information request which revealed that 80 per cent of higher education institutions had still not adopted the definition. I happened to speak to James on the same day that the Community Security Trust published the results of an investigation into university anti-Semitism. They had found 123 instances of anti-Semitism against students and university staff in 34 different towns during 2019. It doesn't sound a lot, until one considers that only about 20 per cent of hate crimes are reported, and that the figure of 123 incidents was 60 per cent higher than the previous year. As we have seen, in Jonathan Boyd's assessment that doesn't imply that anti-Semitism was on the rise that year. But it still doesn't feel good.

The Union of Jewish Students is the umbrella body for the 67 Jewish Societies across the country. Like any university society, the JSocs, as they are universally known, are there to enhance student life and to meet the interests of those who have chosen to join. They may find themselves obliged to respond to anti-Semitism and to lobby their institution to adopt the IHRA definition, but that is not why they were set up, and it is not their *raison d'être*. JSocs are intended as places where Jewish students can meet, connect and socialize with each other. They are, in many ways, senior versions of the youth movements that a lot of Jewish teenagers join.

Jews tend to do things in groups. Not all Jews of course: the proportion of solitary-minded Jews is probably similar to that of the wider population. But Jews are noticeable for banding together. For teenagers this may mean gathering in crowds on a Saturday night or joining vibrant and noisy youth movements. Adults congregate in synagogues or Jewish cultural events; when the state of Israel was founded they settled in *kibbutzim*, the ultimate in socialist living, where even their money and possessions were often pooled. Jews seem to have a pronounced and enthusiastic herd mentality. It's one of the reasons why synagogues are more vibrant than churches. Jews are probably no more religious than any other group, but Jews go to synagogue to meet, probably more than they go to pray. It's why they have a *kiddush* at the end, a tipple and a snack, where they can chat with each other without the nuisance of praying. The Hebrew word for synagogue means 'meeting house', and the word 'synagogue' is its Greek equivalent.

JSocs exist to make Britain's 8,500 Jewish students feel that they belong to a community on campus, a community that James Harris describes as extremely vibrant and diverse. The societies are probably best known for their Friday night dinners, Friday night being the traditional time for a family meal. But they are more than a student dining club. They organize inter-faith and social events and run social action campaigns, coordinating, for example, with other organizations on behalf of the victims of the Ukraine war and the persecuted Uyghur minority in China. Systematically subjected to genocide, forced into labour camps and tortured, the suffering of the Uyghurs is all too familiar to anyone with an awareness of Jewish history. Groups like UJS and the small human rights charity René Cassin are taking the lead in the British Jewish community's response to their persecution.

The Jewish media regularly run stories about anti-Semitism on campus, about how difficult it is to be a Jew at university today. James told me that the problem is aggravated by university complaints processes, which he says are just not working. He puts it down to poor administration rather than anything more sinister. He says there is an element of learning as well, that clearly many of the people involved in managing the complaints processes have never met a Jew in their life and do not really understand the issues. 'But I'd say anti-Semitism is definitely growing. The evidence shows that it has been growing quite significantly over the past five years. During the pandemic, between January and June 2020, there was a 38 per cent increase in anti-Semitic incidents on campus, compared with the same period in the previous year.'

And the figure might have been higher, had it not been for the pandemic, because a lot of the anti-Semitism that had occurred on campus had moved online.

Anti-Semitism is the biggest challenge that the UJS finds itself confronting, but it is not the only one. On a more practical level, James says there are ongoing issues related to religious freedoms: exams and lectures that clash with Jewish holidays, and the availability on campus of kosher food. These are not new matters; they have always been part of Jewish student life. But they are time-consuming and frustrating to deal with, and quite unnecessary. After a century or more of these problems recurring, one might have hoped that by now the combined intellectual power of Britain's universities and Jewish communal leaders would have come up with solutions.

Collectively, Jewish students actively ally themselves with the LGBT community's fight against hatred and phobia. So it came as a shock when a scandal broke out at St Andrews University, in Scotland, involving a Jewish fraternity. All-male, elitist, triumphalist and identified (for reasons that make very little sense) by letters of the Greek alphabet, fraternities are relatively unknown in Britain. They are an American concept that has tried to make inroads into British student life, with limited success. Because the early fraternities excluded Jews, just over 100 years ago American Jews established their own one. They called it Alpha Epsilon Pi, eschewing the Hebrew alphabet in favour of the Greek, unaware that in so doing they were setting themselves firmly on the wrong side of an ancient Jewish quarrel between the now defunct Hellenists and the omnipresent rabbis.

St Andrews University is a major centre for American students visiting Britain on exchange programmes. Alpha Epsilon Pi established a chapter of its predominantly Jewish fraternity there. In July 2020 several women made allegations of rape and sexual assault against fraternity members. The fraternity immediately responded, expressing its abhorrence and saying it had known nothing about the accusations before they were made public. It claimed to have suspended several students. Members of the St Andrews Survivors group challenged their statement, saying that the fraternity had known what had been going on for a long time. The Union of Jewish Students didn't mince their words. They called the fraternity's statement 'a dangerous attempt to change the narrative' and broke off all relations with them.

9

Migrations

Religiously, the Jewish nation considers itself to be in exile. It has been in exile since the Romans destroyed the Jerusalem Temple in 70 CE. Much of the exile has been horrible, blighted by poverty, persecution, pogrom and holocaust. But today, for most Jews, in countries where they are to be found, exile is not so horrible. In fact, it is quite a comfortable, prosperous and enjoyable exile.

Israel, the ancestral Jewish homeland, is not a place of exile. But many Israelis, seeing the comfortable exile that other Jews enjoy, have decided that is where they would rather be. Between 2000 and 2010, 50 per cent more Israelis moved to Britain than Britons moved to Israel. Given that one of the aims of establishing the state of Israel was to absorb Jews from all over the world, the net migration out of the country is striking.[59]

Chief Rabbi Ephraim Mirvis describes the influx of Israelis into Britain as the third great wave of Jewish immigration. The first, he says was when Cromwell allowed the Jews to return; the migrations of the eighteenth and nineteenth century was the second wave. This, he says, is the third wave.

It troubles him because so many do not define themselves as Jews. He told me of an occasion when he was taking part in an inter-faith project in a Catholic church, handing out food parcels. 'And in the churchyard were three mothers with toddlers, all talking Hebrew. So I put my box down, I went over to them, and spoke to them in Hebrew. I said, "Hi, how are you, what are you doing here?" And they said, "Oh, well, we've just collected our kids from the kindergarten here, from the church kindergarten." I asked: "And why did you choose this one?" They looked at me like I was crazy. "What do you mean, why did you choose this one? This is the one closest to our home." And they didn't bat an eyelid. And that's what's happening.'

There are 80,000 Israeli passport holders living in Britain today. It is the second largest expatriate Israeli community in the world, the largest of course being the USA. The figure does include people born in Britain who emigrated to Israel, took out Israeli citizenship and then, for one reason or another, returned to the UK. So if we are talking about native-born, Hebrew-speaking Israelis who have chosen to leave their homeland, the figure is somewhat smaller. But it is still a lot, for a small country like Israel. And, like other Jews, Israelis are aware that they are different, that they are a minority in Britain. But they feel this not because they are Jews but because they are Israelis. They are far more matter-of-fact and confident about their Jewish identity than most diaspora Jews. It is the fact that they are Israeli that makes them feel different.

Israelis live in Britain for many different reasons. Some came as students, fell in love and stayed. Others come for economic reasons: because their job brings them here, or they've been recruited by a British company or maybe even to set up their own businesses. Some come here to work in the religious communities, as rabbis, cantors, scribes or educators. And others are here for political reasons. Anat Koren, who runs *ALondon* magazine, 'the voice of Israelis in London', says that many came in the late 1980s, during the Palestinian intifada, because they did not agree with the political situation in Israel. And until Brexit, Britain was a prime destination of choice for those Israelis who had ancestral European passports and could settle here freely.

Anat has been in Britain for 30 years. She has seen a steady increase in the number of Israelis living in Britain, and she accepts that, although she would like things to be different, on the whole they do not consider themselves to be part of the British Jewish community. There are exceptions of course: some Israelis are here because they married into local families, and have become fully absorbed in local Jewish life. Religious Israelis become involved with their local community through the synagogues and religious institutions they attend. Those who live in small communities often become more involved, because they have few compatriots locally to socialize with. And since the vast majority of British Jews have friends or family in Israel, it is generally easy for Israelis to make local Jewish friends if they want to. They have something, however slight, in common. The interconnectedness of Jews around the world may excite the fantasies of deranged conspiracy theorists, but it is a fact nonetheless. As the medieval biblical commentator Rashi asked, when remarking on how to deal with those who have no relatives to help them with their debts: 'Do you know of any Jew who has no relatives?'[60]

As a result, Anat says, when the Israelis began arriving in Britain they expected the Jewish community to welcome and embrace them. They were disappointed to find that generally they did not. Not because of any hostility but because British Jews, like the British in general, are not a demonstrative people. Some probably felt quite positive about the growing Israeli presence. And they would have been quite pleasant and charming if an Israeli family moved in next door – as long as they didn't make too much noise. But they weren't going to make a song and dance about welcoming them. Any more than they did about welcoming any member of the other Jewish communities that have settled in Britain in recent decades.

And there were some British Jews who positively discouraged Israelis from settling in Britain. The Zionist organizations, those whose *raison d'être* was to encourage and support immigration to Israel (despite remaining in Britain themselves), were very disparaging of those Israelis who chose to leave their homeland. It was as if they held each Israeli personally responsible for fulfilling the Zionist dream, and woe betide those who didn't. Anat recalls how they reacted in the 1980s, when the Israeli presence in Britain started to grow. 'They didn't like us. They used to say to us: "Why are you here? You are embarrassing us. You don't speak the way we speak. You don't behave the way we behave, you don't have the same manners. We've tried for years to integrate into English society and now look what you are doing to us!"'

Irrespective of personal relationships, the Israeli community in Britain is little different from any other expatriate community. They share a common language and culture with other Israelis, but not with native British Jews. In the 1980s, when Anat decided to set up a publication for Israelis in Britain, she looked at the Greek, Cypriot and other expat communities, saw what they were doing and created a publication for Israelis, written in Hebrew and focusing on expat life in Britain and its challenges.

Like any expat community, the Israelis organize their own cultural and social activities. The Israeli Business Club puts on lectures and events for London-based Israeli professionals: there is an Israeli film festival; musicians sing popular Israeli songs; comedians deliver performances in Hebrew. Anat Koren's publication *ALondon* started out as a listings magazine, but she discovered that her audience really wanted to read stories about other Israelis, their lives, their achievements and how they manage to succeed as foreigners in British society. So she turned *ALondon* into an online magazine, with a print edition twice a year, that gives Israelis a sense of belonging to a vibrant and successful diaspora. The magazine reaches 20,000 people each month.

The Israeli American Council, a powerful lobbying body backed by some very wealthy supporters, claims to act on behalf of the half a million Israelis who live in the USA. There is no equivalent body in Britain. And even though the Israeli community in Britain is large, much larger than any synagogue or communal organization, since it lacks a formal representative body, it is not represented on the Board of Deputies. Anat Koren says that she has frequently lobbied for an Israeli delegate at the Board, arguing that it makes no sense for them to ignore the Israeli community. But she keeps coming up against constitutional barriers. The Board of Deputies requires its delegates to be elected by its member organizations, and without an Israeli membership organization there can be no elected Israeli representative. The Board maintains close relations with the Israeli Embassy and is resolutely partial in its advocacy for Israel. But this does not translate into a formal communal recognition of the Israeli Jews in Britain.

The void between the Israeli and British Jewish communities is not unbridgeable, and there is no doubt that the presence of Israelis is beginning to influence Jewish life in Britain. Some Israelis have begun to be appointed to leadership roles in Jewish charities. The charities appoint them to help draw Israelis into their donor network, and this in turn exposes the expats to the needs and priorities of the established Jewish community. At the moment there are only a handful of these Israeli communal leaders, but they meet in a forum every three or four months to discuss wider communal issues. It may be the beginning of a more formal leadership body for the Israeli community, one that would connect it more closely to wider Jewish society and perhaps even win it a coveted seat on the Board of Deputies, constitution permitting.

And then there are the kids. Over half of Israeli families send their children to Jewish schools. The proportion is almost identical to those from native Jewish families. Their schoolmates, of course, pay no attention to which community their friends are part of. Assuming they remain in Britain as they grow up, these second-generation British-Israelis will feel far closer to the native Jewish community than their parents do.

But there are disincentives to Israeli children choosing to remain in Britain when they grow up. Anti-Israeli feeling can be quite strong, especially at times of conflict in the Middle East. All children from minority backgrounds experience prejudice in one form or another; it is a fact of life in a Britain growing noticeably less tolerant. But Israeli children suffer a double helping of prejudice: the low-level anti-Semitism that all Jewish kids are vulnerable to and an additional helping of anti-Israeli prejudice, by virtue of where they were born.

Nevertheless, Anat Koren believes that British Jews and Israelis will start to grow closer once the Israelis become more settled in Britain. At the moment, they tell her, they are in Britain for a few years to enjoy themselves, to do something different as an interlude in their lives, before going back to Israel. They don't see their future here. But things will change, Anat believes, as their children integrate. Once they have been here for a few years, the kids may not want to go back to Israel. They will have established their own social networks, and may well feel more British than Israeli. What started off as a temporary family excursion, to experience a different culture for a few years, may well turn into something more permanent. That will make a difference.

British Jews are, in the main, supportive of Israel. They could hardly be otherwise. The idea of Israel is central to the Jewish faith, and centuries of rootlessness and exile have idealized the notion of a return to Israel as a Jewish homeland. Most British Jews believe in the importance of the Jewish state, have friends in Israel and take pride in Israel's achievements.

British Jews, and indeed those elsewhere in the diaspora, know that the world's media deal with Israel differently from other countries, that they often treat it as a rogue state. Mainly because Israel's open society makes it far easier for journalists to report from there than from the real rogue states, from countries like Iran, Saudi Arabia, North Korea, Libya and all those other places we rarely hear of because journalists have little idea about what's going on in them. They understand that the terrorist organizations who periodically fire rockets into Israel or conduct incursions into Israeli territory are not freedom fighters at all but proxies for Iran in a geopolitical power struggle. They know that Hamas fire their weapons at Israel from residential blocks in Gaza, endangering the civilian population. And they suspect also that much of the anti-Israel rhetoric that periodically erupts in the West, the boycotts and demonstrations and invective, are fuelled as much by anti-Semitism as any genuine political considerations.

But, for all this, many Jews in Britain have profound reservations about some of the things that happen in Israel. They cannot comprehend how, given the history of the Jews, the far right can flourish in Israel, how voices can emerge that call for the expulsion of all Arabs, and worse. They become disenchanted with Israel when they read about corruption in high places, senior government figures on trial, and sometimes in prison, for fraud and abuses of power. They don't understand why the military do things to the Palestinians that are counterproductive, that can only aggravate relations further, why they destroy the homes of the families of suspected terrorists, knowing full well that this will only lead to further resentment, to fresh waves of violence and killings. Or why provocative settlers are allowed to settle in Arab towns, to take over Arab houses; they fail to understand how anyone can imagine that polices of annexation, discrimination and segregation can ever lead to peace. Few British Jews are persuaded by the Israeli response that they would think differently if they lived there. That may be the case. But equally, by being on the outside, it may just be that Britain's Jews are able to take a more objective and constructive view.

Professor Robert Winston is one of the Jewish community's most eminent voices. He recalled Chief Rabbi Jakobovits, who in the 1980s stood alone against most of his rabbinic colleagues worldwide in arguing that Israel should give up land in exchange for peace. Robert extols Lord Jakobovits's position, saying that it was something that needed to be said and has not been said enough. 'My view, as a Jew, is that the rabbinical authorities have let us down consistently by allowing what is essentially an antagonism towards Muslims. I think it does great harm, I think we've allowed ourselves to go back to an eighteenth-century Ashkenazi enclave, where we're under such threat that we can't see the other side, we can't see the *goyim*. I think it's damaging to Judaism. And it's all very well for us to talk about the righteous of all nations inheriting the world to come. But actually, you know, we don't really believe that, or at least a lot of our colleagues don't.'

He says he seriously thought about settling in Israel when he first went there in the 1950s, when it was still an agricultural state, but he couldn't see himself picking oranges or tilling the ground.

Diaspora support for Israel is predicated on many things, but two stand out. One is a sense of solidarity with fellow Jews, a recognition that, even if we don't live there, it is a country where we have friends and family, and where we have the right to settle should we choose to. The other is that Israel is a place of refuge for Jews. History tells us that we need it. Had Israel existed in the 1930s, millions of lives may have been saved. Nobody can be confident that another catastrophe may not occur one day; the troubled state of the world in the twenty-first century (the fifty-eighth, according to the Jewish calendar) should leave us under no illusions about what may happen one day.

The trouble is that, as the Shoah recedes into the vaults of history, the memory of why Israel is necessary fades. And as diaspora Jews, in Britain as elsewhere, become increasingly assimilated into their home cultures, the idea of solidarity with fellow Jews living in their own independent state loses its potency. This explains why many young British Jews have no attachment to Israel, and why future generations may have even less. Particularly if negative perceptions of the occupation and Israeli politicians outweigh pride in Israel's achievements.

Amos Schonfield sees a generational split in attitudes to Israel. It is not an absolute split: many older people align with the view ascribed to the younger generation, and many younger people adopt the older generation's view. But in simple terms, those who remember Israel's foundation or its early years, before the 1967 war changed the landscape, regard Israel as a homeland, a refuge for the Jews, a small, isolated nation surrounded by enemies. They see its very existence as miraculous, even more so the achievements that have propelled it in less than 75 years from a fledgling pioneer nation to a global leader in science, technology, agriculture and medicine. They admire the fact that Israel is the only democracy in the Middle East, that in less than a century it has greened the desert, built a resilient economy and created a viable lifestyle for a population largely descended from refugees, Holocaust survivors, victims of expulsions and idealistic pioneers. Though many of this older generation disagree, often quite strongly, with its policies towards the Palestinians, by and large they accept that the occupation of Palestinian land is the result of intransigence on both sides. There are no simple solutions to the conflict between Israel and Palestine, particularly when neither side seems to feel any urgency about dialogue.

Those who do not remember Israel's foundational years, and are not drawn to it religiously, see things differently. They don't remember the nation's pioneers or their achievements. Those who are in their thirties or younger had their political awakening during the Gaza wars. For them it is not Israel the plucky underdog fighting for survival; it is Israel the occupying power with very little interest in pursuing peace, accused of being an apartheid state. At best, for them, Israel is just another country, albeit populated by Jews; at worst, it brings Jewish values into disrepute and is the catalyst for anti-Semitism across the world. They may believe in the idea of Israel, and defend its right to exist. But they are deeply disappointed with the political direction it has taken.

The days are past when Israel relied on the diaspora. It no longer needs diaspora money for survival and it doesn't need diaspora Jews in high places lobbying on its behalf. But the diaspora needs Israel. Israel, along with religion, culture, humour and food, is a key influence in shaping Jewish identity. A diminishing attachment to Israel does not bode well for the British Jewish community. That doesn't mean supporting Israel right or wrong. But it does mean that, just as those who see Israel's flaws are prepared to defend their views against those who support it uncritically, so too should they be prepared to defend Israel's right to exist against those who dispute it. Ultimately, the polarizing of opinions about Israel undermines the Jewish community's confidence in itself. If a young, passionate, left-wing British Jew believes that the Jewish community is uncritically supportive of Israel, or if a strongly committed Israeli patriot believes that the community is ideologically opposed to his point of view, then communal cohesion, energy and creativity are the losers.

Louise Jacobs, chair of the UJIA, which educates young Jews about Israel, says her organization's role is to ask them to look at Israel in the context of their whole Jewish identity. 'We're not saying Israel is the be-all and end-all of your Jewish identity. But if you want to feel Jewish, in a world which can offer so much, one way to connect is through a relationship with Israel. If you look at the story of the Jews, there's no doubt that Israel plays a part in that. And that's what we're trying to ask people to think about. It doesn't take away your commitment to being a British Jew or to being proudly Jewish in Britain.'

Israel has never been devoid of a Jewish presence; some native families trace their history in the country back over generations. But the great majority of its Jewish population arrived after 1948, when the new state of Israel was founded. Since then, immigration from Britain has been slow but steady, reaching a peak in the 1980s, when just over 7,000 British Jews made *aliyah*, literally 'going up', to the land of Israel. There are now around 20,000 Jews living in Israel who were born in the UK.

Eylon Aslan-Levy was one of the 20,000, though he is not any more. His profile is somewhat different from most other Israelis. He was born and raised in England, in a Jewish family whose English roots are much deeper than most, stretching back to the eighteenth century. His family was British, but both of his parents were born in Israel. Growing up with dual nationality and an Israeli first name, in a family who spoke Hebrew among themselves at home, he thinks of himself as a second-generation immigrant, with a hyphenated British-Israeli identity.

Eylon moved to Israel in 2014, after completing his Master's degree. He went because he wanted to fulfil his obligation as an Israeli national to serve in the army. Every young Israeli man or woman has to do so. He left Britain at the end of what he describes as a difficult summer. The Israeli army had been conducting a military operation in Gaza, generating a wave of anti-Israel protests and a spike in anti-Semitic incidents in Britain. He says that he didn't feel as if he was leaving Britain to get away. 'But I would say the events of 2014 certainly meant I left with a bad taste in my mouth. Even though I never felt that I was being pushed out of Britain, I felt that I was being attracted to Israel.'

When he arrived, he had no plans to settle in Israel; he had simply gone to do his military service and try living there. But one thing led to another: he found a job as an anchor on an English-speaking TV channel and has remained in Israel ever since. He then worked in the publishing industry, translating newly published Hebrew books into English. And he now has been appointed to be the International Media Adviser to Israel's President, Isaac Herzog.

He speaks of Britain nostalgically, contending that life in Britain is very good and that British Jews are very fortunate. 'I really think that there are few places in the world, right now or throughout the course of history, where it's been better to be a Jew than modern Britain. It's a broadly liberal and tolerant society. And where else is it better to be a Jew? Israel, the USA, Canada, Australia, maybe. But there are really not very many places. When you compare it to the rest of Europe, Britain is where Jewish life flourishes the most.'

Like many young people I spoke to, Eylon did not agree with the often expressed view that the anti-Semitism in Corbyn's Labour Party posed an existential threat to British Jews. 'Obviously, that was an unpleasant period, and it was quite distressing that many people, particularly those who saw themselves on the side of progress and justice, had such a blind spot for this man. But I was never convinced by the forecast that, if Corbyn won, Britain was going to see a very large exodus of Jews. Those threats always seemed slightly overblown to me. And not because Mr Corbyn wasn't a thoroughly nasty character. But because life in Britain is good for the Jews. Yes, there are anti-Semitic incidents, but not of the scale and ferocity as in other countries. I look back on life in Britain with a lot of nostalgia and longing.'

Matthew Anisfeld also grew up in Britain. He too now lives in Israel, where he is studying to be a rabbi. He says that he chose to study there rather than in Britain because Israel offers far greater opportunities to those who want to immerse themselves in serious religious study. Jewish religious education in Britain, he says, aims to encourage less observant people to live a fuller Jewish lifestyle, but it doesn't provide serious students of Judaism with the tools to enable them to explore the Jewish tradition for themselves. He is not alone in that view; it is almost de rigueur these days for people from the religious communities to spend a year or two studying at advanced religious colleges in Israel before going to university or beginning their careers. With the exception of the strictly orthodox Gateshead *yeshiva*, based around a rabbinical college established in 1929, there are no similar opportunities in the UK.

David Newman is Professor of Geopolitics at Ben-Gurion University in Israel and has a personal interest in the history of British Jewry. He comes to Britain frequently and was awarded an OBE for promoting scientific cooperation between the two countries. He told me that he thinks British Jewish life is more dynamic in all respects than it ever was. There are still disagreements and quarrels, mainly in the religious sphere, but that is the nature of any Jewish community. They do not compare in intensity to the communal divisions that he remembers from his youth, as the son of a United Synagogue rabbi at a time when intercommunal relations had never been worse.

'I would never have dreamed at that time,' he said, 'that the British community could create Limmud. This would have been the last community you would have imagined could do that. America yes, Israel yes, but Britain? Never. And when you think of the people who created it, they were the mavericks, the people on the margins. And I'm sure they never thought it would take off as it did.'

He believes the relationship between the British Jewish community and Israel has changed. 'Britain has always been a very Zionist community in the sense of being supportive of Israel. OK, it's always had its dissenters, on the far left, or in the *haredi* community. But overall, as a community, it's been strongly supportive of Israel. But in my day and age, being a religious Zionist meant going to live in Israel. After we married, my wife and I went to live in Israel. I think today, it tends to mean you have a second house in Israel, because it's so easy to do. But you see yourself as part of the future leadership of the Jewish community here.'

There are many appealing reasons for settling in Israel. But it doesn't work out for everyone. Nic Schlagman, who works at the West London Synagogue, lived in Israel for several years. He went in his early twenties, sufficiently open to the possibility of settling there that he took out citizenship. Several of his friends went at the same time. But many of them, Nic among them, came back. Some found it too difficult to get a job; they'd arrived during a period when the Israeli economy was struggling. Others, like Nic, found that their worldview was incompatible with the Israeli government at the time. And some came back for family reasons, because they had parents to look after or partners who did not want to live there. Emigration from Britain to Israel is rarely a one-way street. One survey suggests that, in the first years of the twenty-first century, over half the British migrants to Israel subsequently returned. The figure has decreased somewhat since then.[61]

Surveys show that many British Jews feel a strong bond with the Jewish state. Yet only one or two out of every thousand British Jews emigrate to Israel each year. The low rate of emigration may reflect the disadvantage of moving to a land permanently in conflict with its neighbours, weighed against the stability and security of life in Britain. Despite a strong affinity for Israel and an overwhelming belief in its importance in fostering Jewish identity, British Jews are in no hurry to leave. Our exile is just too comfortable to make us want to get up and go.

In January 2015 Islamist gunmen killed four Jewish shoppers in a kosher supermarket in Paris. Two days earlier terrorists had killed 12 people and left 11 injured at the offices of the satirical magazine *Charlie Hebdo*. They were the latest in a series of terrorist incidents in France, many directed at Jews.

Over the course of the next year media around the world reported on an exodus of Jews from France, mainly to Israel and the UK. The impression they gave was that French Jews were fleeing because of anti-Semitism. Indeed, the events of 2015 certainly encouraged many Jews to flee, fearful that they were no longer safe in France. But anti-Semitism is only one reason why Jews have been leaving France. And it is not the main motivation for those French Jews who choose to move to London. For French Jewish immigrants the main appeal of Britain was economic. René Pfertzel, a French rabbi in London, recalls an interview that he gave to BBC News. 'They asked me, "Why do Jews move to London?" And the answer that they wanted was for me to say, "The Jews are fleeing France because of anti-Semitism." And it's true that a few years ago a lot of Jews moved to Israel because of anti-Semitic attacks in France. But in my experience, the Jews I know in

London did not leave France because of anti-Semitism. They left because of the economic situation.'

Simon Tobelem, who was born and spent much of his life in the French community, before moving first to Israel and then to the UK, broadly agrees. He sees emigration from France within the context of a long-term decline in the country's Jewish population. Between 1990 and 2015 the Jewish population of France decreased by 13 per cent, from 530,000 to 460,000. Over the same period the total population of the country increased by 14 per cent.[62] There is little doubt that much of the decline of the French Jewish population has come about because Jews did not feel comfortable in the country. But Simon agrees that most of the emigration to Britain in recent years has been for economic reasons.

Before Brexit there were no barriers to Europeans working in Britain, and with London as a major financial centre many French Jews took the opportunity to come to the city to work in finance. Simon explains that France excels in producing highly skilled mathematicians and engineers, and that finance today is all about algorithms. 'So it made sense for banks to hire this French guy, and the guy, instead of making €100,000 as an engineer in France, he's going to make £500,000 as a banker in London.'

Rabbi René thinks that proximity was a big factor for those Jews who chose to live in Britain. While moving to Israel is an ambition for many Jews, and a powerful statement about commitment to Jewish identity, it is a big decision. The lifestyle is different, the physical distance from friends and family left behind is great and the security situation is a continual worry. London, on the other hand is only two hours from Paris. It is far easier for French Jews to return home to see their families, or even to move back altogether if deemed necessary. Yet as a community, like the Israelis, French Jews have yet to make a significant impact on the nature of Jewish life in Britain.

The French Jews' willingness to emigrate and settle elsewhere is connected to their history in the country. Although there has been an almost continuous Jewish presence in France for over 1,000 years (marred only by periodic expulsions), the majority of today's French Jewish families arrived from the former colonies in Morocco, Algeria and Tunisia, after they gained independence in the 1950s and 1960s. The France they moved to was a predominantly Ashkenazi community, who had been slaughtered in great numbers during the Shoah and were still reeling from their experiences. The newcomers from North Africa were outsiders on two counts, both as immigrants to France and as foreign Jews with different customs, and different memories, from the Ashkenazim. They only became dominant as immigration increased and they began to outnumber the native community. With the memory of exile and resettlement still relatively fresh in their minds, the prospect of upping sticks and moving from France to Britain may not have daunted them in the same way as it might those from longer established communities.

There are cultural differences between the new French communities and the native British Jews. René Pfertzel told me about a family who had asked him to conduct their son's barmitzvah service. 'They were a typically French, Sephardi family, with a lot of relatives who had come over from Israel. We had the barmitzvah at the Liberal Jewish Synagogue in St John's Wood, which is one of the cathedral synagogues in England: very British, very reserved. And the family were making a lot of noise, and the father came in late to the service on his mobile phone: "Sorry, rabbi, I need to finish this call…"

They were taking pictures, selfies, all typically Sephardi. And I could see the English members of the congregation saying, "What is going on?" I really saw a clash.'

The cultural differences are also evident in the relationship that many French Jews have with the major community organizations. Simon Tobelem explains that in France the communal bodies are political organizations which liaise with the national authorities on budgetary and statutory matters, very different from the British model, in which they are integrated into the practical life of the community. 'The idea of the community as a club is not a very French thing. The French Jews are both French and Jews, in a more individualistic way. They will definitely contribute to charity, but they will do so as a personal initiative, rather than as part of an organization.'

Ezra Margulies, who comes from an English family and grew up in Monaco, says that the cultural bond between British Jews is stronger than that between the French, particularly among the religiously non-observant. Non-observant Jews in France are far less likely than their British peers to live in Jewish areas or to be concerned about having Jewish friends. This may explain why, despite his best efforts, Rabbi René Pfertzel has never managed to establish a French Progressive community in London. Progressive Jews, who tend to come from Ashkenazi backgrounds, tell him that they do not want to come together as French Jews in London. They'd rather integrate with the existing British communities. 'I don't have many French friends,' he says. 'It's not something we do. We don't try to find each other and to create little bubbles. Unlike Israelis, who I think do tend to stick together.'

But as with all things Jewish, there is a contrary narrative. In prosperous St John's Wood, Anshei Shalom is an orthodox community of Sephardi French Jews. They do club together as French Jews, they have a French-speaking rabbi and they preserve the customs of the community they left behind in France.

Living in central London, Simon Tobelem initially found it difficult to join in with the native community. He describes the Jews of central and north-west London as understandably very cliquey. They are a community of people who know each other, whose children have grown up together and who are connected through family relationships and social groups. Coming from a different culture and background, he was an outsider. Until he made a point of becoming active in the mainstream Jewish community. For several years he took a leadership role on the Mahamad, the governing body of his ancestral Spanish and Jewish community. He now sits on the board of major Jewish charities. He has integrated into British Jewish life, but he had to make a conscious effort to do so. He runs a successful business in London, with shareholders and colleagues from the native Jewish community. 'That creates a completely different aura. People say: "OK, this guy is here to stay, he is integrated, is contributing, is giving to charity." So obviously, people start behaving towards you differently.'

I asked Simon whether he considered France to be his home. He adamantly rejected the idea. His kids went to school and university in Britain; for them, going to France is a holiday. 'Home is here, and going to France is a holiday. I could say in some way that I'm happy to be home, when I go to Israel, but I think that many Jews would say that. It's not something which is specific to me.'

The French Jews came because Britain's membership of the European Union made it easy both to come and to go. But they are just the most recent in a continuing mid- to late twentieth-century stream of immigration to Britain, Jewish immigrants who managed to arrive, settle and prosper. Communities like the Egyptians who arrived after Suez, the Hungarians who came in the wake of the Soviet invasion, South Africans disgusted with apartheid and Iranians after the fall of the Shah. They weren't the first Jews to find their ways to Britain's shores and, like the French, they won't be the last.

The website Sephardi Voices UK is a treasure trove. It features over 100 video interviews with British Jews who arrived here from the Middle East, North Africa and Iran. They started coming to the UK after 1948, the year in which the state of Israel was founded and the exodus of Jews from Islamic countries began. As the interviews demonstrate, the contribution of these former refugees to British society has been remarkable, their successes spanning business, academia, science, philanthropy and the arts.

The website itself contains interviews in roughly the same proportion as the numbers who arrived from each country. About half are with Jews from Egypt, a quarter with Iraqi Jews and the remainder are with those who arrived from elsewhere in the region. Interviewees speak about their early lives in their native countries, their arrival in the UK, what it was like for them to adjust to their new country and the extent to which they have tried to pass their heritage on to their children and grandchildren.

One might imagine that a website called Sephardi Voices UK would be a record of testimonies from a homogeneous community, that the word 'Sephardi' describes Jews who share common ethnic characteristics. But 'Sephardi' is a very non-specific term. It is the Hebrew word for 'Spanish', and it was originally nothing more than an adjective describing those Jews who lived until the end of the fifteenth century in Spain and Portugal. When they were expelled from Spain in 1492, and from Portugal shortly afterwards, many Sephardi Jews travelled across the Mediterranean, settling among the Jewish communities of the Ottoman Empire in North Africa, Turkey and the Middle East. As the refugees from these lands arrived in Britain after the founding of Israel, they became known as Sephardi Jews, even though only a proportion of them could trace their ancestry back to Spain. And despite there already being a long-established and prominent genuinely Sephardi community here.

So although Jews from Spain, Portugal and the Ottoman Empire each have distinct origins, they are frequently lumped together under the same Sephardi umbrella. It is confusing, and it is one reason why the old established Sephardi community, which has been here since the seventeenth century, refers to its synagogues as Spanish and Portuguese, rather than Sephardi. And why Mizrachi, or 'Eastern Jews', is a more accurate way of referring to those from the old Ottoman Empire.

Daisy Abboudi, the Deputy Director of Sephardi Voices UK, insists that one cannot speak of Sephardi or Mizrachi communities as a block. Mizrachi Jews originate from dozens of different communities, stretching from Morocco to India. When they arrived in the UK, they retained, as best they could, the distinctive characteristics of the towns and villages they came from. There are more than 30 synagogues in Britain that are lumped together as Mizrachi, yet each follows its own distinctive customs. Some communities were large enough to establish their own synagogues, retaining the unique practices of their former homes. Other communities amalgamated, to set up synagogues together. Many individuals chose to blend in with the long-established

Spanish and Portuguese communities. The decision about whether to try to remain as a unique, distinct community or to throw in one's lot with others often depended on numbers and location.

The desire of the Mizrachi immigrants to retain their own communal identity can be traced back to the Ottoman societies they came from. In the Ottoman Empire the Jewish communities were semi-autonomous, responsible for their own welfare and administration. It didn't matter how religious one was: in civic terms a Jew was a Jew, whether they liked it or not. Things were very different in the pre-war European Jewish communities. One could easily forgo one's Jewishness and drift off into wider society without anyone being the wiser – at least, until the anti-Semites found you.

When the pre-war German immigrants arrived in Britain, they found themselves in an Ashkenazi religious and social environment not very different from the one they had just left. Contrastingly, the Mizrachi Jews discovered they were in an alien world, in which they tried as best they could to retain their own identity, despite their small numbers.

Dr Bea Lewkowicz is the Executive Director of Sephardi Voices UK. She also runs the testimony archive for the Association of Jewish Refugees, which documents the experiences of the survivors of the Nazi genocide who found refuge in the UK before and during the Second World War. She is in a good position to compare the different experiences of the German and Mizrachi refugees.

Bea compares the experience of Mizrachi immigrants in Britain with those in the USA. The numbers in each community are much larger in the States, with, for example, huge Syrian and Iranian communities in Los Angeles. It is much easier for them to retain their unique ancestral identity.

And they marry within their communities, not across them. In Britain, where the numbers are so much smaller, even within those Mizrachi communities which have managed to preserve their own sense of identity there is a continual feeling of being an outsider, and of being under pressure to fit in.

Like the Mizrachim, the German refugees also established their own synagogues. Some of their congregations have managed to retain aspects of their Germanic identity, while others have morphed into the wider community. But the big organizational difference between the two groups came about because many of the wartime German Jewish refugees were interned in Britain as enemy aliens.

In 1941 the Association of Jewish Refugees was established to support the new arrivals and to advocate on behalf of the internees. Eighty years on, the Association has become primarily a welfare organization, taking care of the needs of the surviving wartime refugees, and helping the descendants of those who arrived to discover their heritage. Those descendants have created Generation2Generation, a charity that encourages the descendants of Holocaust survivors to tell their family stories, to keep alive the memory of the events so many of their parents were unable to speak about.

Unlike the German immigrants, the Mizrachi communities did not arrive during wartime and did not have the same need for a protective, refugee support organization. That may be changing now: the Harif advocacy charity was established recently to preserve the memory of the old communities and to advocate for the rights of Jewish refugees from Islamic lands. A far cry from the long-established Association of Jewish Refugees, with its professional staff and sophisticated campaigns, Harif is a small volunteer organization that is just at the beginning of its endeavours.

Although the German and the Mizrachi refugees arrived within a couple of decades of each other, the two groups rarely if ever engaged. It was little different in 1956, when the Egyptian refugees who came to the UK in the wake of the Suez crisis found themselves placed in refugee camps in Kidderminster and in Birmingham, alongside Hungarian Jews fleeing the Soviet invasion of their country. The two groups were in the same camps, but they did not mix. Of course, there was a language barrier, but it was bigger than that. They had nothing in common with each other. When it came to building personal relationships, the fact that they shared a Jewish heritage didn't count for very much at all.

The children of the Mizrachi immigrants had a very different experience in Britain from those of the German refugees. Daisy Abboudi, whose grandparents came from Sudan, says that because there is no Mizrachi community organization it is her generation that is mobilizing to preserve the memory of the old communities. For, when she grew up in south London, she didn't meet anyone who could even contemplate having Arabic-speaking, Jewish grandparents.

'It was mind-blowing to people. Then when I got a bit older, I went to a youth group. I had no idea of half of what they were talking about in the groups because all the terminology was in Yiddish. I couldn't even follow the prayers. It was assumed that I would understand what was going on, but I had no idea how to learn it all. I didn't fully understand the culture.' When she is not working on Sephardi Voices UK, she runs Tales of Jewish Sudan, a website dedicated to the culture and history of the old Jewish Sudanese community.

She uses the term 'Ashkenormativity' to describe the assumption within the mainstream British community that Ashkenazi culture is the norm. 'I think it's to do with the way

British Jewry has been historically assimilated. In the past, and also to an extent today, it can be dangerous to appear "foreign" or different in British society. It was safer to blend in – to look, act and sound the same as the white majority. And then these other Jews appeared, coming along with their Arabic accents and their strange food; I don't think it was the face that British Jewry wanted to publicly portray. And there's a cultural element as well. In my grandparents' generation the mentality was very much, "Let's just move on, forget about the past. It's happened, it's gone." And I think that was because historically many of these families moved around the Ottoman Empire a lot. They did move around quite a lot.'

Dame Margaret Hodge, who came to Britain from Egypt as a child, is a different generation from Daisy but had a similar experience of being an outsider. Her parents moved from Germany to Egypt when the Nazis came to power. After the state of Israel was founded, and it was no longer comfortable to be Jewish in Egypt, they moved to Britain. And even though they went out of their way to assimilate and to be seen as British, Margaret says she has always felt like an immigrant. Her children are the first generation in her family who have not had to flee persecution. Her story reinforces the belief of many British Jews that Britain is an ideal place to live.

One might think that, with her history and her sense of being an outsider, Margaret might have kept her head down and lived an anonymous life. But that would be to overlook the drive, ambition and sense of purpose that power the lives of so many immigrants. Long before she confronted Jeremy Corbyn over anti-Semitism, Margaret was rarely out of the political headlines. Yet she says that it was an accident that she entered politics at all. 'I had always been a member of the Labour Party, because of being Jewish, and I was active in CND and anti-apartheid, and against the Vietnam War, and I was doing international research since I speak four or five languages. And in those days when you started having children, you were supposed to give up work. I still went to Labour Party meetings and a friend of mine at those meetings who was on the council had to move up to Birmingham. She said to me, "Go on, Margaret, go on the council. It'll keep you sane while you're changing nappies."'

Over and again in this book I have referred to the British Jewish community. It is a common enough phrase, a shorthand for the commonality of Jews who live in Britain, but it is not very accurate. Because one of the things this book suggests is that Britain's Jews cannot truthfully be described as a community. Granted, there is a communal infrastructure that caters for all of Britain's Jews, but for many people it is only when they need it that they start thinking of themselves as part of a unified community. British Jewry is made up of many different communities, originating in different parts of the world, all trying, to a greater or lesser extent, to retain their distinctive identities.

And Britain's Jewish communities are not just demarcated by places of origin. Communities coalesce around many different things: synagogue membership, religious denomination, political outlook and social networks, to name just a few. To talk about the Jewish community is a generality; it is a little like talking about 'the taxpayer' or 'the motorist'.

It wasn't always so. The early immigrants, who lived cheek by jowl in the poorer areas of the large cities, did feel connected to each other. And their children and grandchildren inherited the same sense of affiliation. But as they prospered and moved further afield, the bonds weakened. Successive waves of immigration, variations in religious practice and the growing multiculturalism of Britain all played their part in fashioning an expanding patchwork of Jewish identities. Slowly British Jewry evolved into what is now a mosaic of different communities. It is not a bad thing. It feels like a strength, not a weakness.

A report published in 2000 by the Institute for Jewish Policy Research was headlined 'A Community of Communities' and described Britain's Jews as a community in transition. Social change has created even more communities today. But the transition seems to be crystallizing, approaching maturity. We may not be able to speak accurately about a British Jewish community. But we can certainly talk about Britain's Jewish communities. Almost without exception, those who make up these various communities are far more confident than ever before of who they are, of what they have to offer, of what they need and of their place in British society.

The maturity of Britain's Jewish communities is one of the recurring features of this book. Fully integrated into British society and confident in who they are, they are no longer afraid, as were previous generations, to poke their heads above the parapet, to stand up for themselves. But arguably that confidence has wavered recently, in the perceived resurgence of anti-Semitism in Britain.

Wise voices in this book have tried to put anti-Semitism into perspective; there is no doubt that more incidents of anti-Semitism are being reported, but that is not to say that more incidents are taking place. There has always been low-level anti-Semitism in Britain, just as there has always been every other sort of racism and prejudice. We just notice it more because social media have thrown everything into the spotlight. But over and again those who I have spoken to have said Britain is one of the best places in the world for Jews to live. I wouldn't argue with that.

Because of our history we tend to place anti-Semitism into a different category from other sorts of racism; but in all respects bar one, Jews in Britain are no more vulnerable than any other minority. That one respect is the ever-present threat of terrorism fuelled by the Israel–Palestine conflict. It has led to the installation of elaborate security systems and the physical presence of protection officers at every synagogue, Jewish school and building. And if that is not worrying enough, there is the moronic abuse from those whose ingrained anti-Semitism extends their hatred of Israel to all Jews or, conversely, projects their hatred of Jews onto Israel.

It is that danger which makes many British Jews anxious. Confidence and anxiety may appear to be incompatible bedfellows, but they are both hallmarks of British Jewry in the 2020s.

As for the future, there are, of course, challenges. Top of the list is probably assimilation, the gradual drift of people integrating into the wider community, paying little or no attention to their Jewish identity and passing even less of it on to their children. Assimilation is not new, it has been going on for centuries, but it has assumed far greater proportions in our time. Very few people consciously choose to assimilate, consciously turning their back on their Jewish community. Instead they just drift away, and are quite happy to do so.

For most of British Jewry's history, the darkest feature of assimilation was intermarriage, or marrying out as it is usually called. Families would sit *shiva* – the traditional mourning period – if one of their children married someone not Jewish.

But intermarriage has become a fact of life in multicultural Britain; it can happen even in the most religious of families. And although it may have consequences in religious law, intermarriage need not be a cultural fissure. As we have seen, in contemporary Britain it is possible to express one's Jewish identity in many different ways. Very few who leave the cradle of Judaism deny their Jewishness completely.

The response to assimilation must lie not in mourning those who have married out or drifted off but in finding ways to keep the connections open. Rather than wringing our hands, Britain's Jewish communities should remain open to those whose Britishness is more important to them than their Jewishness, whose universalism trumps their particularism. Assimilation is only a problem for those who remain behind; it is not a concern for those who go. A confident Jewry should be able to find ways of responding positively to it. Some of the religious outreach groups, like Chabad, are already doing so.

An equally tricky challenge is that of polarization – the growth of the *haredi* community, at one end of the spectrum, and secularization, at the other – with the consequential shrinking of the centre. Historically, British Jewry has been defined by its centre. Like Britain itself, Britain's Jews have tended to tread a moderate path; extreme opinions have rarely done well in Britain either in politics or in religion. But like assimilation, polarization is only a problem for those whose world is challenged by it. Secular Jews are, by and large, happy with their choices; so too are most *haredi* Jews. It is the centre that is worried because that is where the attrition seems to be. Nevertheless there are fears that, as the *haredi* population grows, tensions with the mainstream, centrist community may arise. It has happened in Israel and, to a lesser extent, in the USA. A 2020 Jewish Policy Research report urged that the underlying causes of potential tensions be addressed expeditiously, with structures established to facilitate better means of cooperation between different parts of the Jewish community.[63]

The story of Jewish life in Britain is a relatively tranquil and contented one. Close to 400 years since the first Jews returned to the country, Britain's tangle of Jewish communities have squared the circle of being fully integrated into national life while retaining their own identity. They are mature, confident and settled, and have a much better idea of how to see off their enemies.

Of all the people I spoke to in writing this book, it was Chief Rabbi Mirvis who shone the most radiant light on the quality and nature of the Jews of Britain. 'We have,' he said, 'a great Jewish community today in this country. A wonderful community, our *hesed* [charitable kindness] is extraordinary. The fundraising activities during Covid were mind-blowing. We started Covid thinking we were all in trouble financially. The opposite has happened. Such *gutte neshames* [good souls], such wonderful people. And yes, we've got our challenges, and we've got our *broigeses* [quarrels] and the polarization, but those are details within an overall narrative which is one of a highly successful, wonderful Jewish community.'

Glossary

aguna A 'chained' woman, unable to remarry, either because her husband refuses to divorce her or because it is uncertain if he is dead.

aliyah Emigration to Israel (literally, 'going up').

bet din Rabbinic court.

broiges A quarrel or falling out.

Chabad Hasidic sect notable for their outreach work and concern for all Jews.

challah A plaited bread eaten on the sabbath (literally, 'loaf').

frum Religious.

gefilte Stuffed (as in *gefilte* fish: 'stuffed fish').

gemilut hasadim Acts of kindness or charity.

golus The Jewish diaspora (literally, 'exile').

goy (*pl.* goyim) Non-Jew, gentile.

gutte neshame A good soul.

halacha Jewish law.

hamantaschen Sweet pastries eaten on the festival of Purim.

hanukkiah Eight-branched candlestick lit on the festival of Hanukkah.

haredi (*pl.* haredim) Strictly Orthodox.

hasid (*pl.* **hasidim**) Member of pietist branch of orthodoxy.

hesed Kindness.

huppa Wedding canopy.

kashrut 'Kosherness'.

kibbutz (*pl.* **kibbutzim**) Residential community in Israel often run on socialist or collective principles.

kiddush Short ceremony at the table or in synagogue to consecrate the sabbath.

kippah (*pl.* **kippot**) Skullcap.

Kol Nidrei The service at the beginning of the Day of Atonement. Also the name of a prayer.

kolel Advanced Talmudic study group.

lockshen Noodles.

malchus shel hesed A beneficent kingdom.

matzah Unleavened bread.

mensch A person of integrity.

mikveh Ritual bath.

minyan Quorum of ten required for certain prayers.

misnagdim Eighteenth- and nineteenth-century opponents of *hasidim*.

nebbish A pitiful person.

nu, voss naiyes 'So, what's new?'

parve A category of food that contains neither dairy nor meat products.

rebbe A hasidic rabbi.

Satmar The largest hasidic sect.

schmaltz Of food: fatty.

schmuck An incompetent or foolish person.

seder Evening ceremony and accompanying meal at the festival of Passover.

shabbat The sabbath.

shiva Seven-day mourning period observed in the home.

shtiebel Very small synagogue, prayer room.

shul Synagogue.

simcha Celebration, typically a wedding, bar- or batmitzvah.

simchat torah Joyful festival held in the autumn.

Talmud Torah Orthodox school for religious study.

tikkun olam Social justice, charitable acts (literally, 'repair of the world').

tzedakah Charity.

yeshiva Rabbinic or Talmudic college.

Acknowledgements

The genesis of this book was a lunch that I had with my wonderful publisher, Robin Baird-Smith, in February 2020. Robin, who is probably the most prolific publisher in Britain of books of Jewish interest (though they are only a proportion of his output), said he would like me to write something that looks at the life of the Jewish community in the UK.

This book is the result. It is the sixth book of mine that Robin, backed by the Bloomsbury team, has published, and I have never failed to be impressed by their high quality of production, marketing, publicity and, most importantly, author support. My grateful and appreciative thanks to Robin and his team, to Sarah Jones who did all the hard work in bringing the book from first draft to publication, to Jessica Gray in publicity and Sarah Head in marketing, to Matthew Taylor for his ever-watchful and precise copyediting, Sarah Bance for proofreading and Rosemary Dear for indexing. It is a delight to work with you all.

Of course, it would not have been possible to write this book without the dozens of people who willingly gave up their time to speak to me. Not everyone wanted to be mentioned by name, but for all those who were happy to be quoted, my grateful thanks goes (strictly in alphabetical order) to: Daisy Abboudi, Matthew Anisfeld, Eylon Aslan-Levy, Rabbi

ACKNOWLEDGEMENTS

Charley Baginsky, Rabbi Tony Bayfield, Nick Beck, Georgina Bednar, Luciana Berger, Rabbi Miriam Berger, Richard Bolchover, Ephraim Borowski MBE, Dr Jon Boyd, Rabbi Shoshana Boyd Gelfand, Moshe Braun, Rivkah Brown, Daniel Carmel-Brown, Russell Conn, Mark Cunningham, Rabbi Dr Andrew Davis, Richard Ferrer, Dr Leonie Fleischmann, Jonathan Freedland, Hadley Freeman, Mark Gardner, Rabbi Herschel Gluck, Neville Goldschneider, Jonathan Goldstein, Henry Grunwald OBE, James Harris, Dame Margaret Hodge MP, Ed Horwich, Josh Howie, Alan Jacobs, Louise Jacobs, Dr David Katz, Marion Kinshuck, Anat Koren, Daniel Kosky, Professor David Latchman, Lord Michael Levy, Steven Lewis, Dr Bea Lewkowicz, Adrian Litvinoff, Ezra Margulies, Chief Rabbi Ephraim Mirvis, Bernie Myers, David Newman OBE, Sir Trevor Pears, Rabbi René Pfertzel, Rabbi Michael Pollak, Stephen Pollard, Dr Nicola Rosenfelder, Claudia Rubenstein, Philip Rubenstein, Eve Sacks, Lionel Salama, Nic Schlagman, Amos Schonfield, Rabbi Zahavit Shalev, Raymond Simonson, Chaya Spitz OBE, Eli Spitzer, Rabbi Bentzi Sudak, Simon Tobelem, Arnold Wagner OBE, Michael Wegier, Vivian Wineman, Lady Lira Winston z"l, Professor Robert Winston, Rabbi Raphael Zarum and Jonathan Zenios.

Sadly I must single out one name from the above list: Lira Winston, my good friend and neighbour, who passed away suddenly, unbelievably and at far too young an age, just as I was completing this book. She spent much of her working life as a leader in professional Jewish roles, and was a fount of information and good advice as I was writing the book. Lira was one of those people who always saw the best in everybody; her passing has left a huge void in her family, and the world is a darker place without her sparkle, her good humour, her energy and her positivity.

My thanks also to those who didn't contribute a word to the book but who helped me write it. By being there, by taking an interest, by talking about it and putting me right when I so often got it wrong. Chief of all is my wife, Karen, who is an unflagging support whenever I write. My kids and stepkids, Josh, Mollie, Sam and Dan, in-laws and out-laws Melody and Louis. They have all given me valuable information and advice, particularly about what is going on in their generation and in the fields in which they work. And then, of course, there are Eli, Bonnie, Leo and Dylan. They have all had something to add (even if some of them can't read yet), and they are, of course, the next generation of Britain's Jews. Thank you to you all.

Notes

1 Philip Roth, *The Counterlife* (Vintage, London, 2016), p. 304.
2 Naomi Alderman, *Disobedience* (Penguin, London, 2007), p. 55 (emphasis in original).
3 Isa. 40.1.
4 Richard Bolchover, *British Jewry and the Holocaust* (Littman Library of Jewish Civilization, London, 1993).
5 Some joke that it derives from Gen. 28.10: 'And Jacob went out …' As if Jacob would go out without a hat!
6 *Jewish Chronicle* (15 and 22 September 2006).
7 'Protocols of the Elders of Zion' was a notorious anti-Semitic hoax that first appeared in Russia in 1903.
8 Norman Lebrecht, 'I Am Having My Fill of Bad Jewish Music', *Jewish Chronicle*, 27 July 2020.
9 In the Talmud *apikoros* is a generic term for a scholarly heretic who is able to argue against Judaism on its own terms.
10 'Social and Political Attitudes of British Jews', Institute for Jewish Policy Research, July 1996.
11 David Graham, 'The Political Leanings of Britain's Jews', Institute for Jewish Policy Research, London, 2010: https://jpr.org.uk/publication?id=3002; Andrew Barclay, 'The Political Consequences of Anti-Semitism? The Party Preferences of Britain's Jews': https://blogs.lse.ac.uk/politicsandpolicy/party-preferences-british-jews/
12 *Mail Online*, 23 August 2018.
13 Seth Stephens-Davidowitz, 'Hidden Hate: What Google Searches Tell Us About Anti-Semitism Today': https://cst.org.uk/data/file/a/b/APT%20Google%20Report%202019.1547210385.pdf.

14 Harry Defries, *Conservative Party Attitudes to Jews, 1900-1950* (Frank Cass, London, 2001).

15 Est. 3.8–9.

16 *Jewish Chronicle*, 27 July 2018, 8 and 15 November 2019.

17 https://www.medialens.org/2018/charges-without-merit-jeremy-corbyn-anti-Semitism-norman-finkelstein-and-noam-chomsky/

18 https://qz.com/407157/less-than-2-of-the-us-population-is-jewish-so-why-is-41-of-the-countrys-packaged-food-kosher/

19 The biblical hero Daniel, in the first chapter of the book named after him, refused to drink the king's wine.

20 https://jpr.org.uk/documents/Coronavirus_paper_1.5.Unemployment_redundancies.Final.pdf

21 Chaim Bermant, *The Cousinhood* (Eyre & Spottiswood, London, 1971), p. 202.

22 See my book *Reason To Believe: The Controversial Life of Rabbi Dr Louis Jacobs* (Bloomsbury, London, 2020).

23 *Jewish Chronicle*, 21 June 2019.

24 *Sunday Times*, 25 April 2021.

25 *Jewish Chronicle*, 19 May 2017.

26 https://www.theus.org.uk/aboutus

27 *The Diary of Samuel Pepys*, 1663. https://www.pepysdiary.com/diary/1663/10/14/

28 Michael J. Harris, *Faith without Fear: Unresolved Issues in Modern Orthodoxy* (Vallentine Mitchell, London, 2016).

29 Leonard Cohen, 'Different Sides', *Old Ideas* (2012).

30 https://www.timesofisrael.com/jewish-psychedelics-movement-blasts-off-with-first-ever-conference/

31 'Torah on Tyne: How Orthodox Jews carved Out Their Very Own Oxbridge', *The Guardian*, 22 December 2019.

32 https://elispitzer.com/2020/11/03/the-politics-of-exile/

33 http://nahamu.org/what-is-nahamu/

34 Susan A. Glenn, 'The Vogue of Jewish Self-Hatred in Post-World War II America', *Jewish Social Studies*, vol. 12, no. 3, 2006, pp. 95–136.

35 https://www.theguardian.com/books/2014/nov/06/how-i-stopped-being-a-jew-shlomo-sand-unchosen-julie-burchill-review; https://www.bbc.co.uk/sounds/play/b0b5xh33

36 Tebbit is a British politician who controversially said in 1990 that immigrants who support their native countries at cricket, rather than England, had not integrated adequately.

37 Isa. 47.11.

38 Jerzy Lando *Saved By My Face* (Mainstream Publishing, Edinburgh, 2002), pp. 118–19.

39 https://www.theguardian.com/commentisfree/2020/dec/02/the-government-should-not-impose-a-faulty-definition-of-anti-Semitism-on-universities. *Jewish Chronicle*, 17 and 24 December 2020.

40 https://jerusalemdeclaration.org/; *Jewish Chronicle*, 1 April 2021.

41 Geoffrey Robertson QC, 'Anti-Semitism: The IHRA Definition and Its Consequences for Freedom of Expression', Palestinian Return Centre, 31 August 2018; https://prc.org.uk/upload/library/files/Anti-Semitism_Opinion_03.09.18eds.pdf

42 *The Guardian*, 7 January 2021.

43 The IHRA censors Palestinians by design, not by accident; Ben White, *Vashti*, 23 December 2020: https://vashtimedia.com/2020/12/23/ihra-definition-censors-palestinians-antiSemitism/

44 *The Times*, 21 October 2020.

45 Speech by Ruth Deech to Oxford Jewish community, June 2020.

46 https://www.theguardian.com/commentisfree/belief/2012/apr/27/board-of-deputies-british-jews-revolution; https://jewishnews.timesofisrael.com/hundreds-of-british-jews-sign-letter-criticizing-board-of-deputies-gaza-response/; 'A Community of Communities: Report of the Commission on Representation of the Interests of the British Jewish Community', Jewish Policy Research, March 2000, https://jpr.org.uk/publication?id=702

47 *Jewish Chronicle*, 30 July 2021; *Jewish News*, 27 July 2021.

48 Jonathan Boyd, 'Largest Jewish Populations in the United Kingdom by Local Authority: 2001 and 2011 Comparison', May 2016, https://jpr.org.uk/documents/Largest_Jewish_populations_by_Local_Authority.2001_and_2011_comparison.pdf; Cecil Roth, 'The Rise of Provincial Jewry',

Jewish Monthly, 1950; Board of Deputies: https://www.bod
.org.uk/jewish-facts-info/jews-in-numbers/; *Tablet*: https://
www.tabletmag.com/sections/community/articles/fighting-for
-the-future-in-leeds.

49 Elizabeth Caldwell Hirschman and Donald N. Yates, *When
Scotland Was Jewish* (McFarland & Co., Jefferson, NC, 2007).

50 https://www.scojec.org/resources/files/sjs.pdf

51 http://www.glasspainter.com/synindex.html; *Sunday Times*, 22
June 2008: https://www.thetimes.co.uk/article/john-clark-found
-light-at-the-end-of-a-stained-glass-window-s9mwtv6pk8b

52 *Jewish Chronicle*, 9 December 2016.

53 For example, the secretive, ultra-conservative American organization National Council for Policy, who trumpet: 'We
believe the Founding Fathers created this nation based upon
Judeo-Christian values.' See Anne Nelson, *Shadow Network:
Media, Money, and the Secret Hub of the Radical Right* (Bloomsbury, New York, 2019). Historically the phrase 'Judaeo-Christian tradition' was used to refer to Jewish converts to Christianity or to represent an imagined set of values suggesting
superiority over fascism, communism or, latterly, Islam.

54 Mishnah Gittin 4.3; Tosefta and Talmud frequently.

55 Deut. 16.10.

56 *Jewish Chronicle*, 1 November 1991.

57 L. Daniel Staetsky and Jonathan Boyd, 'The Rise and Rise of
Jewish Schools in the United Kingdom: Numbers, Trends and
Policy Issues', Institute for Jewish Policy Research/ Board of
Deputies, November 2016: https://jpr.org.uk/documents/The
_rise_and_rise_of_Jewish_schools_in_the_United_Kingdom
.pdf; *Jewish Chronicle*, 24 June 2010.

58 https://www.supremecourt.uk/cases/docs/uksc-2009-0136
-judgment.pdf, pp. 90–91.

59 David Graham, 'Britain's Israeli Diaspora: A Demographic
Portrait', Institute for Jewish Policy Research, November 2015.

60 Rashi to Leviticus 25,26.

61 'Immigration from the United Kingdom to Israel', Institute for
Jewish Policy Research, October 2013: https://www.jpr.org.uk/
publication?id=2882.

62 'France', Institute for Jewish Policy Research: https://www.jpr.
   org.uk/country?id=104
63 Jonathan Boyd, *Moving beyond COVID-19: What Needs
   To Be Done To Help Preserve and Enhance Jewish Communal
   Life?* Institute for Jewish Policy Research, March 2021:
   https://jpr.org.uk/documents/JPR_Brief.COVID-19.Mar_2021.
   Final.pdf

Index

A Note on the Author

Harry Freedman is Britain's leading author of popular works of Jewish culture and history. His best-selling publications include *Leonard Cohen: The Mystical Roots of Genius; The Talmud: A Biography*; and *Kabbalah: Secrecy, Scandal and the Soul*. He has a PhD on an Aramaic translation of the Bible and lives in London with his wife Karen. You can follow his regular articles on harryfreedman.substack.com.

harryfreedmanbooks.com
@harryfreedman1